The End of Marriage?

The End of Marriage?

Individualism and Intimate Relations

Jane Lewis

Barnett Professor of Social Policy, University of Oxford, UK

Edward Elgar

Cheltenham, UK • Northampton, MA, USA

Published by
Edward Elgar Publishing Limited
Glensanda House
Montpellier Parade
Cheltenham
Glos GL50 1UA
UK

Edward Elgar Publishing, Inc.
136 West Street
Suite 202
Northampton
Massachusetts 01060
USA

A catalog record for this book is available from the British Library

Library of Congress Cataloging in Publication Data
Lewis, Jane (Jane E.)
    The end of marriage? : individualism and intimate relations / Jane Lewis.
        p. cm.
    Includes bibliographical references and index.
    1. Marriage—Great Britain. 2. Family—Great Britain. 3. Unmarried couples—Great Britain. 4. Individualism—Great Britain. 5. Great Britain—Social conditions—1945– I. Title.

    HQ614 .L48 2001
    306.8—dc21

                                                                            2001033112

ISBN 1 84064 287 4
Printed and bound in Great Britain by MPG Books Ltd, Bodmin, Cornwall

Contents

Figures

Tables

Acknowledgements

This book was written under difficult personal and professional circumstances over the last three years and I am particularly grateful to the following people for their help and support: Sue Bruley, Liz Crosby, Celia Davies, Eddy Higgs, Roberta Linning, Ruth Lister, Mavis Maclean, Jill Pascall, Margaret Pelling, Jenny Stanton and Meta Zimmeck.

The Lord Chancellor's Department provided the money for the empirical part of the research and I am grateful in addition for the interest the Department showed in the findings. Jessica Datta and Sophie Sarre worked as research officers on the project and the empirical research would not have been possible without them.

The author and publisher wish to thank the Office of National Statistics which has kindly granted permission for the use of statistical information.

PART I

1. Introduction: the debate

It has become tempting to write about the 'rise and fall' of marriage in the twentieth century. Marriage became virtually universal in the immediate post-war decades, but was seemingly much less popular by the closing years of the twentieth century. First marriage rates were lower in 1999 than they were at the beginning of the century, and the age at first marriage was higher for men and for women. Remarriage rates were falling. While it would be premature to write off marriage, the pace of family change in the last two decades of the century was dramatic and it is not surprising that the broad trends associated with the decline of marriage and the rise of cohabitation promoted *fin de siècle* anxiety about the future of marriage.

But does it matter that marriage has become increasingly separated from parenthood at the end of the twentieth century, a very different development from the separation of sex and marriage a generation earlier? Anxiety about family change has centred on the implications for children; on the behaviour of men who appear to be more ready to walk away from their family responsibilities; and on women who are often portrayed as bent on fulfilling themselves through their careers as much as devoting themselves to their families. Much of the commentary on family change has emphasised the part played by the pursuit of self-fulfilment and individual happiness over and above regard for marriage vows or for any private commitments that might be made by cohabitants. Individualism has been a driving force in western liberal democracies, but as feminist philosophers have long pointed out, until relatively recently the idea of the individual meant in practice the male 'head-of-household' (Okin, 1979). In other words, in the family, individualism has historically been tempered by economic and legal inequality resulting in the dependence of women, together with the acceptance by men and women of traditional patterns of behaviour.

This book began with a wish to interrogate the thesis of a growing individualism that is often assumed also to be selfish. Is this really what characterises the changes that are going on in families? And how does what is going on in terms of changes in mentalities and behaviour inside families relate to changing structures and norms outside them? The charge of increasing selfish individualism is levied at all aspects of family life, but this book focuses on understandings of marriage, cohabitation and the meaning of commitment inside

3

and outside the family, particularly in relation to the nature of investment of time and money by adult family members. The issue of sexual fidelity as a signifier of marriage is not explored at the level of the individual couple, although the importance of the changes that have taken place in the external sexual moral code are addressed.

The 'facts' of family change are real and are hard to exaggerate. In one generation, the numbers marrying have halved, the numbers divorcing have trebled and the proportion of children born outside marriage has quadrupled. Attitudes have also changed, becoming less traditional on the issues of marriage, divorce, cohabitation and working mothers. By the end of the 1980s, fewer than 50 per cent of 18–24 year olds thought it necessary to marry before having children (Kiernan and Estaugh, 1993). Two-thirds of first partnerships in the early 1990s were cohabitations, compared to one-third 20 years earlier, and 22 per cent of children were born into cohabiting unions compared to 2 per cent 20 years before (Ermisch and Francesconi, 1998). The rate of cohabitation among couples with children reached 13 per cent in 1998. Among those in the lower third or so of the income distribution the rate was almost half as high again, and among couples with children drawing benefits it was more than two and half times as high (Marsh et al 2001[1]). However, it is not possible to deduce changes in values from the statistics of family change. The meaning of the changes, let alone their causes and effects, is extremely difficult to determine and is subject to huge debate, which is inevitably political. In Britain, 'family values' came from nowhere to take a prominent place in the political agenda in the 1990s. The attention of both academics and policy makers has focused broadly on whether family change amounts to family breakdown and on the main outcome of change, in the form of the increase in lone mother families (from 7.5 per cent of all families with dependent children in 1971, to 25 per cent at the beginning of the twenty-first century). There have been remarkably few studies of the changes that have taken place in marriage *per se*, which may be as significant for a full understanding of family change. As H.G. Wells (1933, p. 462) remarked: 'marriage has a false air of having lasted unimpaired throughout the ages'. More recently Giddens (1992) commented on its quality as a 'shell institution'; enormous changes in terms of ideas about such matters as the importance of fidelity and loyalty, and in terms of the division of labour between husbands and wives may be hidden behind its seemingly unchanging façade.

Marriage and the marriage system have changed and there is a real basis for the debate about the implications and the causes. But it is a big jump to conclude that we are all selfish, or that men have become more selfish in their willingness to leave their families, or that women have become selfish in the pursuit of work outside the home. Indeed, some of the changes in behaviour at the level of the family may be exaggerated. For example, women are much more active in the labour market, but this does not mean that they earn enough to be self-sufficient, economically independent individuals. Mentalities, though, may have changed more, not least because expectations are very different. The 'ought' in regard to the behaviour of men and women in families is considerably less specified than it was even a generation ago, in large part because of changes in both the realities and normative prescriptions concerning the labour market and in family law. This in turn has opened up a space for negotiation in families, which may well be positive, but which is certainly no more easy than abiding by the more clear-cut prescriptive economic and legal frameworks that operated in the past. Furthermore, if the gap between expectation and behaviour becomes too great, negotiation may be impossible and relationship breakdown may be swift. It is the argument of this book that changes at the level of the family cannot be understood without considering the much broader social context, and that what might be termed the cultural variable plays a key mediating role. Particularly important has been the erosion of normative expectations associated with the prescriptive frameworks emanating from family law and the male breadwinner model family.

THE DEBATE ABOUT FAMILY CHANGE AND ANXIETIES ABOUT THE GROWTH OF INDIVIDUALISM

For the most part, academic commentators have decided that what happened to the family during the last quarter of the century is problematic. In large measure, late twentieth-century pessimism about the family has been a reaction to the scale and rapidity of the changes in the demographic statistics, which have produced a rethink of divorce and unmarried motherhood. During the 1950s and 1960s, British and American psychological, sociological and medical research concluded that marital conflict was as bad for a child as divorce (Goode, 1956), and that divorce might actually be better for children than living with unhappy parents who were effectively 'emotionally divorced' (Despert, 1953; Nye, 1957). These views were accompanied by optimistic accounts stressing the fundamental stability of marriage and the family: after all, divorce rates were low and the vast majority of births took place inside marriage, regardless of where they were conceived (Fletcher, 1966; Young and Willmott, 1973; Bane, 1976). But, by the 1980s, research findings were drawing much more pessimistic conclusions against the backdrop of rapid increase in both the divorce rate and the extra-marital birth rate. American research began to emphasise the bad effects of divorce on children, launched by the work of Hetherington *et al.* (1978) and Wallerstein and Kelly (1980), and the problems experienced by lone mothers more generally (McLanahan and Sandfur, 1994).

The policy debate seemed disposed to overturn the long-held stress on the importance of the mother–child dyad (reiterated powerfully as late as 1980 by Goldstein *et al.*) in favour of 'bringing fathers back in'. As Davidson Hunter (1991) has commented, the debate over the family has in large measure been a debate over what constitutes the family. British empirical research followed the American in providing evidence of the detrimental impact of divorce and unmarried motherhood on the educational achievement, poverty levels, employment and personal relationships of children and young adults (see, for example, Richards and Dyson, 1982; Maclean and Wadsworth, 1988; Kiernan, 1992). Some American writers have been more circumspect in their judgements (for example, Furstenburg and Cherlin, 1991), but writing in the *Journal of Family Issues* in 1987, Norval Glenn, a respected sociologist of the family, observed that leading American commentators were much less sanguine regarding the prospects of the American family in the mid-1980s than they had been a decade before. There is no doubt that the climate of opinion shifted radically over the course of a quarter of century on both sides of the Atlantic.

Most empirical work and most concern has been about the *effects* of family change, particularly on children. The institution of marriage has long been viewed as the basic unit and bedrock of society, imposing rational bonds on irrational sexual urges, which is why relaxation of the divorce laws has proved so controversial and difficult right through the twentieth century. The married couple has been viewed as the *polis* in miniature. If they could not reach an accommodation, then what chance was there for the wider society? In this view, marriage is a discipline and an order, which also means that it is necessarily a matter of public interest and not just a private relationship. Indeed, the notion of the family, rather than the individual, as the fundamental building block has been central to most western countries, many of which have for much of the twentieth century assumed the existence of a 'male-headed household' and a 'male-breadwinner/female-carer family'.

Early twentieth-century commentators were as convinced as the functional-ist sociologist Talcott Parsons in the 1950s and Fukuyama in the 1990s that the stable, traditional, two-parent family provides the best setting for raising children. Recent accounts have stressed the way in which the traditional family fosters the acquisition of 'social capital' (Coleman, 1988), that is the informal values and norms that permit a group of people to work together. In the context of the family, social capital consists of the relationship between the parents and the children, which gives the child access to the parents' resources, intellec-tual, material and emotional. Older analyses of the importance of the family to the child, such as that of Talcott Parsons, emphasised the mediating role played by the family between the individual and the wider society, and the way in which the traditional two-parent family, with its clearly assigned roles for adult men and women, successfully 'socialised' the child. There have been changes in terms of what kind of family arrangement was considered conducive to the performance of this task. By the middle of the century, it was accepted that a more 'companionate' family that stressed the quality of more democratic relationships between adults and between parents and children, over and above the institution of marriage *per se*, was important to successful socialisation. The main focus for those emphasising the importance of the stability of marriage and the family has been the benefits that are derived by children and thus the wider society, although Marris (1991) has argued the primacy of need for attachment and the way in which marriage in particular protects against depression, and Waite (1995) has argued strongly that the adults involved also benefit in terms of their health and material welfare. However, this is more controversial still, for feminist analysis has long held that traditional marriage works to the advantage of men and the disadvantage of women (Bernard, 1976; Delphy and Leonard, 1992).

Concern about the effects of family change have spread out from the implications for children to the wider society, and as McLanahan and Booth (1989) have observed, has acted as a touchstone for issues that are in and of themselves major sources of anxiety, for example, gender roles, class, race and the role of the state. Thus George Akerloff (1998), an economist, argued that changes in marriage patterns are a more potent cause of social pathology in the form of criminal behaviour and drug abuse than unemployment or 'welfare dependency'. For Francis Fukuyama (1999), family change is part of the 'great disruption' in social norms and values that began in the 1960s and manifested itself in rising crime rates and a decline in trust, as well as in family breakdown. In Britain, Dennis and Erdos (1992) sought to trace the rise of the 'obnoxious Englishman' to family breakdown. Their chief concern was the effect of lone motherhood on the behaviour patterns of young men. Lone motherhood was in their view responsible for at best irresponsible and at worst criminal behaviour in the next male generation. But the possible link between absent fathers and rising crime rates has not been tested for any large-scale British sample. Indeed, the debates over marriage and the family are fraught because cause and effect are so difficult to establish. One of the most recent contributions to the literature on the effects of divorce on children shows that this issue, which has been subjected to careful empirical research, is still far from resolved. Rodgers and Pryor (1998) make it clear how difficult it is to be sure that the outcomes are directly attributable to parental separation, rather than to a range of factors that impinge on families before, during and after separation. The effects of family change are hard to establish, and in a sense it is the uncertainty about where the move away from the traditional married, two-parent family and the stability associated with it might lead that is the problem.

While most attention has been directed at the possible effects of family change, it is not surprising that there has also been considerable reflection as to what might be happening in society to *cause* it. The most pervasive explanation has focused on an increase in individualism in terms of both ideas and behaviour, which is believed to have undermined commitment in intimate relationships. Glenn warned that if a good marriage was to be judged only by hedonistic standards, then marriage might become 'so insecure that no rational person will invest a great deal of time, energy, money and forgone opportunities to make a particular marriage satisfactory' (Glenn, 1987, p. 351). His concern, and that of many others, is about the kind of thinking and behaviour that is associated with lack of permanence and stability.

Swidler (1980) was one of the first to argue systematically that love had become more individualistic and less committed, largely as a result of the pursuit of personal growth encouraged by the therapeutic movement. It would be considered very strange in western countries if a couple proposing to marry did not say that they were 'in love' and did not put love at the top of their list of reasons for marrying. According to Lawrence Stone (1979), the growth of 'affective individualism', which he traced through the rise of more 'companionate' marriage and child-oriented parenting, began in the late eighteenth century, although considerations regarding property and business connections continued to play a conspicuous part in the marriages of the middle classes (Davidoff and Hall, 1987). The idea of marrying for love has undoubtedly triumphed, certainly in the twentieth century, but has still not completely eclipsed all other considerations. Nevertheless, love-as-feeling has tended to feminise it and to isolate and privatise it (Gillis, 1988).

However, the ideal of romantic love does not necessarily lead unproblematically to companionate marriage. Berger and Kellner (1964) portrayed marriage as a forging of a joint identity: couples wrote the marital script together. But there may be a fundamental tension between individual desire and the pursuit of individual happiness on the one hand, and loyalty to the marriage on the other. As Milton Regan (1999) has commented, society attaches a high value to both intimacy and individual autonomy. Individualism is at the heart of the idea of romantic love (Skolnick, 1991; Lystra, 1989) and may just as easily lead to adultery as towards monogamy. In her study of adultery, Lawson (1988, p. 26) wrote of the conflict between the myth of romantic marriage and the 'myth of me', which 'slips out from under' and propels the individual into an affair. As writers from de Rougemont in the 1940s to Luhman in the 1980s have pointed out, marriage with love as its *raison d'être* is inherently unstable. And, as Reibstein and Richards (1992) and Fletcher (1993) have observed, the sexual relationship has become even more important in terms of its exclusivity as sex has become more widely available.

There has been widespread academic support for the idea of increased individualism as a major explanation for family change. Demographers have pointed out the degree to which demographic change has been accompanied by more individualistic values (Lesthaeghe and Surkyn, 1988). Thus Van de Kaa's (1987) theory of a second demographic transition, beginning in the 1960s with the separation of sex and marriage and followed by the emergence of cohabitation, stressed the importance of the accompanying belief in the rights of the individual, especially in respect of personal and career fulfilment. But the degree to which the possible growth in individualism is also selfish and the way in which it is manifested is a matter of debate.

The economics literature has provided the most influential theoretical underpinnings for the idea of the importance of individual rational choice and has applied it to the workings of the family. Neo-classical economists have suggested that as women's capacity to support themselves has increased, so they have been less willing to put up with unsatisfactory marriages (Becker *et al.*, 1977). Gary Becker's (1981) work on a 'new home economics' argued that people marry when the utility expected from marriage is greater than it is if they remain single. Given that women desire children, they will look for a good male breadwinner. Men will look for a good housekeeper and carer. Thus men and women make complementary investments in marriage that result in higher joint gains. In fact there is nothing in Becker's model to make it particular to marriage. Indeed, it may be just as applicable to cohabiting relationships. It is the fact that the law of marriage and divorce together with public policies have historically assumed such a model to exist within marriage that has made it specific to marital relationships. Becker's model assumes that gains are shared equally between husbands and wives (ignoring the possibility of a basic tension between an egalitarian, companionate ideal and the reality of inequalities in behaviour and rewards (Barnard, (1976); Skolnick, 1991)). In Becker's analysis, women's earning power disrupts the balance in the exchange of labour between husbands and wives and causes instability. Economic bargaining models (for example, Lundberg and Pollak, 1996) do not assume that resources are shared equally. Marital investment and exchange must offer both husbands and wives more than they obtain outside the marriage. According to these theories, a rise in women's employment or an increase in their wages will threaten the stability of marriage, because it will no longer offer women unequivocal gains.

The point about these kinds of analysis is that they rely on the idea of individuals making rational choices to maximise their rewards and minimise their costs (Cheal, 1991). However, much more complicated ideas involving desert and reputation (akin to what Offer, 1996, has termed the 'economy of regard') may be involved. Finch and Mason's (1993) study of family obligations stressed that, while Becker was right in perceiving the essence of commitment to reside in the fact that at some point it becomes too expensive to withdraw, the nature of the expense is not necessarily material.

Sociologists have focused much more on mentalities and the search for personal growth and development. Norval Glenn stressed the dangers of hedonism and self-gratification. Robert Bellah *et al.*'s (1985) influential study of 'middle America' argued that the individual is realised only through the wider community and reached very similar, pessimistic conclusions to those of Glenn in regard to the family: 'if love and marriage are seen primarily in terms of psychological gratification, they may fail to fulfil their older social function of providing people with stable, committed relationships that tie them into the larger society' (p. 85). Bellah *et al.* opened their account of middle American life with a statement as to their concern that 'individualism may have grown cancerous' (p. vii). They identified two forms of individualism: first the utilitarian, which amounted to the traditional American desire to 'get ahead' and to be self-reliant; and second, the expressive, which emphasised self-expression and the sharing of feelings rather than material acquisition. In respect of the first, they argued that the values of the public sphere – 'the coolly manipulative style' (p. 48) that is required to 'get ahead' – were invading the private world of the family. In Bellah *et al.*'s view, the contractual nature of commercial and bureaucratic life threatened to become an ideology for personal life. Such an anxiety has a long history. The ideology of separate spheres, whereby the ruthless competition that was thought necessary for the successful operation of the market was balanced by the haven of the family, where women would care for the male worker and also for those too weak to engage in the public sphere, was central to late nineteenth-century social and political thought (Lewis, 1984).

In respect of expressive individualism, the 'therapeutic attitude' threatened to replace notions of obligation and commitment by an ideology of full, open and honest communication between 'self-actualising individuals'. Bellah *et al.* were particularly concerned about the way in which Maslow's (1987) idea of a hierarchy of needs, in which fulfilment of higher needs (for example, love rather than shelter) brings greater satisfaction, had been popularised by the human potential movement and non-directive counselling. Inglehart's (1997) comparative data for economically prosperous countries showed a clear shift from 'materialist' values, emphasising economic and physical security above all, to 'post-materialist' priorities, especially self-expression and the quality of life. Maslow had suggested that self-actualising people, characterised by openness, honesty and self-expression, were simultaneously individualistic and altruistic. They satisfied their needs in order to become 'higher selves', what Maslow referred to as 'healthy selfishness' (Maslow, 1954, p. 156). But critics have argued that the healthy self became the self-in-process, with a constantly shifting identity (Kilpatrick, 1975). As Taylor (1989) has pointed out, in this set of ideas self-realisation becomes the end point and meaning comes to consist only of how we feel. Yankelovich's (1981) work on US survey data confirmed the shift to more 'me-centred' concerns. From this evidence, it seemed that the 'duty to self' was becoming primary.

However, not all academic sociologists subscribing to the importance of individualism as an explanation of family change are pessimistic. Giddens (1992) also argued that late twentieth-century relationships amounted to 'pure relationships', that is, they are 'entered into for [their] own sake, for what can be derived by each person from a sustained association with another; and which is continued only in so far as it is thought by both parties to deliver enough satisfactions for each individual to stay within it' (p. 35). However, unlike Bellah *et al.*, Giddens did not consider such relationships to be inherently selfish; indeed, he believes that they have served to democratise the family. Nevertheless, they are 'contingent' and if a particular relationship does not provide one of the partners with what he or she seeks, then that partner will move on.

When it comes to polemicists and politicians, there has been a tendency to start from the dramatic statistics, and to assume that they provide a sufficient demonstration of selfish individualism at work. Love requires trust (Seligman, 1997) and it is certainly possible to suggest that the risk of trusting and investing emotionally has become greater as employment opportunities have opened up for women, and as the stigma attaching to divorce and unmarried motherhood has been eroded, making it easier for men as much as or more than for women to 'move on'. But the way in which the idea of individualism has been taken up and popularised more often rests on assertion and does not hesitate to allocate blame. The American sociologist, David Popenoe (1993, p. 528), has read off motivation from the aggregate statistics and has argued that the data show that 'people have become less willing to invest time, money and energy in family life, turning instead to investment in themselves'. David Blankenhorn (1990), founder and president of the Institute for American Values, believes, like Fukuyama, that the statistics indicate a decline in values. Much of the debate about the family in the late twentieth century has in fact been a struggle over the meaning of the statistics (Hunter, 1991), with little attempt to refer to the admittedly limited research on the changes that have actually taken place inside family relationships, or to investigate them further. However, simple assertions as to the power of selfish individualism have had a significant effect on policy making on both sides of the Atlantic. For example, in the course of the Parliamentary Debates on the 1996 Family Law Act, Baroness Young said that 'for one party simply to decide to go off with another person ... reflects the growing *self-first disease* which is debasing our society' (*House of Lords, Debates,* 29 February 1996, c. 163 8, my emphasis).

The selfish individualistic behaviour that is held to have resulted in the erosion of marriage and the traditional two-parent family is said to have manifested itself in a variety of ways. Both men and women have been blamed by politicians and polemicists. The most frequently cited cause of family change is the increase in women's employment. As Oppenheimer (1994) has pointed out, the idea that women's increased economic independence has an effect on their marital behaviour is widespread, possibly because people with very different politics can buy into it. Thus feminists have been as likely to endorse a theory that stresses the importance of women's economic independence as right-wing polemicists, but they have stressed women's right and/or need to work. From a rather different political perspective George Gilder (1987) in the US and Geoff Dench (1994) in Britain have seen the increase in women's labour force participation and attachment as something that has stripped men of their traditional breadwinning role with the family, and they blame women for pursuing self-fulfilment in the form of a career at the expense of their families. Dench (1994, pp. 16–17) argued strongly that family responsibilities are an indispensable civilising influence on men: 'If women go too far in pressing for symmetry, and in trying to change the rules of the game, men will simply decide not to play ... The family may be a myth, but it is a myth that works to make men tolerably useful.' In this interpretation, as much blame is attributed to women for undermining the traditional male role of breadwinner as to men themselves. The influential journalist Melanie Phillips (1997, 1999) has also concluded that it is the erosion of the male role that has created 'yobbish men'.

On the other hand, not since the early part of the century had as much attention also been paid to the behaviour of men in families. By the early 1990s the political debate was dominated by those who stressed the selfishness and irresponsibility of men as well as of women. Akerloff (1998) pointed out that the proportion of US men aged 25–34 in families declined from 66 to 40 per cent over the period since 1968. Either they were leaving their families or they were not joining in the first place. Feminists expressed anxiety about 'male flight from commitment' (Ehrenreich, 1983), alongside Conservative politicians railing against male irresponsibility. Michael Howard, then Home Secretary, said in a speech to the Conservative Political Centre in 1993:

> If the state will house and pay for their children the duty on [young men] to get involved may seem removed from their shoulders ... And since the State is educating, housing and feeding their children the nature of parental responsibility may seem less immediate. (Howard, 1993)

The father's duty to maintain was argued not only on the grounds of the importance of the role model it provided for children, but also in terms of fairness to the taxpayer. According to an editorial in *The Economist* (9 September 1995): 'A father who can afford to support only one family ought to have only one.'

Many commentators believe in addition that the state has exacerbated the situation by permitting and even encouraging selfish, individualistic behaviour on the part of men and women. Social policies (in Britain and the US) are also believed to have helped cause the rise in the number of lone-mother families by allowing unmarried and divorced women to draw welfare benefits (Murray, 1984; Popenoe, 1988). At the same time, tax policies are seen to have disadvantaged the two-parent, married family by eroding the married man's allowance and introducing independent taxation for husbands and wives, which in turn has provided incentives to women to enter the labour market (Morgan, 1995). Reform of family law, particularly the relaxation of the divorce laws, is also widely believed to have allowed men to behave irresponsibly (Cohen, 1987; Posner, 1992). Cohen (1987), working within a neo-classical economic framework, pointed out that investments in marriage are front-loaded for women because of child bearing. The relative decline in the value of women on the marriage market thus exposes them to the risk of the expropriation of their greater investment in marriage – their 'quasi-rents' – by their husbands. In Cohen's analysis, it was the introduction of no-fault divorce that permitted men to follow their 'natural' inclinations and behave opportunistically – typically by leaving their middle-aged wives for younger women. From a critical, feminist perspective, Estin (1995) agreed that the nature of the reform of family law was a cause of family change, but suggested that the move to no-fault divorce was directly influenced by the priority accorded by economists to exchange and bargaining models. Men and women were treated increasingly as self-interested actors, which ignored the extent to which marriage was rooted in love and obligation, sharing and sacrifice, and thus served to contribute to selfish behaviour. Treating people as if they are self-interested may indeed encourage self-interested behaviour (Le Grand, 1997).

The underlying anxiety about increasing individualism, whether expressed in the value-neutral language of the neo-classical economist, the value-conscious language of the sociologist, or in terms of the practical concerns of the politician and the polemicist, centres on its implications for the sources of moral commitments. The atomised individual is unlikely to engage fully with either family or community, which results in an 'emptying out' of these fundamental building blocks of society.

Bellah *et al.* (1985) suggested that the therapeutic attitude begins with the self rather than an external set of obligations and that love between 'therapeutically self-actualized persons' is incompatible with self-sacrifice. Agnes Heller (1979) has argued that feeling was linked to morality until the late nineteenth century; it is only as it has become 'psychologised' that it has also been separated from both morality and reason. The strong belief in the freedom of what is assumed to be the rational individual actor to choose unfettered by regulation that characterised the long period of Conservative government in the closing decades of the twentieth century also played a major part in this process of 'emptying out'. Reflecting on the politics of Thatcherism, Marilyn Strathern (1992) identified the emergence of a 'hyper-individualism'. Morality, like everything else, became a matter of individual choice and preference. Morality was to come from within, 'but the interior has itself no structure' (ibid., p. 159). As Sandel (1982) had already suggested, a person without constitutive attachments is a person wholly without character. Strathern (1992) severely questioned the effect of fetishising individual choice on the person, arguing that individuality becomes fragmented in the face of such a consumerist ideology (see also Gergen, 1991).The difficulty of exercising choice in a moral and social vacuum has become an increasingly dominant theme in the literature.

This compelling and frightening picture of a world in which there is no vision of the common good and in which rampant individualism is in the process of destroying the very foundations – the family and the community – on which the market and modern liberal democracies depend has been widely echoed. While polemicists railed against what they perceived as selfish behaviour, philosophers began to try and find ways to talk about the importance of 'social glue'. Thus Coleman (1988) used the concept of social capital as a way of challenging the rational individual action paradigm. Social capital as a set of informal values and norms permits co-operation and fosters trust (Coleman, 1988; Fukuyarna, 1999). Trust and co-operation are held to be learned in the private sphere of the family (and in civil society; Putnam, 1993) and pass from there into the public sphere of politics and the market. Feminists have long insisted upon the importance of connection and the relational self to women's moral sense (Gilligan, 1982; Held, 1993; Griffiths, 1995). The new-found attention to social capital represents a wider appreciation of the extent to which no one is an 'unencumbered self' (Sandel, 1996), and stresses interdependence and hence the obligations people have towards one another.

Thus the discussion of individualism as a cause of family change and the nature of the concern it evokes is diffuse, focusing on changing mentalities and behaviours at the individual level. Changing behaviour in the form of greater female labour market participation or male 'flight' from the family is taken as a manifestation of selfish individualism. But the meanings of such behaviour need closer scrutiny and they need to be understood in a wider context of social change that includes structures, institutions, norms and values. The point of what follows is not to attempt to come to firm conclusions regarding the key variables that might explain family change. As Gottman (1994) has observed, each variable impacts differently on the couple depending on expectations and circumstances. The argument develops an approach that explores the part played by mentalities and norms in social change. It is not intended to be definitive, but rather, to view the complex issue of family change using a different lens. Not only are there important links between mentalities and patterns of behaviour at the individual level to be considered, but these need to be located in regard to changes in norms and values, and in structures and institutions at the collective level.

THE EMBEDDED INDIVIDUAL

At the micro-level of the family, marriage in the twentieth century certainly appeared to be an individual choice. Yet as Regan (1999, p. viii) has observed, it also 'generates connection whose significance is not fully captured by the idea of consent'. In Regan's analysis, the neo-classical economist's view of marriage fails to take account of this sense of connection in the form of attachment to, identification with and commitment to care for others that is also highlighted in feminist writing on the family (Gilligan, 1982; Held, 1993; Griffiths, 1995). The notion of connection makes marriage a community with associated obligations. The literature on marriage has always exhibited considerable confusion as to how to characterise the nature of the marital relationship, whether in terms of two individuals who enter into a contract, or as a status, or as a sacrament. Late twentieth-century socio-legal literature in particular has been divided on how far to treat marriage as a contract pure and simple.

Do intimate relationships consist merely of two independent individuals who agree to an association for whatever reason, or does the sum of the relationship amount to more than its parts, and if so, is this more true of marriage than cohabitation? Intimate relationships are socially embedded. In the first place, intimate association results in more than just the satisfaction of the interests of the individual. After all, divorce would not be so painful if there were no sense of connection and attachment. Furthermore, expectations of intimate relationships in respect of both the individual and 'the relationship' are embedded in wider social structures. Changes in these may affect the balance between the concern for self and other and are likely to provide the context for understanding both decision making and tensions in family life. This book pays particular attention to two of the issues that have been most discussed as being part and parcel of family change: changes in the gendered divisions of labour, and in the law governing marriage and divorce, both of which historically helped to enforce traditional ideas about the role of men and women in marriage.

In the main, the argument that we are seeing increasingly selfish individualism on the part of adult family members has been deduced from the statistics on family change and associated with particular behaviours, in particular, the growth in women's employment, aided and abetted by legal change. There have certainly been major shifts in thinking and behaviour at the individual level and in law, but it is very difficult to understand the reasons for them and the nature of the causal relationships. Increased female employment, for example, affects not just women's own choices but the whole balance of activity in the family. The male breadwinner model family not only described a dominant pattern of behaviour, but also provided an accepted framework for marriage. As much critical feminist analysis has pointed out, the unwritten 'marriage contract' (enforced only at the point of breakdown) relied on the gender-specific roles that were assumed by the model. Changes in women's economic behaviour are therefore likely to carry implications for what has been a major prescriptive framework in respect of marriage and the family, but how and with what effects has not been explored. Similarly in the case of legal change, the strict external moral code that encompassed traditional gendered patterns of behaviour in the family and underpinned family law has been eroded. This pattern of change has been complicated in terms of cause and effect in relation not just to behaviour, but, again, normative prescription. Law has an expressive function (Sunstein, 1997) and cultural as well as behavioural consequences (Pildes, 1991). Again, these aspects of change need to be explored: legal reform may be a response to changes in normative expectations as well as behavioural change, and may seek to consolidate or modify social norms as well as to recognise changes in behaviour.

The Erosion of the Male Breadwinner Model

The traditional male breadwinner model family has described, with varying degrees of accuracy, gendered patterns of paid and unpaid work between men and women at the micro-level of the family during the twentieth century. It has also been as or more important in prescribing the normative expectations of men and women in families as to how their affairs should be arranged, probably for a majority of couples for the first three-quarters of the century. Its erosion is fundamental to understanding family change, but it is nevertheless very difficult to interpret.

Whether academic or popular, the literature drawing attention to increased individualism focuses on individual actors, in terms of their behaviour and/or mentalities, and in particular to the importance of women's increasing labour market participation. However, the meanings of these are not always what they seem. For instance, Giddens (1992) has argued, albeit without empirical investigation, that individualism renders personal relationships more democratic, which is as plausible as the idea of individualism as a corrosive influence. In their economic analysis of divorce, Becker *et al.* (1977) took the fact that the majority of petitioners for divorce are female as evidence of women's growing economic independence and autonomy. However, there are many other explanations for the numbers of female petitioners. Men tend to react to breakdown with violence or by walking out of the relationship, leaving women to seek divorce (Phillips, 1988). As the economically weaker partner, women usually need to try to get the financial arrangements settled (Smart, 1982; Maclean, 1991). In other words, the meaning of petitioning for divorce cannot be assumed. It may be that their increased participation in the labour market has only an indirect effect on women's marital behaviour. Cherlin (1981) argued that women's increased labour market participation had not caused an increase in divorce, but rather had facilitated it. Similarly, de Singly (1996) suggested that it is not women's employment *per se* that is responsible for their greater readiness to consider divorce, but rather the awareness it creates of tensions with the marriage. This indicates the importance of considering the complex interplay between mentalities and behaviour at the level of the family, but it is also important to locate decision making at the micro-level in the wider context of structural and normative change.

The concept of 'individualisation' endeavours to locate the choices made by individuals. It refers to the way in which people's lives come to be less constrained by tradition and customs and more subject to individual choice, which in turn can only be understood against the background of changes in the labour market and in social provision by the modern welfare state in particular (Beck and Beck Gernsheim, 1995; Kohli, 1986; Buchmann, 1989). Elizabeth Beck Gernsheim (1999, p. 54) has described the effects of individualisation on the family in terms of 'a community of need' becoming 'an elective relationship'. Elias (1991, p. 204) expressed a similar idea in the following:

> The greater impermanence of we-relationships, which at earlier stages often had the lifelong inescapable character of an external constraint, puts all the more emphasis on the I, one's own person, as the only permanent factor, the only person with whom one must live one's whole life.

The family used to be a community of need held together by the obligations of solidarity. But women's increased labour market participation has resulted in a new division between biography and family. Burns and Scott (1994) have made a similar point in their discussion of the way in which male and female roles in the family have become 'decomplementary'. In essence, it is difficult to mesh the labour market biographies of two adults with family life. Individualisation thus pulls men and women apart (although Beck and Beck Gernsheim, 1995, argue that they are also pushed together again in new relationships, because as traditions become diluted, so the attractions of a close relationship grow).

This kind of analysis is broad-brush. But it does highlight the importance of the effects of the decline of the traditional male breadwinner model family – which has been underpinned by both increased female labour market participation and the safety net provided by the welfare state – on intimate relationships. However, it is hard to generalise about any part of the developments described by Beck and Beck Gernsheim, while the assumptions made by those who assume that female labour market participation has resulted in female economic independence are suspect. In the UK, variations on the theme of a 'one-and-a-half-breadwinner model' have emerged, whereby women work part-time (often for very few hours) and use a variety of child-care arrange-

ments involving husbands and other kin at the informal level, as well as publicly
and privately provided services.

The issue is what these patterns mean in terms of what they signal about the
priorities of the men and women involved and their impact on the stability of
the family. Given the degree to which women continue to be economically
dependent on men, it is unlikely that all partnered women with children who
are in the workforce are motivated by self-development and self-interest. Indeed,
Catherine Hakim (1996) has suggested that there are two populations of women
workers: a minority who want a full-time career and a majority who continue
to put home and family first. However, in the British context it is likely that
structural constraints in the form of lack of child-care also play a prominent
part in explaining female labour market behaviour (Joshi and Davies, 1992).

Nevertheless, a majority of women may be responding primarily to the
dictates of the family economy and supplementing it to whatever extent is
deemed necessary. This is one of the oldest established determinants of
women's paid employment (Tilly and Scott, 1975), and may point more to the
economic *inter*dependence of family members than to autonomy and independence.

Simple calculations at the individual level of economic self-interest are
unlikely to be sufficient explanations. As a result of their examination of the
position of British lone mothers, whose labour market participation declined
in the 1980s, Duncan and Edwards (1999) have suggested that women do not
abide solely by the dictates of economic rationality in making decisions about
marriage, divorce, motherhood and employment. If we take the question: are
women who work full time and earn a reasonable wage more or less likely to
marry and/or divorce? part of the answer will lie in the domain of economic
behaviour outside the family, but part will also depend on gendered divisions
inside the household, where the key factor may be the woman's priorities and
preferences, or the man's selfishness, irresponsibility or mere inflexibility. Arlie
Hochschild's (1990) interview data have documented the way in which women
have experienced difficulty in dealing with the 'double shift' that has resulted
from the fact that, while they have increased their labour market participation,
men have not significantly increased their contribution to unpaid work. Ferri
and Smith's (1996) survey data have shown the extent to which British men
are content with such a pattern and women are not.

It may be, as Oppenheimer (1994) argued, that with the decline of the male
breadwinner model the whole meaning of marriage and partnership has changed.
Given that two incomes are now necessary to meet household expenditure (particularly mortgages), career women may be more marriageable and may help
to secure family stability rather than jeopardise it, *pace* Becker (Oppenheimer
and Lew, 1995). Oppenheimer (1994) has suggested that instead of positing
the old specialisation of men as breadwinners and women as housewives and

carers, relationships are now based on the ability of each partner to make a contribution, unique or similar, and to pull his or her weight. If this constitutes a new set of assumptions about behaviour in intimate relationships, then again women's employment will not necessarily pose a threat, although male selfishness and/or inflexibility may well do so. Indeed, it is possible that women's employment may affect fertility rates more than divorce rates.

But in respect of understanding the causes of change in marriage and the family, the point is that it is not enough to consider individual choices (which may or may not be driven by selfish individualism) even when they are located in their structural context, as Beck and Beck Gernsheim strive to do. It is also necessary to pay attention to assumptions as to what is considered to be appropriate behaviour. Value systems (shared goals) and norms (shared goals specifying functions, that is, rules regarding the 'ought' supported by sanctions[2]) are a crucial part of the context of the individual actor. They are part of both cause and effect in respect of increasing individualism. The erosion of what I have called the normative prescriptions which accompanied the established, traditional economic and legal frameworks that dominated marriage and family life for the first three quarters of the twentieth century, in the form of the male breadwinner model and the imposition of an external moral code, has left a vacuum.

Oppenheim Mason and Jensen (1995) have drawn attention to the way in which the micro-theory of the neo-classical economists does not recognise or allow for collectively generated or agreed upon norms and sanctions. Thus culture often remains absent from, or peripheral to, explanation. For example, while Fukuyama (1999) acknowledged the importance of culture, arguing that it allowed Japan and Korea to stave off 'the great disruption', he could see no means of explaining why 'attitudes' in western countries should have begun to change rapidly in the 1960s unless they were driven by something else. He preferred therefore to explain family change in terms of social and economic variables: namely, the increased use of artificial birth control and women's greater labour market participation. These in turn changed the norms that constrained men's behaviour and allowed them to behave more irresponsibly. Thus, Fukuyama's explanation prioritised social and economic behaviour; attitudes and norms played a secondary part in the story. He may well be correct, but his relegation of cultural factors to second place meant that, as is commonly the case, little attention was paid to the precise way in which they worked.

It is noteworthy that those who successfully demolished the argument that state welfare benefits had 'caused' lone motherhood concluded at the end of empirical work that considered only quantifiable variables and found them wanting, that 'our hunch is that the real force behind family change has been a profound change in people's attitudes about marriage and children' (Bane and Jargowsky, 1988, p. 246). Inglehart (1997) has argued that while major divorce law reform happened suddenly in most western countries (at the end of the 1960s and during the 1970s), it followed a long process of attitudinal change. However, Oppenheimer (1994) has pointed out that American panel data show that women's changing attitudes towards divorce between 1962 and 1977 had no significant effect on whether their marriages broke down. Rather, the strongest determinant of attitudinal change was whether a woman experienced divorce or separation in that period. It is no more easy to trace a causal relationship between changes in attitudes and individual marital behaviour than between the latter and women's increasing capacity for a measure of economic independence. Sociologists are divided, for example, on whether increased female employment is linked to more egalitarian gender role attitudes (Haller and Hellinger, 1994; Alwin, Braun and Scott, 1992).

Furthermore, the relationship between attitudes and values is far from simple, just as in the case of the relationship between behaviour and attitudinal change. Van Deth and Scarborough (1995) argue that attitudes are empirically measurable whereas values are not. Indeed, value systems may stay the same while behavioural norms change. Thus people may continue to believe in the importance of traditional family life, and possibly express attitudes in keeping with this, and yet divorce (Scanzoni *et al.*, 1989). Norms in respect of family behaviour have undoubtedly changed; the stigma attaching to divorce and unmarried motherhood has eroded in the post-war period, slowly at first and rapidly from the late 1960s. Rules regarding the order in which people have sex, have children and marry are no longer firm and there are few informal sanctions (formal sanctions in the form of law do exist; for example, cohabiting fathers do not have the same rights in respect of their children as married fathers, but people are often blithely unaware of such distinctions). Nevertheless the vast majority of people still say that they value family life (Scott, 1997).

A major divide in the literature is between those who see culture as integral to explanation and those who view it as exogenous. Rational choice theorists such as Jon Elster (1991) may acknowledge the existence of norms, but use them only as a residual form of explanation, to be invoked to explain the awkward bits that are left when the rational choice analysis is completed. Sophisticated economic approaches, such as that using the idea of the 'convention', interpreted by Sugden (1998a, p. 454) in terms of tacit agreements or common understandings giving rise to shared expectations, acknowledge the importance of the cultural variable, but stop short at the idea that norms are internalised. Sugden has argued that conventional practices can generate normative expectations, which may in turn be significant for the stability of conventions. Others insist that norms and values are embedded in society and are part of the framework within which choices are made. Norms by definition are not chosen, and a decision to abide by them may be made consciously or seemingly without any conscious interrogation of alternatives.[3] Thus Sunstein (1997) has insisted that individual choices are a function of norms, meanings and roles, and that individuals may therefore have little control over them. Puzzles of rationality, he argues, are the product of social norms and moral judgements.

Processes such as individualisation are linked to norm-change. The male breadwinner model did not merely describe a pattern of economic activity in the family. Because it was internalised by a majority, certainly in the immediate post-war years, it also conditioned expectations within marriage. The decline of the model in respect of the changing labour market behaviour of women might be expected at some point to have been accompanied by a shift in normative expectations on the part of people and legislators, which may turn out to be more radical than the actual change in behaviour. As Lessig (1996, p. 285) has observed, when norm violation increases, then the meaning of obeying the norm also changes and at some point 'obeying the norm makes one a "chump"'. Stacey (1990) commented that young working-class men in late twentieth-century America were not sure whether to regard one of their number who becomes a breadwinner as a hero or a chump. This is in large measure because normative meanings and expectations are far from clear. The norm may now be that women will engage in paid work. Attitudinal surveys have shown consistent increases in the acceptance by men and women of female employment. But to what *extent* – full-time or some form of part-time – is not entirely clear. Nor is it clear what the accompanying assumptions are in respect of unpaid work. Beck and Beck Gernsheim (1995) have suggested that it is no longer possible to know what marriage and family life mean. The norm is no longer unambiguous, and this opens up a space for negotiation.

This is where the importance of the link between changing structures and norms at the collective level and changing mentalities and behaviour at the individual level begins to become apparent. In regard to the increase in women's employment, which has been identified by so many as important in explaining family change, the mechanisms by which this happens are hard to elucidate. In all probability there are many, but one promising line of inquiry would seem to involve the way in which the increase in women's labour market participation helps to effect a shift in the male breadwinner model, which in turn shakes the whole fabric of gender roles that have been widely assumed – by government and by people – to flow from it. Lesthaeghe (1995) referred to the importance of the erosion of normative prescription when he stressed the significance of the emergence of a sense of individual autonomy, which in his view had nothing to do with egocentric behaviour, but meant only that the individual no longer takes externally supplied norms and morality for granted, relying instead on his or her own judgement. At some point, the gap between practices and the normative expectations flowing from the male breadwinner model becomes too great. The rupture gives rise to a new set of normative expectations. Thus, female employment is expected, although to what degree is unclear. Nevertheless, expectations may actually run ahead of behavioural change, aided and abetted by changes in social policies. Thus at the end of 1990s, the British government swung towards treating all women, including lone mothers, as paid workers for the purposes of the social security system, regardless of the fact that a majority of mothers work only part-time.

It is possible to suggest that late twentieth-century marriages, based on romantic love and increasingly bereft of the prescriptions that accompanied major normative frameworks, such as the male breadwinner model family, became not just more fluid in the sense of movement in and out of them, but also more open to negotiation in terms of their organisation. As part of a theoretical model for comparative gender research, Pfau-Effinger (1998) has suggested that negotiation takes place when a gap opens up between the gender culture (in the form of norms) and the gender order (that is inscribed, for example, in social policies and labour markets). It may be, as so many insist, that behaviour has driven social change in respect of the erosion of the male breadwinner model, but it is in all probability the change in 'normative expectations' that has opened up the space for negotiation. Once normative expectations change, they will cease to reinforce the behavioural dimensions of the male breadwinner model. But negotiating the gap that results is not easy and at the level of the couple breakdown may occur. At the level of policy making, new problems arise when governments begin to make assumptions based on a more egalitarian set of normative expectations about women's paid work that may be almost as out of touch with the social reality as the old assumptions that adult women were housewife/carers in the male breadwinner model family.

The Erosion of an Externally Imposed Moral Code

Defenders of a strict law of marriage and divorce have usually regarded it as a means of stopping people from exercising their individual preferences regarding the formation of intimate relationships and thus threatening family stability. But how far family law could be used to uphold the discipline and order of marriage became an increasingly contested issue, first in the 1920s and again in the 1960s. The relaxation of the divorce law followed (in 1937 and 1969), but even at the end of the century, neither cohabiting nor married people were fully individualised in the eyes of the law.

Changes in family law, which has historically been based on an externally imposed moral code, have been identified alongside changing labour market behaviour as being particularly significant for understanding family change. Irène Thèry (1994), a French sociologist, has captured the nature of the relationship between change at the individual level and legal change in a rather different way, using the idea of 'demarriage', by which she means the disengagement of the institution of marriage from other social structures, such as the law. This idea has some parallels with Beck and Beck Gernsheim's concept of individualisation and gives meaning to the oft-cited idea among sociologists of marriage moving from institution to relationship (proposed first by Burgess and Locke, 1953). Marriage obviously remains an institution, but it is important to realise the extent to which it has broken free of major prescriptive frameworks and in that sense has become more of a private relationship.[4] The process of 'demarriage' does not necessarily affect the number of people who choose to marry, but makes it easier for people to move in and out of marriage. Whereas the vast majority of people's lives only a generation ago looked rather simple in terms of family patterns – marriage followed courtship and death ended marriage – today the patterns are increasingly complicated. The vast majority cohabit before marriage and one in three divorce. These may go on to cohabit again and/or marry and possibly divorce again. Marriage has become a discretionary adult role (Bumpass, 1990), whereas it used to be compulsory if certain other things were to be achieved: a home of one's own and children.

Again, it is questionable whether the effect of legal reform on family change, that is, on behaviour, has been direct. Dror (1959) concluded that legal changes had more direct impact on emotionally neutral and instrumental areas of human activity than on expressive and evaluative arenas such as the family. In respect of divorce in particular, Rheinstein's (1972) comparative socio-legal study argued that marital breakdown could be high, even in the absence of divorce. Similarly in his comparative historical study of divorce, Phillips (1988) insisted that levels of marital breakdown have not been dependent on legal change. However, Rheinstein called attention to the importance of what he called the 'cultural climate', arguing that the incidence of breakdown increased in times of accelerating social change 'with the unsettling tendencies towards anomie' (p. 311), thus making the connection between marital behaviour, the socio-economic context and mentalities. It is also likely in the case of family law that legal change not only contributed to a shift in behaviour but was also related to a shift in normative expectations. Weitzman (1985) suggested that when the rules were changed regarding what was expected of husbands and wives on divorce, so this also changed norms in respect of marriage. Like social policies in respect of cash benefit entitlements, it is likely that family law facilitates rather than causes behavioural change at the individual level, but, because it has historically been underpinned by an external regulatory moral framework, relaxation of divorce law may serve to legitimate changes in behaviour. Phillips (1988, p. 617) concluded that 'it seems probable that divorce does breed divorce', because it becomes part of the cultural climate within which marriages exist and hence the stigma once associated with it disappears.

Hirshleifer (1998, p. 301) has pointed out that a social convention, such as the idea that cohabitation should occur only after marriage, may change partly as a result of conspicuous violations by individuals. At a different level again, if the parents of a cohabiting couple fail to impose sanctions, then other parents may conclude that this is the way that they too will respond. However, it is possible that prior impetus to breaking the expected and accepted pattern of behaviour in regard to cohabitation may have come from public debate and opinion-formers. At some point, possibly before, but more likely after major behavioural change of this kind, official sanction may be given in whole or in part by legal reform. But the relationship between law and social norms is also complicated. The state may impose law from the top down or endeavour to enforce social norms from the bottom up (Cooter, 1997); it may serve to strengthen or weaken norms (Posner, 1996); or it may transform them (Lessig, 1998). The nature of the law is part of the socialisation process and one of the means by which norms are internalised (Dau Schmidt, 1997). The state plays a major role in securing the stability of norms (by imposing legal sanctions) and may also either respond to a behavioural change that instigates norm change or itself act as an instigator by enacting legal reform that actually runs somewhat ahead of behavioural change. For example, divorce law reform in Britain in 1984 adopted the 'clean break' approach, which treated men and women as if they were fully individualised and economically independent when for the most part they were not.

As in the case of the erosion of the male breadwinner model, it seems that more attention should be directed towards the importance of cultural changes. These worked out rather differently in the case of family law, where radical changes in thinking on the part of elite opinion about the desirability and possibility of imposing a strict external moral code played a major part in securing the reform of the strict moral code embodied in the law. But it may be argued again that the erosion of this form of prescription opened up a space for negotiation at the individual level, particularly in respect of whether to marry.

Legal reform that resulted in the progressive relaxation of the divorce laws in particular has been widely characterised as part of a process of 'deregulat-ing' family law. Glendon's (1981) thesis on deregulation has been most influential. She argued that while 'the legal ties among family members are becoming loosened, the web of relationships that bind an individual to his job (and his job to him) is becoming tighter and more highly structured' (p. 1). This analysis of deregulation in the private sphere and more regulation in the public world of work and welfare did not look so convincing by the 1990s, by which time the restructuring of welfare states had moved significantly towards emphasising personal responsibility, while labour markets had become more 'flexible', with more short-term contracts and part-time hours. Indeed, reform in the field of family law was accompanied during the last two decades of the twentieth century by increased uncertainty in the public world of work and welfare. In fact, the idea of deregulation did not quite serve to capture the nature of legal change. The process of liberalisation that began in Britain with the major reform of the divorce law in 1969 has increasingly allowed men and women as husbands and wives to order their own affairs, rather than imposing a strict moral code from above. Thus, family law has effectively assumed the existence of a degree of individualisation. However, it has also put in place measures (such as the 1991 Child Support Act) to regulate men and women as fathers and mothers. Thus during the last part of the twentieth century the prescriptions of an external moral code embodied in family law and designed to operate in concert with the assumptions underpinning the male breadwinner model have been eroded at the same time as economic conditions have undergone major change, again affecting normative expectations regarding employment and the life course for women and men. Family matters have increasingly been left to individual adults, but, at the same time, family law has tried to enforce individual responsibility, which often continues to be defined in traditionally gendered ways.

Habermas's (1996) volume on the theory of law and democracy captures what happens when an established moral code ceases to exist and morality is assumed to come from within: 'under the moral view point of equal respect for each person and equal consideration for the interests of all, the henceforth sharply focused normative claims of legitimately regulated interpersonal relations are sucked into a whirlpool of problematisation' (p. 97). Societal pluralisation and fragmentation mean that it is difficult to agree on an external moral code. But this does not mean that the vacuum was necessarily filled by simple deregulation. Rather, it may be argued that the increasingly popular view that morality should come from within was accompanied by a shift in the nature of regulation: from judging the affairs of the couple according to pre-set criteria, to making sure that the couple takes responsibility for sorting out their own affairs.

Many of those convinced as to the importance of the growth of individualism have tended in the main to read it off from the dramatic changes in the statistics recording family change, and then to link it either to changes in individual behaviour, such as women's increased attachment to the labour market, or to changes in mentalities, such as prioritising personal growth. These studies do not in the main investigate what is actually going on inside personal relationships, even though they are preoccupied with change at the individual level. In addition, change at the individual level will necessarily be affected by what is going on outside the family, for example in the labour market or family law. However, the relationship may not be direct, but may rather be mediated by changes in normative expectations about behaviour, particularly in respect of the nature of the division of labour and the sexual moral code.

It is not the project of this book systematically to review, eliminate and order all the possible variables feeding the idea of 'increasing individualism' as a cause of marriage and family change. Rather, it will seek to examine change in some of the key factors, focusing on the erosion of normative prescriptions emanating from the male breadwinner model and from family law, and on the changes that have taken place inside the relationships of married and cohabiting people, particularly in respect of the division of labour, using both contemporary studies and interview data. Section II of the book pursues the development of the idea of the male breadwinner model and how this, together with the external moral code which was embodied in family law and which served to underpin the gendered nature of obligations associated with the traditional family, have been eroded. It focuses in particular on the mediating effects of changes in prescriptive frameworks and their relationship to law and behaviour. The charting of the debates about marriage and the family serves the further purpose of putting the current anxieties about the growth of individualism into historical perspective. Section III reports the results of a qualitative study of the relationships of married and cohabiting couples with children, and of their parents, which investigated the meaning of obligation and commitment and asked whether cohabitants were more individualistic than married people and whether the younger couples were more individualistic than their parents. The research reported in this section demonstrates how the erosion of prescriptive frameworks has been experienced. As we have seen, the meaning of behaviour labelled individualist may actually be very different when it is contextualised and certainly calls into question the idea that individualism is necessarily selfish. Commitment at turn of the twenty-first century may take different forms, but this does not necessarily pose problems for public policy.

The final chapter of the book addresses the vexed issue of what might be done. Galston (1991) has argued that the liberal state must promote what it believes in: its own concept of the human good, which includes attention to moral issues. When traditional forms of prescription are eroded, it is not surprising that governments begin to talk more openly of morality, but they face the problem that in a pluralist society no one view of what constitutes moral standards will hold. Nevertheless, there is still a strong idea that the state should play a role in setting standards of behaviour. Mead (1997) has identified a more general trend in social politics towards a 'new paternalism', which, for example, proposes to enforce responsibilities and to force people drawing state benefits to take up opportunities, especially in relation to employment. However, it is also possible to argue for more non-intrusive state support for the family, or even for families. Both approaches could be found in British family law and policy in the late 1990s. Some have argued that the market mechanism of contract might be extended to what is perceived as the new individualistic world of the family, for example, through pre-marital and cohabitation contracts (Posner, 1992). However, this has met with considerable suspicion, chiefly on the ground that it would further erode trust (Anderson, 1993), which is an argument that stems in part from a conviction that the private world of the family risks contamination by the public sphere. However, there are many other reasons to question whether the morality of contract is appropriate, not least in regard to the inequalities between the parties to it (Baier, 1986). Many of the communitarians, such as Bellah, who were among the first to raise the alarm about selfish individualism, have expressed suspicion of both an overly attentive state and an unregulated market (Wolfe, 1989; Elshtain, 1995). Thus, Fukuyama (1999) has argued that only a spontaneous regeneration of norms regarding the importance of the traditional two-parent family will do. There is little agreement even on how to begin to address the issue of marriage and family change, or the roles, possibilities and limitations of family law and family policy.

Behind the charge of selfish individualism is the fear that obligations and commitment of adult men and women to each other, and of both to children, have been eroded. There are (empirical) straws in the wind to suggest that this may be too pessimistic a judgement. Cancian's (1987) study of love in America stressed the extent to which individualism was not necessarily antithetical to feelings of responsibility for the welfare of others. Many of the couples in her sample stressed the value of interdependence in the context of greater individualisation. Pahl (1996) has emphasised the importance of distinguishing between individualism and individuality, which carries no taint of selfishness. Interdependent people can value personal growth, individuality, equality and morality that comes from within rather than one that is imposed from without, and yet still feel commitment to one another. Such commitment is not socially prescribed and is in that sense individualistic, although not, as Lesthaeghe (1995) has remarked, necessarily egocentric. The process of individualisation and the erosion of prescriptive frameworks inevitably leave something of a vacuum in the sense that there is no longer a widely accepted 'ought'.

It is in this context that the relational aspects of marriage have come more to the fore, as the working out of intimate relationships has become a more private matter in the first instance. Thèry (1998) has suggested that the meaning of 'the couple', whether married or cohabiting, has changed from '2 makes 1' – the classical idea of marital unity – to '1 + 1 makes 2'. Changes in women's status have certainly been a prerequisite for this change; if not equals, both parties to a relationship are now people to be reckoned with. Both adults expect a 'say'. Indeed, negotiation of the moral and economic aspects of marriage has increasingly been pushed down to the level of the individual couple rather than being prescribed as part of the 'institution' of marriage. But this does not necessarily mean that people will behave selfishly. Academics from a variety of disciplines and political positions have found evidence that people do employ 'moral sense' (Wilson, 1993) and take the issue of their obligations to others seriously (Finch and Mason, 1993; Smart and Neale, 1999). Bauman (1993, 1995) has argued that deregulation and the removal of rules has not meant that people have abandoned responsibility for making ethical choices, just as Karst (1980) found that intimate relationships generate moral obligations even when law does not enforce them. Thus, just because divorce has become easier, it does not mean that moral debate and personal responsibility have been eliminated. Indeed, one of the most suggestive trends in recent empirical work has been the idea that while at the demographic level families and family building are becoming ever more diverse, there is convergence in terms of the negotiated nature of commitment and responsibility (Weeks *et al.*, 1999). This is, on the whole an optimistic picture of change, which the research reported in Section III of this book tends to support. The final section of the book argues that this finding has important implications for family law and family policy, and a particularly important message for those who seek to use the law to put the clock back.

NOTES

1. 1 am grateful to Kathleen Kiernan (personal communication).
2. The definition of norms is recognised to be elusive and varies between the disciplines. Fiske (1992) differentiates further between norms, which prescribe functions and constitute external constraints, and moral standards, which insist on a particular goal as an 'ought'. Cooter (1997), Ellickson, R.C. (1998) and Posner (1996) provide useful reviews from the socio-legal perspective. Of particular importance for this study is the controversy over how far norms are internalised. I believe that they are and that is what explains the prescriptive power of something like the male breadwinner model (see pp. 45–71).
3. The process by which this occurs is complicated; see, for example, Suchman (1997).
4. Laslett (1973) defined privacy in terms of structural mechanisms that prohibit or permit observ-ability in the enactment of family roles. My analysis of the erosion of prescriptive frameworks may be seen as a development of this early work, but Laslett's accompanying idea that as family privacy increased, so 'social control' in the form of legal regulation would decline has not proved to be the case (see p. 24 in this chapter and Chapter 5).

2. Changing patterns: the decline of marriage and the rise of cohabitation

Marriage has been part of the typical experience for adults throughout the twentieth century. During the first half of the century the proportion of women who were or who had been married never fell below 60 per cent, and reached 75 per cent in 1951 and 79.4 per cent in 1971. However, since then the percentage has fallen back again to 1950s levels. The story looks more striking still when told in terms of first marriage rates (Table 2.1). Since the mid-1980s these have fallen precipitously and are now considerably lower than at the beginning of the century. The number of first marriages in the mid-1990s was the lowest recorded this century, despite a much larger population (Haskey, 1995), and the mean age at first marriage for men and for women was at its highest.

During the early part of the century, marriage conferred a higher status on women than spinsterhood. In common parlance, a woman 'failed' to get married. This was particularly the case before the First World War, but marriage remained the normative expectation of women in all social classes. At the end of the century, marriage is still an important event, indeed the amount spent on the average wedding has increased substantially to an average of just over £10 500 in 2000. However, getting married is no longer a matter of urgency. For middle-class women, especially in the period before the First World War, marriage was virtually their only means of financial support because few occupations were open to them. Spinsters faced an often lonely and marginal life in their parents' home or in the households of male relatives. Cicely Hamilton, a leading feminist, wrote bitterly in 1909 of marriage as 'a trade' for women. Working-class women were employed in large numbers, but few commanded wages much above subsistence levels. Marriage has become more of an option in terms of material survival and status, while living alone or cohabiting no longer stigmatises those involved.

Divorce and births outside marriage were relatively rare until the last 30 years of the century. Prior to 1914, divorce was largely confined to the middle and upper classes. Changes in the aid given to poor petitioners in 1914, together with the disruptive effects of the First World War, produced an increase in the divorce rate after 1918, but it was not until 1946 that legal aid became freely available and therefore not until 1951 that divorce petitions began to come from

Table 2.1   First marriages by age and sex, England and Wales, 1901–97

Year	All ages		Mean age
	Thousands	Rate[a]	
Men			
1901	233.9	59.6[b]	26.7
1911	251.7	61.8[b]	27.4
1921	290.6	63.5[b]	27.5
1931	285.5	59.7	27.3
1941	357.1	78.3	26.9
1951	313.5	76.2	26.7
1961	308.8	74.9	25.6
1971	343.6	82.3	24.6
1981	259.1	51.7	25.4
1985	253.3	46.6	26.0
1991	222.8	37.0	27.5
1995	198.5	31.8	28.9
1997	188.3	28.4	29.5
Women			
1901	240.6	57.4[b]	25.3
1911	257.5	58.7[b]	25.8
1921	290.4	55.2[b]	25.5
1931	294.1	54.7	25.4
1941	365.0	74.5	24.6
1951	319.2	76.3	24.4
1961	312.2	83.0	23.1
1971	347.4	97.9	22.6
1981	263.4	64.0	23.1
1985	258.1	58.2	23.8
1991	224.8	46.0[b]	25.5
1995	198.5	40.1	26.9
1997	188.5	35.6	27.5

Notes:
[a] Per 1000 single persons aged 16 and over.
[b] Quinquennia rates 1901–05, 1911–15, 1921–25

Sources: OPCS, *Marriage and Divorce Statistics: Historical Series 1837–1983*, FM2 No. 16 (London: HMSO, 1995) Tables 3.2a and b, 3.5a and b, 3.7a and 3.7b; ONS, *Population, Trends 88* (Summer 1997) (London: Office of National Statistics, © Crown Copyright 1995) Table 23; ONS, *Marriage, Divorce and Adoption Statistics 1987–1997*, FM2, no. 25 (London: Office of National Statistics, © Crown Copyright 1999) Tables 3.7, 3.8 and 3.15.

a cross-section of the population (Rowntree and Carrier, 1958). Prior to the Second World War, working-class couples made use of judicial separation machinery rather than divorce, but the number of informal separations was undoubtedly much larger than the number that came to court (MacGregor, O.R, *et al.*, 1970; Stone, 1990; Phillips, 1988). Table 2.2 shows that the divorce rate began to climb significantly in the late 1960s and trebled during the 1970s. It climbed slightly again in the early 1980s, and has remained high and stable since, falling back slightly in 1997. The extra-marital birth rate increased dramatically during the Second World War, but was due mainly to marriages that were planned not taking place due to conscription, wartime disruption and death. Table 2.3 shows that while there was a significant rise again in the 1960s, the dramatic increase has taken place since 1985. The high rate of teenage births in the UK, most of which take place outside marriage, plays a large role in keeping the total fertility rate well above the European average (Coleman and Chandola, 1999).

Table 2.2   Divorce rate per 1000 married population, England and Wales, 1950–97

1950	2.8
1960	2.0
1965	3.1
1970	4.7
1975	9.6
1980	12.0
1985	13.4
1990	13.0
1995	13.6
1996	13.8
1997	13.0

Sources: OPCS, *Marriage and Divorce Statistics 1837–1983 Historical Series*, FM2 no. 16, (London: HMSO 1995) Table 5.2; *Marriage and Divorce Statistics 1837–1983*, FM2 no. 21 (London: HMSO 1995) Table 2.1; ONS *Marriage, Divorce and Adoption Statistics 1997*, FM2 no. 23 (London: Office of National Statistics, © Crown Copyright 1999) Table 2.2.

Many recent commentators have located the beginnings of the striking change in family structure in the 'permissive' 1960s. However, the story is more complicated than this. There is evidence that sexual activity among the young increased during the 1960s and that the growing use of the contraceptive pill from the beginning of the 1970s strengthened this trend (Black and Sykes, 1971; Bone, 1986; Moore and Burt, 1982; Schofield, 1968; Farrell, 1978). Thus sex was increasingly separated from marriage and increased sexual activity resulted in a rise in both the extra-marital and marital birth rates (Table 2.3). This contrasts both with the war years, when the extra-marital birth rate rose faster than the marital rate, and with the last decade when the extra-marital rate has risen and the marital rate has fallen. In the 1960s there was still a tendency for pregnant women to marry. A majority of births to women younger than 20 years old were conceived outside marriage in the 1960s, but the majority of pre-maritally conceived births took place inside marriage. In 1969, 55 per cent of extra-marital conceptions were legitimised by marriage, 32 per cent resulted in 'illegitimate' births and 14 per cent were aborted (the Abortion Act was passed in 1967) (Lewis and Kiernan, 1996).

Table 2.3   Marital and extra-marital births per 1000 women aged 15–44, England and Wales, 1940–98

	Marital birth rate per 1000 married women	Extra-marital birth rate per 1000 single, divorced and widowed women
1950	108.6	10.2
1955	103.7	10.3
1960	120.8	14.7
1965	126.9	21.2
1970	113.5	21.5
1975	85.5	17.4
1980	92.2	19.6
1985	87.8	26.7
1990	86.7	38.9
1995	83.3	39.4
1998	82.3	40.3

Sources: Office of Population Censuses and Surveys (OPCS), *Birth Statistics: Historical Series 1837–1983*, Series FM1 no. 13 (London: HMSO), 1987) Table 3.2b and c; OPCS, *Birth Statistics: Historical Series 1837–1983*, Series FM1 no. 22 (London: HMSO, 1995) Table 3.1; ONS, *Birth Statistics 1998*, Series FM1 no. 27 (London: Office of National Statistics, © Crown Copyright 1999) Table 3.1b.

It is perhaps therefore not so surprising that there was seemingly little panic about what amounted to a significant increase in the separation of sex from marriage. The fact that a majority of pre-marital conceptions were legitimised and that divorce rates were low (Table 2.2) accounted in large part for a series of optimistic statements about family stability (see, for example, Fletcher, 1966; Gorer, 1971). As late as 1976 Norton and Glick puzzled over the continuing rise in the divorce rate in the United States and speculated (hopefully) that as time went on people's expectations of marriage would become more consistent with experience.

Since the beginning of the 1970s, there have been marked changes in marriage patterns, such as older marriage and substantial declines in marriage rates (Table 2.1) – trends that continue to the present; a dramatic rise in divorce rates that plateaued from the 1980s; and the emergence of widespread cohabitation (Table 2.4). From the late 1970s, the proportion of births outside marriage began to increase slowly at first and then rapidly throughout the 1980s, with signs of stabilisation in the early 1990s at about one in three of all births (Table 2.3). Kingsley Davis (1985) offered a series of tests as a means of demonstrating whether marriage was declining: the postponement of marriage; fewer people marrying; a smaller proportion of adult life spent inside marriage; and a rising preference for competing types of intimate relationship. All these tests now seem to indicate that there is indeed a decline in marriage. In fact, declining marriage rates and increased childbearing outside marriage have been inextricably linked to the growth of cohabitation. Kingsley Davis took the view that cohabitation was not substituting for marriage. The British Social Attitudes Survey for 1994 showed that attitudes towards childless cohabitation had continued to relax; 64 per cent felt that it was all right for a couple to live together without intending to marry. However, a majority (57 per cent) still felt that people who wanted children should marry (Newman and Smith, 1997). Nevertheless, childbearing has increasingly been taking place in cohabiting relationships. As Meuleman (1994) has commented, it is now clear that cohabitation is both sequel and alternative to marriage.

Cohabitation was apparently common in the early part of the twentieth century, when divorce was rare (Gillis, 1986). When separation allowances were provided for the wives of servicemen during the First World War, special provision had to be made for 'unmarried wives' (Parker, 1990). However, cohabitation was probably at its nadir in the 1950s and 1960s, when marriage was almost universal (Kiernan and Estaugh, 1993). Living together as a prelude to marriage began in the 1970s. In the 1990s, typically 70 per cent of never-married women who married had cohabited with their husbands, compared with 58 per cent of those marrying between 1985 and 1988, 33 per cent marrying between 1975 and 1979, and 6 per cent marrying between 1965 and 1969. The proportion of spinsters who were cohabiting more than trebled between 1979 and 1993, from 7.5 per cent to 23.5 per cent. Additionally, in 1993, 25 per cent of divorced women were in cohabiting unions. In the early 1980s, half of first partnerships consisted of people who had married without cohabiting, about a quarter of people who were marrying after cohabiting, and just under one in five were cohabitants. By the early 1990s, over half consisted of people marrying after cohabiting, and the rest were equally divided between those who had married without having cohabited, and cohabitants (Haskey, 1999). The peak age for women to cohabit is 20–24 years; 20 per cent of women in this age group were cohabiting in 1995–6. Cohabitations have tended to be short-lived

Table 2.4 Cohabitation of non-married women aged 18–49 by legal marital status[a] (%), Great Britain, 1979–98

Legal marital status	1979		1981		1985		1991		1995		1998	
	b	c	b	c	b	c	b	c	b	c	b	c
Single	8		9		14		23		26		31	
Widowed	0		6		5		2		[8]		[8]	
Divorced	20	11	20	12	21	16	30	23	27	27	31	29
Separated	17		19		20		13		11		12	
% of all women who are cohabiting	3		3		5		9		10		13	

Notes:
a Women describing themselves as 'separated' were, strictly speaking, legally married, but because the separated can cohabit they have been included.
b Percentage of each group who cohabit.
c Percentage of all 'non-married' women who cohabit.

Source: ONS, *Living in Britain 1998*, (London: Office of National Statistics, © Crown Copyright 2000) Table 5.11.

(under two years) and childless, but during the 1980s children were increasingly being born within these unions. The changing patterns of birth registration provide some evidence of this (Table 2.5). By 1994, 58 per cent of births were registered by couples living at the same address; teenage unmarried mothers are the least likely to be cohabiting.

Table 2.5   Registration of births outside marriage, England and Wales, 1964–98 (%)

	1964	1971	1981	1994	1997	1998
Sole registration	60	54.5	41.8	22.7	21.3	20.8
Joint registration	40	45.5	58.2	77.3	78.9	79.2
Births outside marriage as a percentage of all births	7	8.4	12.8	32.4	37.0	37.8

Source: OPCS, *Birth Statistics, Historical Series 1837–1983*, series FM1 no. 13 (London: HMSO 1987) Tables 1.1 and 3.7; ONS, *Birth Statistics*, series FM1, no. 27 (London: Government Statistical Service 1999) Tables 3.9, 3.1.

Increases in divorce, cohabitation and childbearing outside marriage have all contributed to the separation of marriage and parenthood. This is a very different phenomenon from the separation of sex and marriage that was forecast in the 1920s (Joad, 1946; Russell, 1985) and that was actually observable by the 1960s. Between 1970 and 1990, the percentage of lone-mother families more than doubled (Table 2.6). This was due in large measure to the rise in the divorce rate, which increased almost threefold over the same period, but also, since 1985, to the increase in unmarried motherhood. When cohabiting relationships with children break down, the women usually enter the statistics on lone motherhood as unmarried mothers. In other words, the rise in lone motherhood is to a significant extent the product of a process of 're-labelling' (Kiernan *et al.*, 1998).

Figures on cohabiting relationships with children have only recently become available. Data from the British Household Panel Survey (BHPS), which has followed a sample of 10 000 adults annually since 1991, have shown that, among women born between 1950 and 1962, 9 per cent of those cohabiting had a baby; while the figure for those born since 1963 is 18 per cent. Kiernan's (1999) analysis using 1992 BHPS data showed 17 per cent of women aged 25–29 having their first child to be in a cohabiting relationship (a figure that is still low compared to the 53 per cent for Sweden or 46 per cent for France). BHPS data project that of every 20 cohabiting couples, 11 will marry, eight will separate and one will remain intact and unmarried after 10 years (Gershuny and Berthoud, 1997). Table 2.7 shows that cohabiting couples were the fastest growing group in the 1990s, but only 4 per cent of families are cohabiting

Table 2.6   *Distribution of lone-mother families with dependent children according to marital status, Great Britain, 1971–98 (% of all families with dependent children)*

	1971	1974	1981	1984	1991	1998
Single lone mothers	1.2	1.0	2.3	3.0	6.4	9.0
Separated lone mothers	2.5	2.0	2.3	2.0	3.6	5.0
Divorced lone mothers	1.9	2.0	4.4	6.0	6.3	8.0
Widowed lone mothers	1.9	2.0	1.7	1.0	1.2	1.0
All lone mothers	7.5	10.0	10.7	12.0	17.5	23.0

Note: Estimates are based on three-year averages.

Sources: J. Haskey, (1993) 'Trends in the Numbers of One-Parent Families in Great Britain'. *Population Trends* no. 71: 26–33; ONS, *Living in Britain 1998* (London: Office of National Statistics, © Crown Copyright 2000) Table 3.4.

Table 2.7   *Families by type, UK, 1990–1 and 1995–6 (%)*

	1990–1	1995–6
Married couples		
With dependent children	44	41
With non-dependent children only	11	9
With no children	22	23
All married couples	77	73
Cohabiting couples		
With dependent children	3	4
With non-dependent children only	—	—
With no children	5	7
All cohabiting couples	8	11
Lone parents		
With dependent children	12	13
With non-dependent children only	4	3
All lone parents	15	16
All families	100	100

Source: P. Newman and A. Smith, *Social Focus on Families* (London: Office of National Statistics, © Crown Copyright 1997), p. 11.

couples with children. General Household Survey data show that, in 1998, 10 per cent of all families with dependent children were cohabiting couples.[1]

One of the main issues in respect of all the statistics on family change has been the extent to which they signal a decline in obligation and commitment and a concomitant rise in selfish individualism. Are people just more willing to walk out of relationships, even where there are children, on what earlier generations might have judged to be little more than a whim? The rise in the cohabitation rates has caused particular concern because it has been the driver of change in the late twentieth century and because cohabitation appears to offer a relationship with minimal ties. Mansfield and Collard (1988) described marriage as a 'strategy for the rest of your life', while early research on cohabitation showed that cohabitants saw fewer barriers to ending their relationships (Newcomb, 1981). Rindfuss and VandenHeuvel (1990) have argued that cohabitation is not an alternative form to marriage. Rather, cohabitants more closely resemble never-married people. Newcomb (1981) identified an element of 'Linus-blanket cohabitation' among young cohabitants, indicating both the need for emotional security and dependence. However, Beck and Beck Gernsheim (1995) have suggested that similar needs increasingly characterise marriage. This may be particularly the case with young marriage, something that is much more common in the UK than the rest of Europe.

However, the data indicate that cohabitation is more unstable than marriage, four times more so according to British Household Panel Data (Gershuny and Berthoud, 1997; Ermisch and Francesconi, 1998). Maclean and Eekelaar (1997) found that 80 per cent of the children of the cohabitants in their sample who parted were under five years old, which compares with 31 per cent of the children of divorcing couples (Newman and Smith, 1997). Axinn and Thornton (1992) concluded that cohabitation selects the kind of people who are more prone to break-up. However, others have argued that differences in values rather than characteristics explain the greater likelihood that cohabitants will dissolve their relationships (Clarkberg *et al.*, 1995; Nock, 1995b; Lye and Waldron, 1997). Cohabitants are reported by many to have more egalitarian attitudes and to value independence more highly, although the meaning of independence differs, being associated with wanting a career, control over income and less commitment to sexual exclusivity by some, and with a more diffuse desire for autonomy and self-fulfilment by others (Lye and Waldron, 1997). Newcomb (1987) and de Singly (1996) have highlighted the way in which cohabitation permits both the quest for independence and relatedness. In Drew's (1984) analysis of pre-marital cohabitation, couples were found to be committed to individual aims which they hoped to connect to ones that could be shared together. Askham's (1984) work on marriage identified a very similar tension between independence and relatedness, but the tendency in the literature is to assume that the balance is tipped in favour of the former in cohabitation and in favour of the latter in marriage.

The concern that cohabitation may be increasing at the expense of marriage has been heightened by concern that it appears to be relatively impermanent and a less 'committed' form of relationship, with higher rates of dissolution. Indeed, a Canadian study that attempted to operationalise Giddens' concept of the 'pure relationship', in which the partners are committed only for as long as they feel that they personally benefit, concluded that cohabitants came closest to matching the criteria developed (Hall, 1996). It is tempting to conclude that the process of 'individualisation', which according to Beck and Beck Gernsheim (1995) pulls men and women apart, but at the same time makes a close relationship attractive, would favour cohabitation over marriage.

Nevertheless, there are many different forms of cohabitation and the reasons for each may be very different (McRae, 1997a). In addition, interpretations of the evidence are in any case contested. Pre-marital cohabitation has long been justified as a form of trial marriage. Gillis (1986) has suggested that it resembles older patterns of bethrothal. Certainly the average duration of pre-marital cohabitation is very close to the traditional period of engagement. Cohabitants were asked by the British Household Panel Survey in 1998 what they expected the outcome of their relationship to be, and 70 per cent answered 'marriage', although in fact only 60 per cent go on to marry. American research has indicated that the effect of pre-marital cohabitation on marriage may actually be negative (Thomson and Colella, 1992). Indeed Cherlin (1992), who is considerably less pessimistic regarding family change than many of his US contemporaries, has argued that cohabitation is a relationship that the parties believe should be ended if it fails to provide satisfaction, and that people take these attitudes into marriage:

> Cohabitation comes with the ethic that a relationship should be ended if either partner is dissatisfied, this after all is part of the reason why people live together rather than marrying. Consequently the spread of cohabitation involves the spread of an individualistic outlook on intimate relations. (pp. 15–16)

Rindfus and VandenHeuvel (1990) found that among their young cohabitants, cohabitation was seen as a way of securing intimacy without making any long-term commitment. The findings of Schoen (1992) and Clarkberg *et al.* (1995) were similar, and stressed the liberal values of cohabitants and the way in which these were indicators of preferences for a type of relationship that was essentially different from marriage.

However, Brown and Booth (1996) found on the basis of their national sample survey of US households and families that the relationship quality of cohabitants with children was similar to their married counterparts; it was the cohabitants who did not intend to marry who were different. Kiernan and Estaugh's (1993) British data showed that the attitudes of cohabitants with children were less liberal than those of childless cohabitants and were very similar to those of married parents. The most recent European research by Kiernan (1999a) provides convincing evidence of the similarity between first partnerships that are marriages and those that begin as cohabitations but convert into marriages. Kiernan found very little difference in most European countries between these two groups in terms of the proportion that remained intact after 10 years, which raises a question mark over Cherlin's idea that cohabitation necessarily affects people's approach to marriage. However, the dissolution rate is much higher for first partnership cohabitants who do not marry, especially in Britain. Furthermore, cohabitants with children are less likely to convert into married partnerships and more likely to dissolve. Half of first-time cohabiting parents dissolve their relationships by the time their child is five. All this serves to show that the population of cohabitants must be disaggregated (Manting, 1996).

Some cohabitants may avoid entering a legally constructed relationship in order to make it easier to move on if it does not come up to their high expectations. Some may make a principled decision about cohabitation being more suited to a relationship in which both contribute equally. The idea of the pure relationship is premised upon a degree of equality between the partners, and assumes a large measure of material well-being. Smart and Stevens (1999) have referred to those making a principled decision about cohabitation as 'reflexive'. However, others may be responding to difficult circumstances. Living together is popular among both students and the young unemployed. But cohabitants who do not marry are more likely to have lower levels of education, to have no religious affiliation and to have experienced the divorce or separation of their parents (Kiernan, 1999b). McRae (1993) investigated 228 mothers who had cohabited either before or in place of marriage and 100 never-cohabiting, married mothers. She concluded that cohabitation represented a 'rational response' to low male wages and economic insecurity (see also Ermisch and Francesconi, 1998). Marriage is 'practised most often by those with something to transact' (McRae, 1993, p. 106). In this analysis, it is material circumstances rather than values that are most important in explaining this form of cohabitation. Smart and Stevens (2000) have called this low-income group the (rational) 'risk' takers. BHPS data have shown that among this group a rise in the man's wages means that the couple is more likely to decide to convert the cohabitation into a marriage (see also Smock and Manning, 1997, using US data). In fact the majority of UK cohabitants with children are disproportionately ill-educated, young and poor. In the 1960s, this group may well have had shot-gun weddings, quite possibly divorcing later. Given the rates of cohabitation breakdown, it is now likely that these women become lone mothers by a different route.

It is tempting to write of the 'rise and decline', if not the 'end', of marriage in the twentieth century, with marriage becoming virtually universal in the immediate post-war decades and seemingly becoming much less popular in the closing years of the century. As Smock (2000) has remarked, the key question now seems to be not who cohabits, but who does not. Even remarriage rates, which were high in the 1970s, have fallen dramatically (Table 2.8). The statistics relating to the higher rates of dissolution for cohabitants who do not marry have been taken to signal a greater degree of individualism. In the view of Newcomb (1981), cohabitation meets the desire for individualism and intimacy, but it may just as plausibly be argued that it meets the needs of late twentieth-century young people who became sexually active earlier and remain economically dependent for longer (de Singly, 1996); of young people who are sexually active with no property and few skills; or of women who experience conflict between a desire for autonomy and the sanctions of marriage (Adams, 1998).

Table 2.8   Remarriage numbers and rates by sex, England and Wales, 1961–97

	All ages No. (000s)	Rate per 1000 divorced people aged 16 and over	Total number of decrees made absolute (000s)[a]
Men			
1961	18.8	162.9	25.4
1971	42.4	227.3	74.4
1981	79.1	129.5	145.7
1991	74.9	61.6	158.7
1995	77.0	56.1	155.5
1997	76.8	47.9	146.7
Women			
1961	18.0	97.1	25.4
1971	39.6	134.0	74.4
1981	75.1	90.7	145.7
1991	73.4	49.0	158.7
1995	76.9	45.4	155.5
1997	77.1	41.0	146.7

Note: [a] Each decree absolute creates a divorced man and a divorced woman.

Sources: ONS, *Population Trends* no. 88, (1977), Tables 15 and 22; *Population Trends* no. 47, (1987), Table 15; ONS, *Marriage, Divorce and Adoption Statistics* 1997, Series FM2 no. 25 (London: Office of National Statistics, © Crown Copyright, 1999) Tables 3.7, 3.8, 3.12 and 4.5.

To some extent, all these explanations see the emergence of cohabitation as a rational solution to complicated changes in beliefs and behaviour. It is not possible to make simple links between less marriage, more cohabitation and more individualism. Cohabitation is now both alternative and sequential to marriage. Haskey's (1995, 1999) analysis shows that patterns of marriage, divorce, singlehood and cohabitation are becoming much more complicated within the life-course of the individual. Periods of cohabitation may precede marriage and follow divorce. Whereas in the nineteenth century marriage rates were a reasonable proxy for the employment rate, this was no longer so in the late twentieth century. Better wages together with a national minimum level of welfare secured by the state have ensured that people can adopt the kind of post-materialist values identified by Inglehart (1997). Following the ideas of Beck and Beck Gernsheim, Kuijsten (1996) concluded that there is 'convergence towards diversity' as individuals construct new biographical models involving serial cohabitations, marriages and divorces. Prinz (1995) developed a model of cohabitation with four stages, in which the fourth and final stage is cohabitation with children. He suggested that at this point cohabitation looks like marriage, but largely because marriage has become more like cohabitation. However, such a staged model is tidier than the reality. Indeed, Gillis (1997) has turned the argument around, suggesting that all intimate relationships now resemble conjugal ones. 'The perfect couple', loving and committed, has become the standard for pre-marital and cohabiting relationships. This may be the case at the level of expectations, but the important point is that the meaning of cohabitation varies, just as does that of marriage. In these circumstances, marriage becomes less central as a unifying cultural experience (Nock, 1995b).

The issue remains as to whether marriage, as an institution as well as a relationship, is in some way different and whether it matters. Marriage is a public institution and requires a public declaration of commitment. Schoen and Weinick (1993) have commented on the fact that cohabitation is more informal and that cohabitants emphasise achieved statuses – in the form of education and employment, for example – rather than ascribed (family) characteristics. Cohabitation is almost certainly a more 'private' arrangement, but whether it amounts to an 'incomplete institution', lacking agreed standards and relationships with kin (Nock, 1995) is another matter. It may be argued that it is increasingly an issue as to why people marry at all, given that cohabitation has become normal practice.

The emergence of widespread cohabitation raises large issues for family law and social policies. Increasingly, the separation of marriage and parenthood has been reflected in legal changes; for example, all biological fathers were given the obligation to maintain their children by the 1991 Child Support Act. But there is no general body of law relating to cohabitation in the UK.

Sometimes cohabitants are treated as if they are married, as in the case of means-tested benefits, and sometimes as if they are not, as in the case of insurance-based benefits (Harris, 1996). Family change and in particular the decline in marriage rates, marital breakdown and the emergence of cohabitation, has undermined all manner of legislation that assumed the existence of two-parent, married-couple families and, to a varying degree, the operation of the male breadwinner model. Furthermore, government has to decide whether to codify cohabitation. Interestingly the criteria developed by the social security system for establishing the existence of a cohabitation consisted of public manifestations, for example, a change of name, or taking holidays together. In the 1990s, the Solicitors Family Law Association and the Law Commission (Rodgers, 1999; Gouriet, 2000) have discussed the idea of defining a cohabitation for legal purposes, the latter leaning towards public manifestations and the former towards evidence of personal and financial commitment to the relationship; however, both agreed that the amount of time that it has lasted should be a criterion. From the legal perspective, Brenda Hoggett's (1980) observation almost 20 years ago that the distinction between marriage and non-marriage would become relevant mainly to the childless couple where one partner was inactive in the labour market was prescient. But law-makers (and academics) have great difficulty in working with the grain of family change, and the inclination is often to try and resuscitate older marital forms, which is all the more difficult now that the prescriptive frameworks supporting them have been eroded. Marriage has changed too. It remains a public institution, but it is very more open (to negotiation) in terms of the nature of the relationship between the partners than it was. The expectations people hold of marital relationships and of intimate relationships in general are no longer as sure as they once were. Thus it is not surprising that both negotiation between the partners and a reluctance to make judgements about the behaviour of other couples has increased.

NOTE

1. 1 am grateful to Kathleen Kiernan for this information (personal communication).

PART II

3. The male breadwinner model family

The male breadwinner/female housewife-carer model family has long been promoted as the most efficient and stable family form in which the obligation to maintain was clear for men and the obligation to care was clear for women. The economic dependency of women that this entailed was questioned only by a few feminists until the last quarter of the twentieth century. Nevertheless, the model only ever accurately described the arrangements of a proportion of families – a relatively smaller one at the beginning and end of the century and a relatively larger one in the immediate post-war decades. But as an ideal type it achieved widespread acceptance among ordinary men and women and policy makers until the last quarter of the century, and exercised considerable power in creating normative expectations as to male and female roles that in turn served to reinforce the model.

From early in the century commentators recognised and speculated about the threat posed to the traditional family by changes in the legal and economic position of women. It was feared that this would loosen the bonds of marriage and allow easier exit, or result in greater sexual freedom and more infidelity. A large part of the literature on marriage in the middle of the century consisted of attempts to 'modernise' the male breadwinner model, so as to make it less patriarchal and more 'companionate', in keeping with the social changes that were taking place. As late as the 1970s, there was considerable optimism that the model would have the capacity to evolve into a much more egalitarian form, a prediction that was dashed by the research findings of the 1980s, which reported the extent to which any such quiet revolution in domestic arrangements was 'stalled'.

The first part of what follows examines anxieties about individualisation and the changing presentations of the male breadwinner model. The second part looks at the empirical work on marriage and the family, which in the immediate post-war decades reported findings consistent with the movement towards a male breadwinner, 'companionate' family form. But in the last quarter of the century research documented, first, the effect of changes in the gendered division of paid work on the model, and second, the extent to which normative expectations no longer acted to reinforce it. Rather, expectations increasingly assumed a more egalitarian, individualised family form, which, given the lack of change in the gendered division of unpaid work, opened up a gap between expectation and reality that had to be negotiated.

IDEAS ABOUT MARRIAGE AND THE FAMILY: CREEPING INDIVIDUALISATION AND ITS CONTAINMENT

Anxiety about increasing individualism in intimate relationships is not new. Much of the literature on the nature of marriage and the family over the whole twentieth century has been characterised by a debate as to how far marriage has become and is likely to become more individualistic. There has been a measure of agreement with regard, first, to the idea that the nuclear family of parents and children and later the married pair are becoming more 'individuated' or differentiated from their surrounding kinship structures and from the public world, and second, to the notion that the adults in intimate relationships are becoming more individualistic. The broad trend in the literature has been towards seeing marriage and the family as the dependent variable, adapting to social and economic change and changing from public institution to private relationship (Lewis *et al.*, 1992). Writers such as Bellah *et al.* (1985) have essentially accepted the notion that marriage is a private relationship and have voiced their disquiet at the extent to which the partners seem determined to go their own ways. But the tendency towards individualisation has long been recognised, if not labelled as such, with attention focusing first on the increasing economic independence and political and legal rights of women, and the exercise of sexual freedom by men and increasingly by women. The main issue for those fearing radical change has been how such threats to marriage and the family are, can be, or should be contained. Various degrees of pessimism and optimism have been expressed as to the possibilities.

Turn of the century social reformers attributed considerable importance to family relationships in the work of forging character, which in turn was held to be the only way of achieving lasting social progress (for example, Bosanquet, 1906). Sublimation of self and sacrifice in the name of law, duty and honour was seen as the essence of character and the key to moral action (Susman, 1979; Sennett, 1986; Taylor, 1992). The search for morality, which was seen as consisting of a system of obligations, led inexorably back to marriage and relations between men and women because family relationships were widely believed to give rise to altruistic behaviour. As Collini (1991) has shown, altruism occupied an important place in Victorian social thought. William McDougall's *Introduction to Social Psychology* (1912, p. 66) subscribed to the view that it was the parental instinct that gave rise to the 'tender emotion' and that this was the root of altruism. Edward Westermarck's *Origin and*

Development of Moral Ideas, published the same year, also suggested that altruism began with maternal, filial and conjugal affection and was developed through natural selection. The conjugal family was seen as the place in which obligation was fulfilled and altruism learned, and this was considered to be fundamentally 'natural'. Egotistical behaviour, most obviously in the form of sexual infidelity, was condemned because it threatened the whole purpose of family life.

If individualism was necessary and inevitable in the public world, the altruistic world of the family was needed to provide the required balance. The evolutionary perspective that characterised late Victorian thought highlighted the importance of this 'separation of spheres'. Herbert Spencer (1876) devoted considerable attention to the issue of marriage and the family. He believed that the evolution of society had been accompanied by the emergence of monogamy, a stronger sense of personal rights and a sympathetic regard for the rights of others that extended to women in the family. Evolutionary progress involved separating the family from the public world and the harmonious co-operation of men and women. 'Differences of constitution' between men and women dictated progress towards an 'equal but different' model of separate spheres for the sexes. Women's role in the family provided care for the weak and all those unable to compete in the public world. Spencer's idea of individualism as above all the motor of the competitive market place was controversial. Durkheim, for example, accepted the importance of individualism as a means to freedom and autonomy, while condemning Spencer's idea of individualism as antithetical to collective action as 'morally impoverished' (Bellah, 1973, p. 54). As Lukes (1973) has pointed out, there have always been different notions of individualism. However, the impact on the family of women's claim to increased freedom and autonomy was widely viewed as being particularly dangerous.

Not all writers on marriage and the family agreed with Spencer's idea of what constituted evolutionary progress, but few commentators at the turn of the century questioned the basic evolutionary framework. Spencer clearly attached considerable importance to changes in the position of women in his analysis of the past and future prospects of marriage and the family. He believed that the limits to the individualisation of women would be the natural ones of biology. They would inevitably be intellectually incapacitated because of the antagonism between individuation and reproduction (Spencer, 1892). Spencer did not write about the ways in which separate spheres were institutionalised for middle-class women at the turn of the century by their formal exclusion from higher education, professional occupations and politics. Nevertheless, the implications of the demand by women for more 'equal rights' – in respect of family law as well as political citizenship and the means to economic independence – were broadly understood by social and political theorists, which explained why they were so controversial.

One of the most controversial writers on marriage at the turn of the century, Mona Caird, argued that the institution of marriage represented an invasion of personal liberty. Her attack on marriage prompted a correspondence in the *Daily Telegraph* in 1888 that was terminated abruptly by the editor after 27 000 letters had been received in two months (Quilter, 1888). Caird wrote as a feminist who desired both legal equality and economic independence for women. She viewed marriage as an impediment to both. Like other contemporary radical writers on sexual relations and on the condition of women, Caird blamed the institution of marriage for a wide variety of ills. However, she believed that the problems she articulated were temporary, and represented a 'mere confused stage' between two clearly identifiable orders: patriarchy and individual freedom (Caird, 1897, p. 54). H.G. Wells, who freely acknowledged his desire to 'take sex lightly', felt much the same (Lewis, 1995). Caird and Wells were anxious to get beyond the separation of spheres that Spencer regarded as the 'highest' form of development, to the point at which men and women would become fully individualised. Such radical views on the relations between men and women received some support from one side in the academic debate between anthropologists on the origins and development of marriage that raged during the 1920s. In an argument that echoed Engels, Briffault suggested that matriarchy and group marriage had been overwhelmed by the imposition of patriarchal marriage on women, and that a return to a looser and less stable matriarchal form was likely, while Malinowski argued fiercely for the idea that marriage had always been a voluntary, monogamous relationship between a man and a woman.[1]

In many respects, these early twentieth-century writings had more in common with the preoccupations of the late twentieth century than with those of the theorists of the 1950s. The issue was: what would increased individualism do to marriage? Would it reach some natural, biologically determined limit? Would it strengthen marriage, allowing a more equal, 'companionate' relationship to develop, or blow it apart? On the whole, the early twentieth-century commentators were enthusiastic defenders of whatever changes they forecast, although the kind of analysis offered by Briffault or by those – such as H.G. Wells – who argued for radical reform to increase the individual freedom of women, economic and sexual, occupied a distinctly minority position.

The debate about marriage and the regulation of sexual morality in particular reached a new peak in the inter-war period (see Chapter 4). Count Herman Keyserling published a book of essays on marriage in 1926 that included many of the leading commentators of the day. Keyserling's own assessment of the prospects for marriage were sober. He accepted the ideal of separate spheres, but also saw the possibility for tension rather than harmony between men and women. His own perspective was firmly evolutionary. 'Higher' development, he stated, was necessarily accompanied by a measure of individualism and the more developed the person the more he must experience a 'calling' for marriage, because marriage inevitably required sacrifice. One of the women contributors pushed this argument further. As modern democracies gave women more recognition as individuals, so this would strike at marriage as an institution: 'the institutional character of marriage will decidedly recede into the background as compared with its character of personal relationship' (Unjern Steinberg, 1926, p. 266). Unjern Steinberg also envisaged much more by way of extra-marital relationships in the future, in the same way that H.G. Wells gave an enthusiastic welcome to the idea that free love would accompany individual freedom. Muller-Lyer's (1931) book on marriage (which influenced Sir William Beveridge's thinking on relations between the sexes), again took an evolutionary view of the family as moving from 'primitive love', prompted by 'animal sex instincts'; to 'family love', characterised by the beginning of individualism among men; to 'personal love' as women also became individualised. Personal love, he argued, would inevitably mean growing differentiation between men and women and would entail more freedom in moving in and out of marriage (albeit with due protection for children), but not necessarily more sex outside of marriage.

Thus, by the inter-war years, the individualisation of women in terms of political and legal rights and economic independence was portrayed as going hand in hand with sexual freedom and was no longer necessarily assumed to have natural limits, which resulted in considerable unease. Somewhat later, de Rougemont (1940) wrote strongly about the evils of sexual passion, which he believed to be wholly irreconcilable with marriage. The constant search for passion and the prioritising of *Eros* over *Agape* could only result in marital instability. On the whole, writers in the 1940s tended to be more pessimistic about the prospects for marriage and the family. Sorokin (1941, p. 776) articulated a pessimistic vision of the coming crisis of what he perceived to be a 'sensate culture', with debased and selfish sensual *and* material values that were likely to make the home a mere ' overnight parking place' for sex. Zimmerman's (1949, p. 30) similarly dark picture of a period of atomisation, when individuals 'consider the family a personal or individual arrangement for their own limited specious purposes' was, like Sorokin's, intrinsically linked to the experience of Nazism, which had made a particular family form central to its ideology. A writer such as Folsom (1948) was in the minority in seeing in the pursuit of romantic love the flowering of an individualism that was not selfish and destructive, but rather that expressed the growth of democratic freedoms.

The urge to return to the traditional family at the end of the War was strong. In Britain 'rebuilding' the family was very much part of the post-war political agenda (for example, Marchant, 1946). The underlying threats to marriage and the family were widely appreciated, but how could the changes in the legal and economic position of women and in freer sexual expression, both of which advanced dramatically during the War, be contained?

The classic answer was provided by Burgess and Locke's (1953) text on the family. The basic thesis of the book was once again evolutionary. The family, it was argued, had been in transition from an institution, with family behaviour determined by mores, public opinion and the law, to 'companionship', in which behaviour followed from the mutual affection and consensus among its members. Burgess and Locke illustrated what they meant by the US companionate family in the following way:

> My family, consisting of Mother, Father, and myself, has always been very closely knit. ... The harmony in our family results from the democratic or companionship relationship. My father is the chief breadwinner of the family; however, all of his decisions are reached only after discussions with Mother. Mother shares the financial business of the family by keeping and managing the budget. In late years I have shared the discussions of major importance and have had my part in deciding important questions.
>
> An outsider looking in on us would think that we were a very silly group because of our demonstrations of love for each other ... My father does not show his love for Mother by showering her with gifts ... but rather by sharing all activities with her and spending his spare time with her. Mother is a very affectionate type of person and is always doing minor unnecessary things to add to our comfort and enjoyment ...
>
> It is not very often that our family circle is broken. We never make trips of any distance unless in a body. (pp. 189–90, capitalisation as in original)

Burgess and Locke commented on this case study:

> Unity in this family is very little, if at all, the result of community control, tradition, authority of the head, or participation in a common economic enterprise, as in patriarchal families. The prominent factors in this family are demonstration of affection; sharing of experiences; mutual confiding; sharing in the making of decisions; companionship ... combining as a unit against attack ...

Burgess and Locke described a male breadwinner/female housewife-carer family, shorn in large measure of kin and community supports, and operating as a unified entity to deal with the problems encountered by its members. It was not so dissimilar a picture from Herbert Spencer's notion of the highly evolved conjugal family. It was also a form that had been lauded by social commentators before the First World War as the best way of combining the public interest and private welfare, for example, by Helen Bosanquet, a noted commentator on the condition of the poor, in her book on the family published in 1906. While Bosanquet was sympathetic to extending the political rights of women, she believed that specialisation and co-operation between husband and wife was crucial: 'If the husband is the head of the Family, the wife is the centre' (p. 279, capitalisation as in the original). The fact that the 'strong' family members worked for the weak maximised economic efficiency. Furthermore, nothing but 'the combined rights and responsibilities of family life will ever raise the average man' (p. 222). These responsibilities were widely understood and satirised from the days of the Music Halls to the 'angry young man' novels of the 1950s. As Joe Lampton (in *Room at the Top*) told the employer who advocated early marriage as something 'to work for': ' "That's very true", I said, fighting to keep the anger out of my voice. "It also makes a man easier to handle" ' (Braine, 1989, p. 145).

But while Spencer relied on biology and Bosanquet on an uneasy mixture of something approaching rational economic choice operating alongside careful social surveillance to ensure the future of this family form, Burgess and Locke relied on mutual affection, sympathetic understanding, common interests and democratic relationships. Companionate marriage assumed mutual respect. The ideas of Burgess and Locke mixed the idea of increased individualism, freedom and autonomy with a commitment to the traditional family. In their analysis, the male breadwinner model family was not only a model of social efficiency, it was also *freely chosen*, although they felt that individuals may well need the help of counselling agencies and marriage guidance in constructing their companionate families. This conceptualisation of the family reconciled the tensions between increasing individual rights and freedoms – social, economic and sexual – and traditional marriage, and remained dominant in the post-war literature on marriage and the family, as well as informing the assumptions made by policy makers (Land, 1980), until relatively recently. Sir William Beveridge's blueprint for the post-war welfare state gave an enthusiastic welcome to the equal-but-different ideas inherent in this idea of marriage when he insisted on using the term 'partnership' and drew attention to the importance of women's role in reproduction (at a time when the birth rate was low) (Committee on Social Insurance ..., 1942). As Finch and Summerfield (1991) have noted, 'companionate marriage' had no one clear meaning when it was used in Britain in the immediate post-war years, but the kind of gloss given it by Beveridge was probably the most common.[2]

Most of those writing on the nature of marriage and the family and their development fitted their ideas about past and future trends around their contemporary experience. Thus Spencer's highly evolved family matched the experience of middle-class women at the turn of the century, and Burgess and Locke's companionate family matched that of suburban, middle-class Americans. Talcott Parsons, who had the last word on marriage and the family for many years, also generalised from the suburban American model. Parsons' theory of the family was part of a much broader understanding of societal change as a process of differentiation. Differentiation brings into existence new structures and also tends towards individuation. Parsons saw the conjugal family becoming a specialised agency, more private and more isolated from kin, and, within the family, the roles of men and women also becoming more specialised into the male earner/female carer model (Parsons and Bales, 1955). The classic male breadwinner model was portrayed as supremely functional for the proper socialisation of children. As Cheal (1991) has commented, Parsons assumed that there had to be something to counter the disintegrative process of differentiation, otherwise no society could survive. The male breadwinner model family served as a necessary bulwark in this respect. It was perceived as stable and economically efficient, and able to hold the tensions in marriage and the family. However, Parsons' (1949) early work had acknowledged that the asymmetric roles of men and women, while functional, were 'at the same time an important source of strain' (ibid., p. 243). Confining the major breadwinning role to the husband served to 'eliminate any competition for status' (ibid., p. 245) between husband and wife, which was in turn likely to threaten family stability, but in his work published before the War, Parsons also recognised the tension between the 'feminine role' and the pursuit of equality. That women had jobs rather than careers was part of the accommodation that ensured the health of the male breadwinner system, the importance of which loomed increasingly large in his post-war theory, largely because of the stability associated with it. Parsons' post-war account of the male breadwinner model wrote out the possibility of tension and conflict, as did Berger and Kellner's (1964) influential essay on marriage, which elaborated the way in which companionate marriage within the framework of the male breadwinner model worked for the couple. Berger and Kellner sought to show how the private world of the family provided a place for the creation of identity through the joint project of marriage. It also provided a counterbalance to the forces of modernisation, which led to changes in consciousness that affected the individual's experience of everyday life and resulted in increasing atomisation. The 'continuing conversation' of marriage served to validate identity.

The neo-classical economists' theory of marriage complemented that of the post-war sociologists. Becker's (1981) model proposed that men and women freely chose to marry in order to maximise the gains that followed from a traditional division of labour. It was the desire to maximise gains that ensured that men acted as altruists in sharing their earnings. (Becker ignored the altruism inherent in the unpaid work performed by women. Furthermore, subsequent research provided detailed documentation as to the extent to which men failed to share their income.) Whereas Parsonian theory about the roles of men and women within marriage had a rather static quality, neo-classical economic theory predicted that as the wife's wage rate rose relative to her husband's so the division of labour would change. Becker went on to argue that the increasing economic autonomy of women decreased the gains of marriage that were the product of the traditional division of labour in the male breadwinner model family. This in turn meant that people who were modestly mismatched and who had moderately difficult temperaments were more likely to part. Thus economic theory recognised the possibility that the male breadwinner model would not, under changing circumstances, be able to continue to hold the tensions in marriage and the family.

The criticism of Parsonian theory of marriage and the family grew enormously from the late 1960s, as feminists pointed out the extent to which marriage remained patriarchal and/or 'functional to capital' (Barrett and McIntosh, 1982), and radical psychologists and anthropologists pointed out the ways in which the traditional family could damage individual development (Cooper, 1972, and Leach, 1967). But, possibly because, as many observed (for example, Fletcher, 1966), the traditional family seemed to be surviving the profound cultural change of the 1960s – virtually everyone married, divorce was low and the vast majority of births took place inside marriage – effort was concentrated on pointing out its shortcomings and arguing for its demolition, rather than into producing an alternative theory as to its development. However, in 1980, Neil Smelser, a pupil of Parsons, speculated that the process of dif-ferentiating affective relations would result in marriage being separated from parenthood, meaning that men and women as husbands and wives were becoming relatively more isolated. Smelser thought this meant that experiments within marriage would have less effect on the rest of life than had hitherto been the case. His ideas about further differentiation were broadly in line with what the statistics on family change were to indicate for the 1980s and 1990s: that marriage *was* increasingly being separated from parenthood. But what this produced was in fact more tensions between the roles of spouse and parent. Indeed, the experience of patterns of family change from the late 1970s resulted in a rather different set of sociological ideas about the nature and development of marriage and the family and about the increase in individualisation.

By 1992, Giddens proceeded on the assumption that adult intimate relation-ships had indeed become differentiated from those associated with parenthood. Ignoring parenthood, he focused his attention on the increasingly individual expression of intimacy, from the world of arranged marriages, to the flowering of romantic love and finally, in the late twentieth century of 'confluent love', which he described as 'active and contingent'. If de Rougemont feared the destructive effects of the passion engendered by romantic love, he would have found little comfort in the notion of confluent love, with its dedicated search for the perfect relationship. Giddens gave women the leading role in driving these changes, which, given their restricted scope for action in the late nineteenth and early twentieth centuries, is problematic, although there is a strong case for saying that love became feminised as 'feeling' in marriage and the family became more private and more the preserve of women (Cancian, 1987; Gillis,

1997). Like Folsom's observations on de Rougemont's fear of the effects of romantic love, Giddens regarded recent developments as essentially democratic rather than destructive. His analysis was strongly influenced by the mainly negative reaction to the rapid pace of family change at the end of the century, and by the empirical studies of the family over the last 20 years, which showed the extent to which it was not the harmonious and unified entity described by Burgess and Locke and Parsons, but was, rather, replete with conflict and inequality. The notion of confluent love celebrated the idea of two equal individuals making democratic decisions that may be as likely to involve parting as staying together.

However, Giddens' analysis assumed that full individualisation for men and women had been achieved. There was no consideration of the context of intimate relationships that informed earlier theories. Beck and Beck Gernsheim (1995) differed in this respect. They suggested that it is no longer possible to pronounce what family, marriage, parenthood, sexuality and love mean. Rather, they vary in substance, exceptions, norms and morality from individual to individual, and from relationship to relationship. But Beck and Beck Gernsheim did not see this as an 'ego epidemic', arguing that the degree of individual freedom that had been achieved had been profoundly constrained by the trans-formations in the relationship between individuals and society, particularly the labour market. Labour market freedom in fact implies that everyone is free to conform to certain pressures and to adapt to the requirements of the job market. So just as traditional marriage and family life does not amount simply to restriction, so modern individual life does not necessarily equal freedom. But women's entry into the labour market, together with the social protection offered by the modern state, has made possible 'individually designed lives' (p. 58) that are more likely to be difficult to fit alongside each other. Within this new context and the kind of 'hyper individualism' of consumer choice identified by Strathern (1992), marriage increasingly becomes a place which specialises in the development and maintenance of the individual self. However, permanence and stability are likely to be casualties.

There has therefore been a remarkable degree of consensus as to the importance of the effects of increasing individualism on marriage and the family in the twentieth-century literature on the subject. Perceptions of the precise nature of the threat varied considerably over time, but have related more to women than men, in terms of their economic independence and legal rights and sexual autonomy. Broadly speaking, increasing individualism was perceived as bringing increased freedom. The problem lay in deciding whether this was congruent with the development of liberal democratic societies, or was more likely to undermine them by threatening the 'basic unit' of the family. By the late twentieth century, earlier hopes on the part of some that biology was destiny in so far as women were concerned had been blown apart by technological advance in the field of birth control, while the idea that the two-parent traditional family was 'natural' and too firmly rooted in the culture of western societies to be overturned looked increasingly shaky. The statistics of family change made it impossible to hold on to the idea of progress towards a single family model that managed to be both traditional and modern, while the empirical research on the workings of marriage and the family over the last two decades raised fundamental questions about the basic characteristics of the male breadwinner, companionate family.

EMPIRICAL STUDIES OF MARRIAGE AND THE FAMILY

Corroborating and Refuting the Male Breadwinner Model, 1900s–1980s

The vast majority of those who carried out the empirical studies on marriage and the family prior to the last quarter of the twentieth century accepted the desirability of the traditional male breadwinner model family. Before the Second World War, the main issue was to establish how far the model was being followed: were men acting as responsible earners; were women behaving as 'good' wives and mothers? The investigations were confined to working people, and on the whole, the answers were far from comforting. The more self-consciously sociological studies carried out in the immediate post-war period continued to present a picture of marital organisation far from the companionate ideal articulated by Burgess and Locke (1953). It was not until the late 1950s and the 1960s that social scientists confirmed the existence of something approaching Burgess and Locke's ideal and also began to express optimism about its capacity to adapt to social and economic change, especially in regard to women's increasing labour market participation and the advances in birth control. However, at the same time, others began to use insights from feminism in particular to come to an entirely different set of conclusions about the workings of the male breadwinner model family. Thus while empirical investigation followed the lead of the more theoretical literature on marriage and the family prior to the late 1970s, since then it has played a part in dismantling the myth of harmony and unity that both allowed the model to act as a holding device for tensions in marriage and family, and gave it much of its strength in both sociological and economic analysis. Furthermore, social researchers have more recently begun to show what happens in the vacuum that follows the erosion of the prescriptions that accompanied the model. The picture is much more complicated than the simple growth of selfish individualism.

Early twentieth-century social investigators were above all anxious about the extent to which working-class couples deviated from the male breadwinner model family. Helen Bosanquet (1906), while extremely concerned to promote the traditional family form, endeavoured to take a balanced view of the early twentieth-century working-class family. She was convinced that the enforcement of a strict work discipline was crucial to ensure that the working-class husband and father lived up to his responsibilities to provide, but she cited the numerous books on 'how the poor live' published by Margery Loane, a district nurse, as evidence for working-class men's strong 'natural affection' for their children and for home-life. Working-class women were well-intentioned, but often ignorant of how to run a home and bring up children, something that more education would remedy. These views were widely shared (Ross, 1993; Marks, 1994; Lewis, 1980). The attention of officialdom focused on the wife and mother as the pivot of the working-class household in her role of domestic manager and as the main impetus to her husband's activity in the labour market. As the eminent economist, F.Y. Edgeworth (1922, p. 453) put it, quoting the advice given by a social worker, 'if the husband got out of work the only thing that the wife should do is sit down and cry because if she did anything else he would remain out of work'.

Contemporaries were often struck by the pragmatic quality of working people's domestic lives, which also betokened acceptance of the male breadwinner ideal. As Ellen Ross (1993) has commented, intimacy was by and large lacking, although whether it is correct to go as far as Gillis (1986, p. 259) when he says that 'the long era of mandatory matrimony had utterly failed to transform the myth of conjugal love into lived reality as far as ordinary people were concerned' is another matter. The evidence of one Poor Law visitor made a considerable impact on the members of the Royal Commission looking into divorce which reported in 1912. She told the story of a family taken into the workhouse, the husband and father being 'hopelessly out of work'. On her exit from the house, the wife went to 'live in sin' with another man, defending her action by saying that the first husband 'was no husband for her and one that worked for her she respected' (Royal Commission on Divorce ..., 1912b, Q. 20120). During a period when working-class women faced extremely hard household labour, many pregnancies and an average of five surviving children to care for, they supported the ideal of the male breadwinner model family. A woman who had to add paid employment to her list of tasks was to be pitied (Roberts, 1984). However, the ideology of the male breadwinner model family was no more likely than romantic love to guard against adultery. As the testimony heard by the 1912 Royal Commission showed, in a period when material values necessarily predominated and marriage was more about mutual support and survival than intimacy, the search for a good husband, defined as a good provider, or a 'good wife', defined as a good manager, not uncommonly led to informal separation.

The social investigations of the immediate post-war years continued for the most part to reiterate the basic elements of this picture of a strict male breadwinner model as a widely held ideal, but one that was very far from 'companionate' in practice. The 'sex surveys' of the post-war period provided the largest samples. Mass Observation's 1949 'Little Kinsey' survey of some 3000 professional people and 2000 randomly chosen 'people in the street' reported that 'most people ... have a more or less realistic and mundane view of marriage' (Stanley, 1995, p. 121). Sexual maladjustment in marriage was increasingly touted by medical doctors and by marriage guidance experts in the 1940s as the root cause of marital difficulties (Packer, 1947; Walker, 1957; Chesser, 1964; Mace, 1945), but Gorer's 1950 survey of sex and marriage, based on a stratified random sample, reported that qualities such as give and take, consideration and good temper were the most highly valued. Gorer's second survey, published in 1971, found that intimacy was by then much more important. It was not until the 1960s that respondents began to report sexual intimacy as an issue. However, it is impossible to be sure that intimacy was not an issue prior to the 1960s. Given that it was not openly discussed, it is difficult to interpret the empirical evidence. However, it does seem that it was not accorded the kind of attention that it was given later on. The picture of the factory worker in *Saturday Night and Sunday Morning* one of the 'angry young men' novels of the 1950s, revealed little by way of genuine affection, or companionship, or intimacy between the sexes. The hero deplores the possibility that he might 'unwittingly and of course disastrously – find himself on the dizzying and undesired brink of the hell that older men called marriage' (Sillitoe, 1994, p. 156), but nevertheless falls into marriage like the rest of his peers.

Chesser's survey of the sexual, marital and family relationships of 3800 married women in 1956 reported that only 6 per cent said that they were unhappy or very unhappy. The vast majority of all the respondents felt strongly that they had a duty to run their homes. The community studies confirmed a picture of at best sober and conventional expectations. Mogey's (1956) work on two working-class neighbourhoods in Oxford, one old and established, and the other a new housing estate, concluded that while the romantic ideal was 'firmly held', it was 'usually tempered by a sense of reality' (p. 52). In working-class Bethnal Green, younger fathers pushed prams (Willmott and Young, 1957) and in middle-class Woodford, husbands did the washing-up (Firth *et al.*, 1970). In all these examples the basic adherence to a male breadwinner system was the same, but there was a little more evidence pointing towards companionability. Dennis *et al*'s., 1956 study of a Yorkshire mining community, however, was considerably more bleak. The expectation of a 'businesslike division of labour' (p. 183) between husbands and wives was strong. Any failure to fulfil it, for example if the wife offered her husband fish and chips rather than cooking him a 'proper' meal, was understood by both parties to be likely to result in acrimony. Rightly or wrongly, the book is probably best remembered for the picture of angry miners throwing their dinners on the fire. The authors of the study commented explicitly on the separate lives led by husbands and wives and on the lack of companionship in their marriages. The impression was left of marriages that hung together only because in a small village where economic opportunities were few and sexual reputation was closely guarded, there was no alternative. Komarovsky's (1962) study of 'blue collar marriage' in the US gave a less extreme, but not dissimilar picture of fairly segregated lives, traditional roles and minimal communication. She reported that in response to a vignette of a wife who complained that her husband watched too much television and did not talk to her, 37 per cent of her sample of 58 couples denied there was any problem and a further 37 per cent thought there was a problem, but did not necessarily blame the husband.

However, Mogey's study of Oxford commented on the degree to which marital relationships between the working-class couples on the new housing estate were different from those in the old established neighbourhoods. The former were more 'family centred', while the latter were more 'neighbour-hood centred', in the manner described by Young and Willmott (1957) for Bethnal Green or by Kerr (1958) for the people of Ship Street in Liverpool, where mothers seemed to be more important than husbands to the younger married women. Mogey commented on the differentiation of the family from the wider kin group and from the community that was taking place. One element of Burgess and Locke's definition of the companionate family seemed to be emerging.

Bott's extremely influential qualitative study of marriage and the family, published in 1957 and based on intensive interviewing with 20 couples, took this a stage further. She suggested that close-knit family networks were accompanied by segregated – in the sense of complementary or independent – roles for husbands and wives. As Turner (1967) pointed out, it was not clear whether the networks themselves were also sexually segregated. Loose-knit networks were accompanied by joint sex roles. Bott argued that the lack of close kin meant that husbands and wives had to seek emotional satisfaction in each other, with the result that their relationships were more joint in terms of organised shared interests and the greater importance attached to sex. Close-knit networks were most likely to be found when the husband and wife had grown up in an area and continued to live there after marriage. Given increasing social mobility, the trend was towards greater 'individuation' of the nuclear family. Bott thus drew a picture of marriage becoming more companionate and 'joint', and more isolated.[3] The picture she presented was more in tune both with the dominant account of the trend in marital relationships in the theoretical literature, and with the more generally optimistic picture of marriage and family that was current in the 1960s. Bott's findings were in line with Berger and Kellner's (1964) picture of marriage as a mutual project. In their view, with increasing equality, husbands and wives might be expected to build a marriage together; individual identity becoming submerged in the marital relationship.

Further evidence of companionate families came from the study of the 'affluent [male] worker' carried out by Goldthorpe *et al.* (1968) which focused on the position of men in the workplace and found that manual workers in a period of full employment had an instrumental attitude towards work and retreated from workplace-based activities into a more consumer-based domesticity.[4] A different style of marriage made family life more rewarding, both men and women were involved in a 'family project' (p. 177). Again, the picture was of a more isolated and inward-looking conjugal unit, which the authors termed 'companionate'. However, Elizabeth Roberts' (1995) oral history material for the period 1940–70 suggests that, compared to the early part of the century, women's role as household managers had become devalued with increasing affluence. She found more strong women in her sample for the pre-war period.

Nevertheless, Young and Willmott's (1973) findings from their study of work and leisure in London took the optimistic view of a 'modernising' male breadwinner model a stage further. They felt justified in rejecting the term companionate, and suggesting instead that 'jointness' was becoming 'symmetrical'. Young and Wilmott reported partnership in leisure pursuits, increased paid work on the part of women, and more 'help' from men in respect of unpaid work at home. They assumed that the division of labour between men and women would become more symmetrical and more equal. However, the Rapoports' (1971, 1976) studies of dual-career families warned that, while women's lack of access to paid work had proved to be the 'bottleneck' of the 1960s, the unequal division of unpaid work was proving to be the bottleneck of the 1970s. Still, they, like Young and Willmott, were optimistic on this score, believing that any problems of adjustment and unhappiness would prove to be 'transitional'. By the 1970s, then, empirical studies of marriage and the family were suggesting not only that companionate marriage was common among people of all social classes, but that the model would be able successfully to adapt to further social and economic change.

However, feminist social investigation in particular raised many awkward question marks over this interpretation. Bernard (1976) insisted that marriage meant very different things to husbands and wives; Whitehead (1976) drew attention to acute antagonism between husbands and wives; while Oakley (1974) insisted on highlighting the inequality in the division of labour. The Pahls' (1971) study of managers and their wives showed that, while the couples they interviewed believed that they were 'closer' than their parents had been, this had not been accompanied by any significant change in the division of labour. As the percentage of married women in the labour market increased from 35 per cent in 1961 to 62 per cent in 1981, so more attention focused on this aspect of marriage. Edgell (1980) argued that the unequal division of paid and unpaid work, rather than social networks, was the key issue in terms of understanding the role relationships of middle-class couples. 'Jointness', he argued, rested on the unequal division of work. The inequalities in respect of the division of labour that were central to the concept of companionate, equal-but-different marriage have been especially highlighted by more recent empirical research.

Thus, just as the evidence from empirical studies was being interpreted in such a way as to support the construction of marriage as a joint enterprise and an increasingly companionate partnership, so new studies began to highlight the tensions and inequalities inherent in the model. Askham's (1984) research on marriage took as its starting point Berger and Kellner's analysis, but instead of finding the harmonious building of a joint project, presented a picture of profound conflict between the pursuit of identity and the pursuit of stability. Similarly Hochschild's (1990) study drew attention to the tensions that resulted from the unequal division of paid and unpaid work leading to the double-day for women, and a gap between their expectations of marriage and the reality. Furthermore, the neo-classical economists' view of the division of labour in marriage, whereby the position of husbands and wives is optimised, and husbands share their income with their non-working wives, was shown to be a highly idealised view by the work carried out into the household division of resources in the 1980s and 1990s (especially, Pahl, 1989). In cases where the wife had been subjected to violence during the marriage (estimated to be as high as 25 per cent in all cases of divorce), it was shown that she often found herself better off drawing welfare benefits after divorce than she had been in the marriage. Thus research since the late 1970s has served substantially to demolish the notion of the traditional companionate marriage and to talk instead of the 'stalled revolution'. But whether it has also provided evidence to support the dominant idea of increasing individualism that is also selfish is a moot point.

Evidence of the Decline of the Male Breadwinner Model in the Last Quarter of the Twentieth Century

During the last quarter of the twentieth century, research revealed the extent to which the male breadwinner system no longer described behaviour of a significant proportion of families (Crompton, 1999). But nor have families become fully individualised, with both partners engaged in full-time work and economically independent of one another. The male breadwinner model has eroded but the social reality is still far from a family comprised of self-sufficient, autonomous individuals. Nevertheless, women's behaviour has changed sub-stantially in respect of paid work. Men have changed much less in respect of the amount of either paid or unpaid work they do. The pattern of paid work between men and women in households is now much more difficult to predict, but patterns of unpaid work have not changed so much. The male breadwinner model family never described the social reality for large numbers of families, but it was nevertheless widely accepted as a normative prescription for the way in which men and women should behave in intimate relationships. The extent to which the model has been eroded at the level of normative expectations is as important as the extent to which there has been a change in behaviour.

In the US, Blumstein and Schwartz (1983) have commented on the way in which paid work had become the medium by which adults achieve autonomy. Indeed, Pateman (1988b), a feminist philosopher, has argued that the independence provided by a wage has become the essential ingredient of modern citizenship. Men and women both engage in paid work to an increasingly equal degree in terms of simple labour market participation rates, but as Sorenson and MacLanahan (1987) have documented, their structural position in the labour markets of western countries, in terms of hours worked and rates of remuneration, has remained profoundly unequal. In other words, in terms of behaviour, while the male breadwinner/housewife-carer way of arranging matters within the household is now of negligible importance, this does not necessarily mean that women have achieved individualisation in the sense of economic self-sufficiency.

The extent to which married women and more recently the mothers of young children have entered the labour market is a matter of common knowledge. According to the General Household Survey, in 1975, 81 per cent of men 16–64 were economically active and 62 per cent of women. By 1996, this figure was 70 per cent for both men and women (ONS, 1998, tables 5.8 and 5.9). Married women are as likely to be employed as non-married women. Since the 1950s, the proportion of employees who are female has increased from around one-third to one-half, while there has been a simultaneous fall in the number of male employees (Walby, 1997, table 2.1). Indeed, the contribution by men to family income fell from nearly 73 per cent in 1979–81 to 61 per cent in 1989–91 (Harkness *et al.*, 1996).

In Britain during the 1980s, employment for married women with children, especially younger children, increased faster than among women without children (although the employment of lone mothers declined). But the aggregate data on women's employment hide the fact that employment for women with higher qualifications and employed partners has increased fastest, and that there is a major divide between women working full-time and short part-time hours. The vast majority of the post-war increase in married women's employment is accounted for by part-time employment in the service of the welfare state, most often in jobs involving care work. Table 3.1 shows the economic activity rates of mothers. The most dramatic increases have been for women with children under five years old; the difference in the activity rates between women with and without dependent children has halved in the period 1973 to 1996. However, almost half of women workers are employed part-time. Table 3.2 shows the pattern of women's employment relative to that of men, who still work predominantly work full-time. Eight per cent of men worked part-time in 1998, and most of these were either elderly or students, whereas 44 per cent of women did so (Thair and Risdon, 1999). Furthermore, almost a quarter of women with children under ten work 15 or fewer hours per week (ibid.) and 23.7 per cent of all female employees work under 20 hours a week (Rubery *et al.*, 1998). The proportion of men's hourly wages earned by women who were working full-time rose from 63 per cent in 1970 to 80 per cent in 1995. However, the hourly wage rate of part-time women workers compared to male workers only narrowed six percentage points over the same period and actually worsened relative to full-time women workers (Walby, 1997, tables 2.4 and 2.6). Arber and Ginn (1995) have shown that among dual earner couples, only 6 per cent of employed women earn £40 per week more than their partners and only 11 per cent of married women who work full-time have higher earnings than their husbands.

The precise nature of the erosion of the male breadwinner model is therefore far from clear. Helen Jarvis's (1997) calculations as to the number of earners for a sample of married and cohabiting couples with dependent children, taken from the 1991 Census, showed 55 per cent to have more than one earner, 36 per cent to have a single full-time earner and 9 per cent to have no earners. The point is that while families supported by a single male breadwinner are now undoubtedly in a minority – as a result mainly of women's increased contribution to the labour market, but also of the increased number of lone-mother households – the division of paid work in dual-earner couples takes a variety of forms. Dual *career* couples are relatively rare. The norm in the UK has become a more-or-less 'one and-a-half-earner household'. Because of the high proportion of women working short part-time hours, together with the low hourly rates of pay for part-time women workers, in many dual-earner households the woman does not achieve half the man's income. Ward *et al.*, (1996) found that 78 per cent of 33-year-old women contributed less than 45 per cent of the joint household income and 46 per cent did not earn enough to be self-sufficient. In addition, almost half of their sample of married full-time women workers were financially dependent.

All this has implications for that part of the male breadwinner model that assumed women would do the unpaid work of the household. The division of unpaid work in the home has remained unequal, although Gershuny *et al.*'s (1994) longitudinal data showed an increase in men's participation over the period 1975–87 albeit from a very low base, especially if their partners were in full-time employment. In the male breadwinner model it was assumed, for the most part correctly, that women would carry out the work of care for young

Table 3.1 Economic activity of women of working age (16–59) with dependent children, Great Britain, 1973–96 (%)

Age of youngest dependent child[a]	1973	1979	1981	1983	1985	1989	1991	1993	1994	1995	1996
Youngest child aged 0–4											
Working full-time	7	6	6	5	8	12	13	14	16	16	16
Working part-time	18	22	18	18	22	29	29	32	30	32	33
All with dependent children											
Working full-time	17	16	15	14	17	20	22	21	23	22	22
Working part-time	30	36	34	32	35	39	36	38	37	38	39
No dependent children											
Working full-time	52	51	48	46	47	51	48	46	48	46	45
Working part-time	17	18	18	18	21	22	23	23	22	25	24
Total											
Working full-time	34	34	33	31	33	37	37	35	36	36	35
Working part-time	23	26	25	25	27	29	29	30	29	31	30

Note: [a] Persons aged under 16, or aged 16–18 and in full-time education, in the family unit and living in the household.

Source: ONS, *Living in Britain: Results from its 1996 General Household Survey*, (London: Office of National Statistics © Crown Copyright 1998), table 5.12.

Table 3.2   Economic activity of married couples of working age[a] with dependent children, by age of youngest dependent child, Great Britain, 1996 (%)

Economic activity of husband and wife	Age of youngest dependent child[b]			
	0–4	5–9	10+	All couples with dependent children
Husband working:				
Wife working full-time	17	21	29	22
Wife working part-time	35	44	43	40
Wife unemployed	3	3	2	3
Wife economically inactive	33	20	13	23
Total[c]	89	87	86	87

Notes:
[a] Married couples with husband aged 16–64 and wife aged 16–59 and with dependent children.
[b] Persons aged under 16, or aged 16–18 and in full-time education, in the family unit and living in the household.
[c] Numbers are rounded off.

Source: ONS, *Living in Britain: Results from its 1996 GHS* (London: Office of National Statistics, © Crown Copyright, 1998), table 5.13.

and old as well as housework on an unpaid basis. At the other end of the spectrum, we might anticipate that in the dual-career model, care and household services would be bought in. A small-scale qualitative study by Gregson and Lowe (1994) showed this to be the case, but also found that couples who had previously had a fairly traditional division of labour used paid help to replace the woman's household labour. Those who had previously shared both child care and housework used paid help to modify their division of unpaid work and tended to hire help with child care rather than with housework. Thus even where the male breadwinner model has virtually ceased to exist in terms of labour market behaviour, it was still likely to exercise an influence in respect of the division of unpaid work.

There is very little information on what happens to unpaid work in dual-*earner* families. The vast majority of dual-earner couples rely mainly on relatives and childminders to provide child care; among mothers with children aged 5–11, 37 per cent work only while the children are at school. Where the female earner works long part-time hours or full time, but not necessarily in a job that she regards as a 'career', a large amount of care may be supplied by kin, the state and the market. Where the female earner works short part-time, she will probably continue to provide the bulk of care, together with kin and her partner. The fastest growing provider of child care since the late 1980s has been the private sector (Land and Lewis, 1998). However the most important source of child care, especially for pre-schoolers, remains kin, followed by childminders (Newman and Smith, 1997, table 2.6). Furthermore, the literature on the division of resources in the household has revealed the way in which money earned by the woman tends to be earmarked for expenditure on child care, reflecting the extent to which provision is believed to be the responsibility of the female partner (Pahl, 1989; Vogler, 1998; Burgoyne, 1990).

Thus the statistical data show that we are very far from a fully individualised, adult worker model and this has major implications for social provision more generally. While female labour market participation has increased, women remain economically dependent on men especially when there are children (Delphy and Leonard, 1992).

Both the neo-classical economist and the sociologist working with models of exchange (for example, Becker, 1981; Levinger, 1976; Young and Willmott, 1973) predicted that the male breadwinner model would adapt to changed circumstances. In particular, they predicted a rational allocation of unpaid household work according to who has the most time to do it, which is in turn related to whose market work is more important to the family economy. Blood and Wolfe's (1960) early classic study of the dynamics of marriage suggested that as women entered the labour market their earnings would give them more leverage in respect of achieving a more equal division of the domestic division of labour, a view that was repeated in subsequent American and British studies (Scanzoni, 1972; Blumstein and Schwarz, 1981; Wheelock and Oughton, 1994). However, as Thompson and Walker (1989) concluded from their review of the research findings of the 1980s, most showed that this had not proved to be the case. Husbands did relatively more domestic work in dual-earner households, but mainly because wives did relatively less. Unemployed men did not necessarily increase their unpaid work (Morris, 1985). If earnings were indeed a source of power, then women did not seem to have used them as a bargaining counter.

Thompson and Walker (1989) concluded that this was because more than behavioural variables were important and that gender was in fact the key independent variable. This was similar to Ross's (1987) earlier conclusion that, while changes in the division of labour in the home were set in train by women's employment, further change depended more on a shift in values, particularly in respect of men. Above all, the meaning of paid and unpaid work is different for men and women (Goodnow and Bowles, 1994). South and Spitz (1994) found that married women did more unpaid work than cohabiting women in similar circumstances and concluded that the only explanation for this lay in the idea that the married women were 'doing gender'. It may be that alternative moral rationalities underpin women's greater commitment to family work (Tronto, 1993; Ahlander and Bahr, 1995; Duncan and Edwards, 1999) and that given the choice between even a well-paying job and unpaid care work for a child or elderly relatives, some women would prefer the latter. British Labour Force Survey data report that 90 per cent of women with children who work part-time did not want full-time work (Thair and Risdon, 1999). Hakim (1996) has argued (controversially, because she insists on choice and tends to ignore the operation of constraints, such as the absence of good, affordable child care) that only a minority of women are career-oriented and that most opt for paid work that can be combined more easily with unpaid work (see also Dex and McCulloch, 1997). However, what most of these recent studies have done is highlight the degree to which decisions about the division of labour are socially embedded. As Anderson *et al.* (1994) have pointed out, the allocation of unpaid work is affected by current employment patterns, work histories and the belief systems that couples create through interaction, which in turn modify the options open to them. To this list might be added the influence of peer groups and kin at the individual level and changes in normative expectations at the collective level.

Thus the more recent empirical evidence on the workings of marriage and the family effectively documents the erosion if not the complete fall of the male breadwinner model family in terms of the division of paid labour. The division of unpaid labour, which is also crucial to the model, has not changed nearly as much. The kind of traditional family model pictured by Talcott Parsons or Becker probably prevailed for a majority of the population only in the immediate post-war period and was even less likely ever to have been companionate in the manner described by Burgess and Locke. This way of organising paid employment within the family has declined, and with it some of the accompanying expectations as to the 'ought' of male and female roles in the family. In its place, huge variations in the patterns of earning between men and women, ranging from short part-time, low-paid female dual bread-winning, to equal-earning dual careers have emerged. It is difficult to see any general way of characterising such patterns, even though the increase in women's employment has been taken by many as an important signal of increasing individualism. The evidence does not suggest that women have become equally avid in the pursuit of careers. Some men have begun to do somewhat more unpaid work, especially in respect of child care, but others have undoubtedly opted for what Gerson (1993) refers to as the pursuit of 'autonomy' that is frankly self-regarding.

A huge volume of empirical work has fleshed out this complicated story of the uneven erosion of the male breadwinner model and of the inequalities that persist. Some of the clearest pointers regarding the complex patterns that have emerged and the way in which they are handled at the level of the couple have come from qualitative studies of men, which interrogate the central issue of men's relative lack of change in behaviour. Gerson's (1993) research into how men in gay, married and cohabiting relationships made choices about family and employment categorised them into the 'breadwinners', the 'autonomous' and the 'involved'. The breadwinners made high economic contributions to their families and low domestic ones on traditional lines; the autonomous scored low on both counts; the involved were either high or low on the first, and high on the second. The autonomous were the most individualistic. They were likely to encourage their partners to participate in paid work, but were themselves unlikely to engage in unpaid work. Men who were involved had either started on a fast track at work and left it, or had hit a dead end; thus in contrast to women, period effects were found to be extremely important in determining men's relationship to unpaid work. Coltrane's (1996) findings from his study of fathers were a little different, suggesting that women's earnings may have an influence on the amount of housework that men do, but that men's attitudes are the key to whether they perform child care. In his sample, the men who were more involved in unpaid work were also more likely to be consciously rejecting the attitudes and behaviour of their own fathers. Certainly, men who see women's paid work as secondary will do less unpaid work. As Fassinger's (1993) study of divorced fathers showed, these men did not tend to see unpaid work as their responsibility, whereas the women tended to accept their obligation to perform care work and housework as 'natural'. Thus the interplay between attitudes, expectations and behaviour has been shown to be important and to vary for different groups of men, and between men and women. On the whole men still assume unpaid domestic work to be the province of women, but this may have as much to do with the residual prescriptive power of the male breadwinner model as with an increase in selfish individualism.

Yet studies have suggested that there is remarkably little conflict between men and women over the fundamental modern inequality represented by the division of household work (Pleck, 1985; Komter, 1989, Hochschild, 1990; Thompson, 1991), even though expectations as to the 'ought' of greater equality in intimate relationships does seem to have increased. The British Social Attitudes Survey (Kiernan, 1993) showed growing support for the ideal of equality between the sexes between 1983 and 1991, but only one in four believed in the reality of equal opportunities. Indeed, Scott *et al.*, (1996) have shown that the pace of change in gender-role attitudes slowed in the 1990s in the UK. Nevertheless, it seems that while Young and Willmott's picture of the 'symmetrical' family failed to become a reality, a greater commitment to equality took hold as an ideal. This is important, given that many authors are agreed that relationship breakdown has more to do with failed expectations than with fault (Silberstein, 1992; Bainham, 1994).

The Negotiation of New Patterns

Alongside the newly amassed evidence documenting the erosion of the traditional, male breadwinner model of marriage in regard to behaviour and perhaps even more in regard to expectations, there has also been considerable interest in establishing what then happens to the way in which the partners in an intimate relationship relate to one another in the absence of the kind of pre-scriptive framework that the male breadwinner model provided. The complexity of the patterns raise the issue as to how men and women in intimate relationships negotiate their lives: after all, a majority do not get up and move on in search of the perfect relationship. In the immediate post-war decades the gendered division of work, paid and unpaid, was sufficiently in line with the male breadwinner model to give rise to a set of normative expectations about the roles of men and women within the family, which in turn reinforced the model (Fig. 3.1).

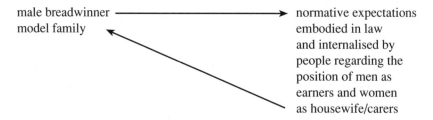

Figure 3.1   The male breadwinner model

During the last quarter of the century, the change in the gendered division of paid work was sufficient to provoke a shift in expectations towards a more egalitarian model. This opened up a crucial gap between expectations and a reality that is still far from adult individualisation, and this has to be negotiated (Fig. 3.2).

Qualitative research has suggested how it is that a majority of couples manage to reconcile expectations and reality and so keep their relationships intact. Backett's (1982) study of mothers showed how they were willing to sustain the myth of their husbands' willingness to perform household tasks, so long as the men recognised the value of the extra work performed by the women. Hochschild (1990) has also suggested that emotional support from husbands is highly valued and will often be sufficient to maintain the idea of sharing, and has also identified the way in which a couple will pretend that their rela-tionship is more equal than it in fact is. In other words, couples invented a myth to fit the new-found belief in greater equality. Unequal relationships could thus be believed to be fair (Regan and Sprecher, 1995). Hochschild suggested that an 'economy of gratitude' operates in marriage. If the husband does a little more than average then the wife is grateful. Similarly, Coltrane (1996), who divided his sample of fathers into sharers, helpers and disengagers in respect of unpaid work, concluded that the economics of gratitude and notions of entitlement shaped the division of labour in ways that could not be predicted by materially based resource or exchange models. In other words, in face of new-found expectations as to greater gender equality, ways have had to be found to gloss the fact that much has stayed the same, particularly on the domestic front.

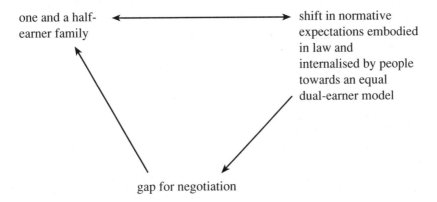

Figure 3.2   Towards an adult worker model

These means of reconciling expectations and reality may cover failed efforts at open negotiation or stand in place of them. Leonard (1990) noted that preferences may not always be articulated. Early work on the deference paid by women to their husbands (Bell and Newby, 1976) stressed the way in which this pattern of interaction derived from power rather than being a prerequisite of power, and, in their view, exemplified sexual stratification rather than explained it. But Gottman (1994) has argued that women are more assertive within the domestic sphere. While in public settings they tend to defer; in marriage they are more likely to confront. Women may indeed be able to use emotion as a resource (Safilios Rothschild, 1970, 1976), and threaten to withdraw love. However, equally men may be able to stifle women's voice in the household (Komter, 1989; Okin, 1989). In addition, Tannen (1992) has stressed the differences in male and female patterns of communication, which in and of themselves may affect the extent to which men and women are prepared to engage in open discussion at all.

Those who are convinced that intimate relationships have become more individualised also assume that the partners are able to engage in open communication about their arrangements and difficulties, 'sustaining trust through mutual disclosure' (Jamieson, 1998, p. 160). But as Askham (1984) observed, while the search for identity required open and honest communication, the search for stability often meant the need for silence and concealment. In fact it seems that it is not possible to predict the relationship between the degree to which the partners are individualised and the capacity to communicate within the relationship. Fitzpatrick's (1988) research on marital communication identified three types: the traditional, who hold conventional values about relationships; the independents, who are non-conventional and seek both freedom and the avoidance of conflict; and the separates, who are conventional in respect of marital and family issues, but who also value individual freedom. She found that in terms of communication the traditional husbands and wives did best at predicting how the spouses saw themselves (an important indicator of satisfaction); independent women also did well, but their husbands did less well; while separate husbands and wives both did poorly. There was less conflict and more disclosure among the traditionally married couples. This, of course, may signal a considerable degree of intimacy, but not necessarily negotiation. The main point about traditional relationships, after all, is that there is little to negotiate. It is newer, more fluid patterns of activity in intimate relationships that pose more complicated issues for negotiation.

It is clear from both quantitative and qualitative research that the traditional ideal of the male breadwinner model family that was the basis of post-war ideas about the companionate family, even if it never accurately captured the actual division of work or degree of domestic harmony for a significant proportion of the population, has substantially disappeared among two-parent families. A range of patterns of behaviour in terms of the division of labour have emerged in the last quarter of the century. There has been no simple, straightforward adjustment to changing circumstances. It is now widely assumed by policy makers and people that women are in the labour market 'like men', but women are still economically dependent and do more unpaid work. Indeed, there is a tendency on the part of policy makers to share Giddens' assumption that the 'ought' has become an 'is' and that men and women in intimate relationships are fully individualised. In the 1990s, both Conservative and Labour governments constructed social welfare policies on the assumption that all adults, male and female, should and would be in the labour market. Individual attitudes have probably moved further towards a belief in equality than is reflected in behaviour, although 'doing gender' remains powerful especially in respect of unpaid work. The growing gap between ideal and reality has to be bridged somehow. Again, those who assume a greater degree of individualistic behaviour than there is actually evidence to support also assume full and open communication, but negotiation may be difficult to achieve. What is clear is that the male breadwinner family model which carried such clear prescriptions for the behaviour of men and women within it, and which was a shared ideal if not a reality for many women as well as men during the first half of the twentieth century, is now neither ideal nor reality. In its wake new accommodations must be reached. These are explored at the individual level in Chapter 7. Similarly, as the next two chapters show, there is a vacuum left when the other main prop of the traditional family in the form of an externally imposed moral code is dismantled.

NOTES

1. This debate entered the public arena with a series of radio broadcasts (Briffault, 1931).
2. It should be noted that the term companionate marriage has been applied to historical periods other than the post-war years. Lawrence Stone (1979) used it to describe the growth of 'affective relations' between husbands and wives in the eighteenth century. An American judge, Ben Lindsey, whose writings crossed the Atlantic in the 1920s, also used it to describe a new form of trial marriage for the childless (see Chapter 4).
3. The importance of kin has been a relatively neglected topic since these early post-war studies (Pahl and Wilson, 1988). However, women's female friendships have been argued variously to be a safety valve in cases where the marriage is unhappy, or a means of increasing autonomy (Lees, 1993; O'Connor, 1992).
4. This observation is not so dissimilar from that of Stedman Jones (1974) regarding the increasing domesticity of the regularly employed and relatively well-paid 'aristocrats of labour' at the end of the nineteenth century.

4.   From public to private morality

The other main holding mechanism for traditional marriage during most of the twentieth century was the law of marriage and divorce and the imposition via this body of law of an external moral code, which was justified as a means of stopping people giving free rein to their preferences regarding intimate relationships and which also (as the next chapter will show) incorporated the assumptions of the male breadwinner model family. In 1985, Schneider argued for the US that there had been a diminution in the moral discourse of the law in respect of the relations between family members, particularly in the previous two decades. He suggested that a transfer of many moral decisions from the law to the people had taken place, most notably of course with the move towards no-fault divorce. Schneider saw four main reasons for this development: the changing nature of moral beliefs with increasing pluralism and tolerance for heterodox moralities; the ideology of liberal individualism; the legal tradition of non-interference in families; and the rise of 'psychologic man', by which he was referring to something very similar to Bellah *et al.*'s 'therapeutic culture'. Psychologic man judged things by what worked rather than by what was right, as emphasis on self-control and the importance of character gave way to self-expression (see also Susman, 1979) and 'no-guilt' underpinned 'no-fault'. Furthermore, his emergence complemented an increasingly pluralist culture. Schneider's interpretation is controversial, but his analysis is important for the way in which it directs attention to the importance of the debate about the use of the law to secure the imposition of an external moral code. By the end of the 1960s traditionalists in this respect had pretty much lost the argument. Decisions about the 'ought' of intimate relationships in particular were increasingly privatised to the couple, which inevitably blurred the boundary between marital and non-marital relationships. The liberalisation of family law that followed changed the nature of divorce and this in turn had a significant effect on understandings of marriage. Its significance for this study lies in the way in which it opened up a vacuum comparable to that left by the erosion of the male breadwinner model family. The debate as to whether people are prepared and able to strive to make moral decisions rather than act selfishly, or can be trusted to do so, continued to rage at the end of the century.

The law of marriage and divorce has regulated entry into marriage and exit from it, but as Weitzman (1981, 1985) has observed, by so doing has effectively also prescribed a particular idea of marriage. In the first place sex was to be kept inside marriage. Until 1937, the grounds for divorce were confined to adultery, and, alongside unreasonable behaviour, continued to be cited by the vast majority of those petitioning for divorce at the end of the century (Davis and Murch, 1988). Thus the imposition of an external moral code had much to do with sexual morality. In the view of Pateman (1988b), a feminist philosopher, the marriage 'contract' is fundamentally a sexual contract which controls male access to female bodies, a view that gains support from the fact that rape in marriage was legally impossible in the UK until 1992. Certainly, it has been above all female sexuality that has been defined by marriage (Gay, 1986). In his analysis of the double moral standard, which persisted in an extreme form until mid-century, Hugh Thomas (1959) concluded that a woman's chastity was not hers to dispose of, rather it was owned by her parents or husband. At the end of the century, O'Donovan (1985) also pointed out that the fact that gay marriage has not been permitted historically signals that marriage should be seen as a public institution for heterosexual intercourse. However, the law has also underpinned other forms of traditional obligation between men and women in marriage. The notion that marriage involves male financial support for women and children and female performance of domestic and caring duties – the essence of the male breadwinner model – has been reflected in what happens when marriage ends (Weitzman, 1981; Smart, 1984).

These ideas about patterns of sexual and financial obligation in marriage survived the slow steps towards the legal emancipation of women. Even though individualisation has been more marked in respect of legislative change than in labour market behaviour, it too remains markedly incomplete, especially in public law. So long as middle-class women in particular were substantially economically dependent on men and so long as the male breadwinner family model remained an ideal, then the imposition of an external moral code through family law acted in concert with it. Both holding mechanisms declined in the post-war period, with change accelerating after the 1960s.

A majority of commentators have attached more importance to economic change, particularly in terms of women's increasing economic independence, and to the changing technology of birth control in providing greater sexual freedom than to the changes in the law and in ideas about morality (for example, Posner, 1992; Fukuyama, 1999). Certainly, the relationship between law and behaviour is a vexed one. There is relatively little support for the idea that behavioural change follows legal change, for example in respect of divorce (see, for example, Burgoyne *et al.*, 1987). Haskey (1996) concluded that the main effect of the major relaxations in the law in 1969 and 1984 was to allow a backlog of petitioners to divorce, with the result that there was an immediate, but one-off surge in the divorce rate. However, Castles and Flood's (1993) examination of cross-national data on divorce rates gave a much more prominent role to the state of the law. While a simple causal relationship between law and family change is as difficult to establish as that between the latter and changes in women's employment or in the availability of state benefits, it is likely that the law *facilitates* and, additionally, *legitimates* particular kinds of behaviour. At the individual level, Mnookin (1979) made the influential but controversial suggestion that couples with marital difficulties bargain 'in the shadow of the law'. From his comparative analysis, Phillips (1988, p. 617) concluded that it seems possible that 'divorce does breed divorce' in that it becomes familiar and socially acceptable. Socio-legal commentators have referred to this as the 'expressive' function of law, pointing out that the cultural consequences of legal change may be as or more important than its effect on behaviour (Sunstein, 1996; Pildes, 1991).

Indeed, just as changes in normative expectations played a significant part in the erosion of the male breadwinner model, so changing ideas about marriage and the marriage system, albeit that they originated at the level of opinion makers rather than people, have been an extremely important part of the story of the erosion of the kind of family law that sought to secure the operation of an external moral code. The changes in ideas were an important intervening step between changes in law and behaviour. The point about the old fault-based family law was, as Rheinstein (1972) observed, that it said one thing on paper, setting out a clear and strict moral code, while permitting something else to operate in practice. In the early part of the century, the poor who had no property decisions to make ignored it and not infrequently separated informally, going on to 'live in sin'. By the inter-war period, the better-off were increasingly able and willing to work round the law, coming to an agreement to secure evidence of adultery. It has often been assumed that when the gap between the law on paper and the law in practice became too blatant – in other words, when the hypocrisy became too great – reform resulted. However, there was also a change in thinking about marriage and in particular questions were raised about the desirability of imposing an external moral code via family law. This made what Rheinstein called 'dual law' – on paper and in practice – untenable, the process illustrated by Figure 4.1.

Increasingly an influential body of opinion insisted that morality could only come from within and that it was impossible to impose an absolutist moral code. This meant that the couple would have much more say over whether to end a relationship, and indeed over whether to formalise it by getting married in the first place. Once the thinking about the marriage system no longer supported the law as it existed on paper, then the balance was tipped in favour of reform. The decisive shift in thinking began in the 1920s, but then went underground during the war and post-war years, to re-emerge in the 1960s. Thus it is probably helpful to think in terms of the mutually reinforcing role played by the two holding mechanisms of the male breadwinner model and family law prior to 1970, just as during the last part of the century legal reform and changes in the household economy have also reinforced one another.

Mona Caird, the late nineteenth-century feminist campaigner on marriage, was one of the first to observe that 'the tendency will be gradually to substitute internal for external law' (Caird, 1897, p. 125). The main justification for the imposition of an external moral code rested on an appeal to the public interest. The family was believed to be the source of moral obligation and the family

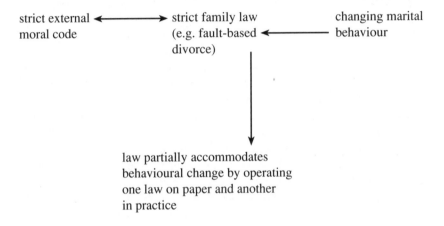

Figure 4.1   *Tensions in the operation of a strict external moral code*

rather than the individual was perceived by many to be the fundamental unit of society (see above, p. 6). Its functioning in this respect was widely believed to be 'natural', and yet there were fears that it was fragile. Certainly, the traditional family form and the roles of men and women within it required reinforcement. Durkheim captured this way of thinking when he stated firmly that members of a moral society have obligations to one another; that those obligations take on a legal character when they become important; and that 'free unions' are ones in which obligations do not exist and are therefore immoral (Traugott, 1978). The family was of course also later credited with the production of children who were fully individualised (Parsons and Bales, 1955); the problem was that egotism on the part of its adult members posed a threat to this process. Nevertheless the question as to why autonomous adults should not choose for themselves rather than have morality thrust upon them became increasingly urgent. As Caird (1897, p. 126) put it: 'In the marriage contract, the state has a deep concern, but it does not follow therefrom that it has a right to interfere.' The conceptualisation of marriage and the family as the 'private sphere' added to the difficulty of justifying public regulation in the form of a strict moral code.

Durkheim argued that people needed rules for their own happiness and that marriage regulated, moderated arid disciplined, but this did not address what became the critical issue in the debate: whether people needed rules in order to enforce their obligations to other family members. The debate about the existence of an external moral code raged first during the 1920s, chiefly among a radical and influential, but small, minority, and re-emerged decisively in the 1960s. The debate in the 1960s was decided largely in favour of the view that a prescriptive moral code was very difficult to impose in an increasingly secularist and pluralist society, especially as it had already been acknowledged that the traditional code had served to inscribe men's independence but not women's and had been maintained in form rather than substance. The aim of those arguing for a morality from within did not do so on the basis of the right of the individual to exercise his or her preference. For the vast majority of reformers, the aim was to achieve a 'higher morality'. Self-expression would result in a more genuine concern for the other. This may have been a naïve and/or pious hope, but it was sincerely held. Nor was it argued that parental, as opposed to spousal, obligations should be de-regulated. During the 1990s, the issue of morality and law has come on to the agenda again, the debate centring on whether government should not once more seek to involve itself in the imposition of moral behaviour. A torrent of complaint has associated family change with a decline in moral standards and with rampant individualism.

ARGUING FOR A PRIVATE MORALITY IN THE EARLY TWENTIETH CENTURY

Morality was at the heart of Victorian concerns, indeed Himmelfarb (1986) has suggested that the English made a religion of it. The ideal type of morality consisted of a system of obligations. While human inclination tended towards selfishness, it was believed to be all important to strive to obey the call of duty (Collini, 1991). George Eliot was unable to believe in God, but retained her faith in duty. The moral and the social were continuously conflated, whether in the search for the cause of social problems such as poverty (Hennock, 1976), or in the optimistic faith in progress that derived from the use of an evolutionary framework (see above, pp. 47–50). The tendency was, first, to see an all-important connection between the quality of the relationship between husband and wife and the fulfilment of obligations in the wider society. Second, the vast majority of early twentieth-century writers on sex, marriage and morality, whether in favour of legal reform or not, supported the idea of making marriage a 'higher relationship', whether as a means of raising the moral standard of society or, more narrowly, the position of women. Radical reformers, however, saw no reason to make any link between public and private morality, or to aim to raise the quality of marriage, emphasising instead the importance of individual freedom and power of self-determination (most controversially for women as well as men) in intimate relationships. By the 1920s, this minority view was stated openly and strongly. More moderate reformers also stopped making the case for morality in terms of the demands of the public sphere, preferring to base their argument on the needs of the couple, but in relational rather than individualist terms, insisting that a more privately negotiated morality would raise rather than lower the quality of marriage.

The basis of marriage posed certain fundamental issues. Commentators worried about the extent to which it may be based on sex rather than love. After all, the only grounds for divorce recognised by the Church had to do with adultery. At the turn of the century, the sex instinct was widely deemed to be a 'low impulse' on two counts. First, it was associated with animal behaviour. Herbert Spencer (1892, p. 463) wrote that unbridled sexual passion 'severs the higher from the lower components of the sexual relation'. Mankind evolved towards the practice of chastity. In the absence of chastity, affection and sympathy failed to grow. Second, sex was fundamentally egotistical behaviour and therefore a lower impulse. As Collini (1991, p. 89) commented at the end of his article on the important place of altruism in Victorian social thought: 'it is hard not to hypothesise about the ways it [altruism] may have been related to a kind of distancing of the sexual instincts'. Certainly Comte saw the sex instinct as the most disturbing egotistical propensity and the least capable of being transformed (Wright, 1986).

Women were commonly acknowledged to have a special gift for cultivating the feelings that were the source of moral behaviour, which gave them an unusually powerful voice in the early twentieth-century debates. They stressed the importance of a high, single moral standard and a sense of mutual obligation as a means of purifying relationships between men and women and raising them on to a higher plane, and as a means of laying a firm foundation for public life (Bland, 1995). There was in fact a fine line between arguing for a higher morality in the family as a necessary basis for public life and as a mere support for a façade of civilised behaviour. Rebecca West (1912), radical feminist and lover of H.G. Wells, charged Mary Ward, the popular Victorian novelist and anti-suffragist who believed strongly in a strict law of marriage and divorce, with hypocrisy in this regard. West argued that Ward's morality depended more on taboo than honesty. This was to become a much more insistent refrain during the inter-war years. Positions on the issue of sex, morality and marriage were often complicated. For example, Beatrice Webb wrote in her diary about the importance of a higher impulse in marriage in the form of both spirituality and duty, but these ideas seemed to co-exist with a much more traditional view of sexual morality that tolerated a degree of hypocrisy (Lewis, 1995).

However, most early twentieth-century writers on marriage adopted a high moral tone. Very few followed the older and coarser arguments, for example those of W.E.H. Lecky (1884), who accepted that men's sexual passions were frequent and irregular while women's were not, and that prostitution was therefore inevitable. As Mary Ward put it in her novel *Eltham House*, in which she punished its hero, a Liberal MP, for consorting with a married woman: 'what we have to deal with is the general tightening up for men – of the connection between public service and private morals' (Ward, 1915, p. 134). The message in Mary Ward's popular novels was the need for mutual fidelity; with wives exerting their moral power within the home and husbands protecting the women they married, no matter what faults were committed by either partner. Social theorists, sexologists and feminists were all committed to seeking a higher relationship between the sexes. Indeed, science and morality were widely held to be working hand-in-hand to lead men and women beyond mere animal passion. The 'higher' races were thought to hold chastity in greater regard. As a pupil of Herbert Spencer, Beatrice Webb, wrote: 'I cling to the thought that man will only evolve upwards by the subordination of his physical desires and appetites to the intellectual and spiritual side of his nature and unless this evolution be the purpose of the race, I despair' (Diary 30 November 1901 f. 2461). Even an enemy of the social purity movement like George Bernard Shaw 'looked forward to a time when, in the course of evolution, ecstasy of intellect would replace sexual passion' (Holroyd, 1989, p. 256).

Thus, reformers and conservatives were for the most part united in wanting to elevate marriage, although they differed profoundly on how this should be achieved and on what reforms to the law might be necessary. The Reverend James Marchant, who became secretary to the National Council of Public Morals in 1904 and who played a leading role in calling for the rebuilding of the family in the late 1940s, said that the sexual impulse:

> is a part of human nature, destined to subserve the propagation of our race. Clearly, in the normal condition of things, it is not to be extirpated, but regulated and purified. The animal and passionate element in it is to be freely subordinated to the spiritual, and so made to subserve not only the physical but the moral life ... the union of marriage not only serves the lower purpose, but creates the highest and dearest moral relations – the relation of husband and wife, of parent and child, of brother and sister – relations which exemplify, as it were in miniature, the greater relations which bind all human society together. (Marchant, 1904, pp. 20–1)

The proper mixing of the physical and spiritual elements resulted in what Peter Gay (1986) has called the 'tender passion', and what many contemporaries identified as 'love'. The perfect melding of soul and senses produced a relationship that was invested with considerable moral power. L.T. Hobhouse, the theorist of New Liberalism, devoted two of eight chapters in his *Morals in*

Evolution to marriage and the position of women. He wrote of marriage as an 'ethical sacrament'. At its best, marriage was characterised by 'perfect love, in which ... men and women pass beyond themselves and become aware through feeling and direct intuition of a higher order or reality in which self and sense disappear' (Hobhouse, 1906, p. 231).

Most of those stressing the importance of achieving a high moral standard in private relationships were extremely critical of sexual relationships outside marriage, although they differed as to how far they favoured a strict law of marriage and divorce as a means of achieving this. Ethel Snowden (1913) (n.d.), wife of the Labour MP, was unusual in suggesting that so long as selfishness was avoided and the higher aim of mutual service was kept firmly in view, any sexual relationship in or outside marriage could be considered moral. This view was not dissimilar to that held by some of those who hoped that men and women might achieve the higher aim of a spiritual relationship, which in the view of sexologists in particular might be found outside marriage. For example, Havelock Ellis, the leading early twentieth-century sexologist, felt that chastity was a useful means to a desirable end, but that to make it a rigid imperative risked overestimating the importance of the sex instinct. However, Millicent Garrett Fawcett, the constitutional suffragist campaigner, and Mary Ward, who was against women having the vote, both wanted to 'level-up' moral behaviour, for example, by making divorce more difficult for men rather than easier for women (Royal Commission on Divorce ..., 1912b, Q. 21732). Ward had a strong sense of the fragility of civilised relations between men and women and of what might happen if male protection was withdrawn; the treatment meted out to militant suffragettes showed that her fears were not without foundation (Vicinus, 1985). In this view, marriage was an order and a discipline for men as much as or more than for women.

Nevertheless, there was a growing number of voices arguing that it was up to adult men and women to work out their own arrangements for their private, intimate relationships. Mona Caird took a radical, libertarian position and opposed any state interference in marriage: 'the right of private contract is a right very dear to a liberty-loving people; yet in the most important matter of their lives they have consented to forego it!' (Caird, 1897, p. 58). Havelock Ellis (1910, p. 471) was also in favour of legal reform, but he did not believe that it was possible to make marriage a true private contract. Nor did Shaw, who satirised the attempt to draw up a marriage contract in his play *Getting Married*. Westermarck's (1926) work on the origins of marriage, first published in 1908, portrayed the two-parent family as the natural basic unit of society, which would be perpetuated by deep-rooted 'instincts' and 'sentiments' (rather than biology as *per* Spencer), but he was pessimistic about the problem of male sexuality, which, while it 'may be modified by reasoning and even lose its character of a moral question, is too deeply rooted in man's emotional appre-

ciation of virgin chastity to allow the problem to be solved in a purely intellectual fashion' (Westermarck, 1936, p. 147). For all his conservatism about
the origins and importance of the traditional family, Westermarck saw the
solution in terms of a more relaxed law of divorce. The only way to preserve
the institution of marriage was to allow freer exit from it. If it was not possible
to impose stricter sanctions on sexual behaviour outside marriage, then the
growing 'voice' exercised by women as they gained legal and later a measure
of economic independence lent credence to Westermarck's solution. By 1920,
Ellis, together with Bertrand Russell (1916) and H.G. Wells (1902, 1905), had
all come out in favour of some form of consensual union for adults who did
not have children.

However, there was something rather different about Russell's and Wells'
arguments in favour of a private morality. In the first place, Russell (1916) and
G.E. Moore (1968) both denied that a moral standard and hence an estimation
of progress could be derived from social evolution or the history of morality in
the manner of Spencer, Hobhouse or Westermarck, but rather depended upon
a judgement grounded independently of them. Moore stated clearly that ethics
were unable to give rise to a list of duties, while Russell wrote of all human
activity springing from impulse and desire, a far cry from duty and obligation.
Himmelfarb (1986) has noted that the Bloomsbury group practised what it
preached, their rejection of the importance accorded to public duty being
paralleled by private promiscuity. Second, the rejection of duty resulted in a
tendency to take intimate relationships a lot more lightly. H.G. Wells refused
to see the search for a 'higher relationship' as either necessary or desirable
(Lewis, 1995). Rather, sex was natural, inevitable and, perhaps most radical of
all, fun. In his autobiography, Wells (1966, pp. 467, 475) insisted that he had
merely wanted to ask ' "Why not?" ', to question Victorianism and to condemn
the hypocrisy of 'chastity which is mere abstinence and concealment'. In his
novel *Anticipations* (1902), he asserted that the old ethical principles of chastity,
purity, self-sacrifice and sexual sin would no longer do. Wells lived outside
the rarefied atmosphere created by the new ethics in Oxbridge and Bloomsbury,
but he reached a wide audience and was particularly influential with the young.[1]
Wells may be read as merely justifying his own sexual adventures. Certainly
his antipathy to divorce (Wells, 1930) probably signalled a degree of acceptance
of the double moral standard, but he insisted equally on women's desire for
sexual freedom and suggested that this rather than greater male continence
would put an end to prostitution, something that had never been openly
suggested before. His position opened the door to the 'lower impulses' and
threatened to undermine the argument that linked a high standard for morality
in marriage to the cultivation of altruism in private and public life, and finally
to the welfare of state and nation.

The emphasis on the intimate link between private and public morality was not ubiquitous in the years following the First World War, as it had been before. Bertrand Russell played a key role in advocating the exercise of individual freedom in respect of intimate relationships. In *Marriage and Morals*, published in 1929, he acknowledged love to be more than the desire for sex; sex without love was mere experimentation. But 'love can only flourish as long as it is free and spontaneous; it tends to be killed by the thought that it is a duty' (Russell, 1985, p. 94). Mary Ward's stereotypically Victorian emphasis on the importance of maintaining a marriage no matter what happened to the feelings of the partners was abhorrent to Russell. Like Fukuyama (1999) at the end of the century, he referred to women's emancipation and birth control as the major drivers behind the 'new freedom'. Women were no longer prepared to do all the adapting in marriage, while birth control had made possible the separation of sex and marriage. Professor Joad (1946) had made the same point a few years earlier than Russell, arguing that the increased economic independence of women and the practice of birth control would militate against a uniform morality. He predicted that:

> as the clear-cut line of demarcation between married and unmarried unions becomes obscured by the increase in the number of the latter, it will no longer be either possible or necessary to put the unmarried mistress as completely beyond the pale of decent society as has been customary in the past. (Joad, 1946, pp. 42–3)

In cases of childless marriage, Russell was in favour of easy exit. He approved of the American Judge, Ben Lindsey's (1928) ideas for promoting stability in the sexual relationships of the young by introducing a new form of marriage (which he called 'companionate', but which bore no relationship to the later use of the term by Burgess and Locke, 1953), whereby the use of birth control would be permitted and a couple would be able to divorce by mutual consent so long as they remained childless. Where there were children, Russell believed that the responsibility of the parents should continue, although this did not necessarily mean that other sexual relationships were excluded. In other words, very early on Russell made the jump from seeing that technology had made the separation of sex from marriage possible, to the possibility of separating marriage and parenthood, something that did not occur until the late twentieth century (see Chapter 2). Russell remained convinced that the parental relationship was a crucial foundation of society. If women were to share the upbringing of children with the state rather than with men, he argued, it would eliminate the only emotion equal in importance to sex love in men's lives and they would probably be less productive and retire earlier from work, an echo of the early (and indeed also late) twentieth-century conviction that men's incentive to work was provided chiefly by their responsibility to maintain.

In the US, Walter Lippmann (1929) was deeply perturbed by Russell's thinking on marriage and the family. He recognised only too well that 'the whole revolution in the field of sexual morals turns upon the fact that external control of the chastity of women is becoming impossible', but expressed grave reservations about the possibility of separating 'parenthood as a vocation from love as an end in itself ... this is the heart of the problem: to determine whether this separation, which birth control has made feasible and which law can no longer prevent, is in harmony with the conditions of human happiness' (ibid., p. 288). Lippmann believed that:

> If you idealize the logic of birth control, make parenthood a separate vocation, isolate love from work and the hard realities of living, and say, that it must be spontaneous and carefree, what have you done? You have separated it from all the important activities which it might stimulate and liberate. You have made love spontaneous but empty and you have made home-building and parenthood efficient, responsible and dull. (Ibid., p. 305)

In Lippmann's view Russell's scheme for changing the 'conventions' or normative expectations governing marriage by separating the primary and secondary functions of sex was impossible.

This was also the view of the majority of English commentators. G.E. Newsom (1932), the Master of Selwyn College, Cambridge, was appalled at the idea that the so-called 'new morality' should advocate the separation of the sex life of adults from parenthood. He reiterated the older idea that sex was a fundamentally animal impulse that was only given a higher moral purpose by family life. Newsom felt that the new morality was too close to the anthropological arguments of Robert Briffault regarding the matriarchal origins of the family, and to practices in the Soviet Union. The separation of sexual and parental love could only mean that 'sexual passion is to be relieved from duty towards social purpose' (ibid., p. 194); the psychology of the new morality was above all egoistic, and sheer selfish individualism could never be moral. Newsom's rather laboured critique of Russell expressed fear about the lack of order that he believed must follow upon the deliberate abandonment of the traditional moral code, as well as abhorrence of the way in which Russell seemed to have little regard for marriage as a higher (spiritual) relationship: 'sex-life released from social purpose will find itself completely at home in a civilisation which has no social purpose at all and is at the mercy of science' (ibid., p. 241). Another Roman Catholic commentator condemned the new morality as mere hedonism and a search for irresponsible freedom, rather than for new mechanisms to secure obligations (Dawson, 1930).

Russell's view of the nature of family change in the future was, to say the least, prescient, but most reformers of the inter-war years tried to steer a less controversial course which reintegrated sex, marriage and parenthood, but which also accepted that an externally imposed moral code was incompatible with intimate relationships based on love. Writers on sex during the inter-war period made it central to marriage. Marie Stopes (1918) employed suitably mystical language and continued to use eugenics and the requirements of racial hygiene to legitimise her writing on sex, but her purpose was in large measure to eroticise marriage. Maude Royden (1921), a feminist lay preacher who wrote widely on sex and marriage after the War, persisted in the view that ideally sex was for procreation only, but nevertheless accepted the use of birth control and the idea that sex was natural and necessary to human relationships. She also accepted the view of 'modern psychology' that women had sexual desires and needed to express them. Some inter-war sexologists began to argue strongly that sex was the foundation of marriage (for example, van de Velde, 1928), something their pre-war counterparts would never have done. A number of more moderate writers acknowledged the impact of Freudian ideas about a link between sexual repression and ill-health (for example, Ingram, 1922), while continuing to stress that self-control was quite different from repression. The 1930 Lambeth Conference of the Church of England cautiously admitted that sex had a 'secondary end' (p. 92), meaning that it had a role in securing marital satisfaction as well as in reproduction.

Royden (1921, p. 39) continued to stress the importance of love as representing the mixing of soul and senses: 'the physical side of marriage becomes simply an expression of the love of the spirit, the perfect final expression, the sacrament of love', but she did not argue that such a basis for marriage was crucial to the stability of the wider society. Of course, once marriage and intimate relationships were regarded more as matters of private than of public significance, women in particular lost an important means of exerting leverage on the public debate. To the extent that marriage became much more of a private relationship, it also became much more difficult to ground demands for change in men's behaviour, or in women's position in the public sphere, in an analysis of private relationships. Royden and other moderate writers on sex and marriage in the 1920s, such as Herbert Gray, one of the founders of the marriage guidance movement, took the view that because love was the centre of marriage, the morality of the marital relationship depended in the end on the nature of the (private) commitment of the couple (Gray, 1923). Thus while they did not seek to reform the structure of marriage in the manner of Russell, they too abandoned the idea that morality was achieved primarily through the imposition of a strict moral code that prescribed sex within marriage and allowed divorce only for 'fault', accompanied by obligations that were clearly gendered. Gray argued that the integration of body and spirit which was what the true Christian attitude required could not be imposed by law. All law could do would be to stigmatise all lapses in a punitive manner, whereas it was love alone that could make intimacy right. Moderates like Gray struggled against the negative, repressive, 'thou shalt not' image of the 'old morality', but in doing so faced the problem of how to defend traditional marriage and, in particular, how to justify keeping sex in marriage.

The *deus ex machina* was the emphasis moderate reformers placed on the importance not of individual freedom, but the development of 'personality'. As Royden (1921, p. 51) put it: 'It is the holding of human personality cheap that is really immoral.' It was the aim of such writing to argue that the full development of personality could only take place inside a committed personal relationship which balanced pleasure and responsibility. Aldous Huxley (1949, p. 141) was predictably sceptical, but still declared that 'myth for myth, Human Personality is preferable to God'. Of course, moderate reformers like Gray and Royden laboured to avoid any such distinction, seeking rather to import ideas about the development of human personality into an updated form of Christian morality. Nevertheless, the emphasis on personality did appeal to more secular commentators. Chesser (1964), a medical doctor, was not alone in welcoming the idea of a new synthesis between scientific knowledge and religion. The philosopher John Macmurray (1935, p. 94) was influential in arguing that personal life was different from both social life and individual life: 'The habit, which we have inherited from several centuries of individualism, of talking about human life in terms of a contrast between the individual and society is a misleading one.' Personal life was not to be lived in solitude and personal development depended on personal relationships. Primary consideration should not be given to the maintenance of marriage and family as institutions; rather, the key issue had to be the quality of the personal relationship which would make or break the institution. Personal relationships, he argued, should be governed by freedom and equality; morality could only come from within. Macmurray agreed that chastity was the true basis for sexual morality, but disagreed that it could be imposed from without. The integrity of the individual had to be the condition of personal relationship, otherwise people became subordinate to function. In common with other writers of the period (see, for example, Fletcher, 1938), Macmurray deplored the hypocrisy surrounding the traditional moral code embodied in family law and pointed out that there was as much sexual immorality within marriage as outside it.

Thus, in this work of a relatively small but diverse and influential group of writers, morality was relocated from the public to the private sphere, but became in this formulation not a matter of exercising individual preferences, but rather an expression of the love that grew out of personal relationships and which thereby fostered full personal development. One of the more popular advice books of the 1930s told young people that true morality was created from within and would properly govern the whole life of the relationship, whereas conventional morality concerned itself only with what happened before and outside marriage (Barnes and Barnes, 1938). In a pamphlet for the Student Christian

Movement, Seccombe (1933) explained that while obligation suggested compulsion which is contrary to the nature of love, in fact love came from within and promoted the highest kind of obligation. A later generation would automatically use the term commitment rather than obligation (see Chapter 6), but it was this kind of thinking that was rediscovered and that became influential among a much wider audience in the 1960s.

ABANDONING AN EXTERNAL MORAL CODE IN THE 1960s

War-time disruption strengthened conservative views about the family and the need for a strong moral code. Rebuilding the traditional family was perceived to be as important as more conventional forms of post-war reconstruction (Marchant, 1946). The increase in the divorce rate and in the juvenile crime rate, together with the fall in the birth rate, prompted many professionals to blame excessive individualism' (Hagan, 1946, p. 122; Spence, 1946). David Mace, the first general secretary of the National Marriage Guidance Council, also looked at the Registrar General's data on pre-marital conceptions for the period 1938–43 and estimated that one woman in six had abandoned the idea of pre-marital chastity (Mace, 1945). Mace and members of the House of Lords, who discussed his figures in May 1946 (*Debates*, c. 1448) regarded them as symptomatic of an unfortunate levelling down of moral standards. The Royal Commission on Divorce, appointed to inquire into the law on divorce and matrimonial causes in the wake of efforts to introduce liberalise the divorce law in 1951, reported in 1956 (Royal Commission on Marriage and Divorce, 1956) and voiced its suspicion of both the effects of women's emancipation and modern psychology. The tendency for policy makers to adopt a conservative position in the face of evidence of major family change was as strong in the post-war period as it was at the end of the century.

However, at the same time, the views of moderate inter-war reformers were being absorbed into new writing that had a substantial impact on some of the most influential actors in the debate over the imposition of a moral code, particularly the Church. Sherwin Bailey (1952, p. i) developed what he called 'a theology of sexual love', which he hoped would reorientate the Church's attitude towards sex and marriage at a time of 'grave sexual disorder'. He reiterated the idea of love as 'personal relation' and defined marriage in terms of the expression of love, the 'institutional end' being procreation but the 'first object' being 'integration and fulfilment' (ibid., p. 107). E.O. James, a University of London professor of the history and philosophy of religion and a member of the Archbishop of Canterbury's committee on artificial human insemination in the 1940s, also wrote of marital intimacy as the means of developing personality, which in turn would ensure a moral community: 'For the individual a new moral sentiment grows through this graded system of personal relationships, extending outwards from the union of husband and wife as the most effective symbiosis in the home, through kin and the tribe or village or nation' (James, 1952, p. 193). This was the classic statement of the reformer's hope for morality from below rather than the imposition of morality from above.

Cancian and Gordon (1988) have observed from their study of marital advice articles in the United States that 'emotion norms' showed signs of modernity in the 1920s, but then went underground until the 1960s. Something very similar seems to have happened in Britain and was indeed recognised at the time (for example, Bentley, 1965). While the 1960s did not see the cataclysmic change in behaviour that is usually attributed to it by late twentieth-century politicians (see Chapter 2), it did witness a major debate on morality and the role of the law. In many respects, the categories of participants in the debate were remarkably similar to the inter-war period. Radical reformers like H.G. Wells and Bertrand Russell found their counterparts in people like Alex Comfort, whose ideas about the importance of personal growth were resonant of the American human potential movement and Abraham Maslow (see above, p. 10). Comfort (1963) argued that any form of personal relationship was all right so long as it was not exploitative. His argument was different from that of Russell in that he allowed any sexual relationship to have a value of its own; sex was a form of healthy sport. His claim that chastity would come to be seen as no more of a virtue than malnutrition, made on BBC television in 1963, was shocking and Acland (1965, p. 32) was not alone in labelling him a 'self-centred individualist'. Like Helena Wright (1968) and G.M. Carstairs, the Reith lecturer for 1962, he was optimistic about the liberating effects of the new birth control technology in the form of the pill and believed that sexual freedom would banish unwanted pregnancy and deepen person-centred relationships.

The views of this group of radicals were both more individualist and more pragmatic than their radical counterparts in the 1920s, and once again they constituted a minority voice. The main debate took place between those who were convinced that morality could only come from within, but that this represented a higher form of personal relationship, and those who continued to defend the imposition of a strict moral code. Those grounding morality in the individual and in the quality of the relationship (like Gray and Royden in the inter-war years) were very far from 'permissive', but as one contemporary commented, the 'rather solemn and high-minded personal relations approach' could in practice be interpreted as sanctioning the sort of behaviour that the radicals favoured (Atkinson, 1965, pp. 86–7).

However, the mainly Christian commentators on morality were all profoundly uneasy with the pragmatic approach of more secular writers such as Carstairs or Edmund Leach, another Reith lecturer (in 1967). Contributors to Alec Vidler's 1963 book of essays, who were in part responding to Carstairs' (1962, p. 55) notion of sexual relations 'as a source of pleasure and also as a mutual encountering of personalities in which each explores the other', were convinced that morality in respect of intimate relationships had to come from within, but returned to the theme that it was not possible to abstract sex from other aspects of the human personality. This continued to provide a basis for opposing sex outside marriage. Thus Douglas Rhymes (1964), the Canon of Southwark Cathedral, commented that the sexual amorality of the hero of *Room at the Top* was simply a reflection of his whole attitude to life. For this group, Leach (1967) also appeared to go too far. He argued that morality was variable and was specified by culture. Indeed, in a changing world moral rules made it hard to adapt to new situations. Leach's notion that moral judgements were about social relations and not facts was not so far from some of the central ideas of the 1960s' version of a 'new morality', but there was no evidence that Leach was striving for a 'higher morality', especially when his comments on morality were linked to his extremely controversial statement about the family with 'its narrow privacy and tawdry secrets' as 'the source of all our discontents' (ibid., p. 44).

Atkinson (1965) observed that while the old rule-based morality was open to exploitation by people who did not transgress the letter of the law, so the new morality based on 'emotional sincerity' was not wholly proof against self-deception. In their eagerness to embrace what they regarded as a 'higher' form of morality, the more moderate reformers, who comprised many eminent churchmen, tended to make extremely hopeful assumptions about human nature. Moderates in the 1960s were positioned on a spectrum between those who espoused what came to be known as 'situation ethics', which played down rule-based morality, and those who favoured a 'higher morality' based on morality from within, while not necessarily abandoning external rules entirely.

Mary Whitehouse (1977, p. 188), the fervent campaigner for traditional moral standards in public life and in the media, referred disparagingly to situation ethics as the 'if you itch – scratch' school of thought. However, the warmth and optimism of the 1960s variant of the 'new morality' was infectious and fitted well with the popular mood. Barr (1969) defined Christian situation ethics as a set of ideas that put people first, made love the ultimate criterion for ethical decisions, and recognised that what love demands depends on the situation. Likewise, Norman Pittenger (1967), a Cambridge theologian, explained that love was the 'clue' that countered the view of Christian life as static, mechanical and formal. Deep personal fellowship was at the heart of the new ideas rather than coercive power. The openness of love as giving and receiving was suited to the progressive modern world. The old rules could only serve as a guide; it was essential to recognise that 'context alters content'. This was the essence of situation ethics, which made sexual behaviour rest on 'free responsible personal decision, with due regard to consequences both personal and social'. Pittenger dismissed the old, external moral code governing sexual ethics as designed 'to avoid conception, infection and detection' (ibid., p. 84).

K.C. Barnes (1958, p. 97) who with his wife published his first advice book on sex and marriage in 1938, argued in a second edition that 'a personal relationship has its own inherent morality, a morality that is not imposed by any rules from the outside. In a relationship that is truly personal you simply *cannot* use the other person without being aware that you are destroying or denying something.' In 1963, Barnes was part of a controversial Quaker group which reported on the issue of homosexuality and again emphasised that sexual morality could only come from within and could only be based on the refusal to exploit another human being (Heron, 1963). The Quaker group's report was published the same year as the Bishop of Woolwich's *Honest to God*, a best-seller, which resulted in the Bishop, John A. T. Robinson, receiving over 1000 letters in the first three months (Edwards, 1963). Robinson was very aware of writing in an increasingly secular society for a post-Freudian audience: 'we all need, more than anything else, to love and be loved. That's what the psychologists tell us' (Robinson, 1963, p. 277). Robinson's belief that it was impossible to condemn anything that was truly based on love, whether pre-marital sex or divorce, was, to say the least, controversial. His views were foreshadowed by his evidence to the *Lady Chatterley* obscenity trial, when he said that while the sexual relationship in the book was not one that he regarded as 'ideal', he felt that D.H. Lawrence was trying to stress 'the real value and integrity of personal relations' and advised Christians to read the book (Rolph, 1961, p. 72). Robinson used the term 'new morality' in the book, which was attributed to him and taken up three months after the book's publication in the debate over the Profumo sex scandal.[2]

Robinson admired the way in which the American Joseph Fletcher had developed his ideas about situation ethics. Fletcher (1966) began his book on the subject with a quotation from G.E. Moore. He denied that his approach amounted to antinomianism; rather, the responsible person decided whether the wisdom of the Church's rules could serve in his or her particular situation. Robinson (1970) said that the new morality merely emphasised love without denying law. Most of those espousing situational ethics were agreed on this, although many were antagonistic to the old moral code. Helen Oppenheimer (1962) felt that rules could be dangerous because it was possible to believe oneself virtuous if the rules were kept. While Christian morality was not 'lawless', love could not be reduced to law. MacKinnon's contribution to Alec Vidler's influential *Objections to Christian Belief* (1963) rejected the idea of Christian morality as a morality of obligation and command. The new morality offered 'ways' that were morally sound, rather than an authoritarian judgement as to what was right: 'it is by trying to please another person out of love that

one can really be set free from self-centredness, not by trying to "be good" '
(Oppenheimer, 1962, pp. 32–3).

The new morality was inductive. Like modern science, the morality of obedience to external absolutes was giving way to the morality of involvement and discovery. Inevitably this was threatening because the answers were not settled beforehand. However, as Monica Furlong (1965), a journalist, commented, openness and lack of certainty was tremendously appealing in a decade that welcomed not only the Beatles and the Rolling Stones, but the television satirical show *That Was the Week that Was* and *Monty Python's Flying Circus*. Deductive morality 'from above' started with the institution of marriage and decided the issue for the individual in advance, but, as Robinson repeated, not all marriages were moral. The decisive thing had to be the presence or absence of love. The approach was people-centred in that value resided only in love: 'Christian ethics or moral theology is not a scheme of living according to a code, but a continuous effort to relate love to a world of relativities through a casuistry obedient to love; its constant task is to work out the strategy and tactics of love, for Christ's sake' (Fletcher, 1966, p. 158).

Neither Fletcher nor Robinson were 'permissive'. Fletcher (1967, p. 91) recognised that 'sex is dynamite. Unchannelled by high character it leads to chaos and destruction', and a true morality from within was held to build character. Fletcher was convinced that with advances in birth control technology it would have to be personal conviction rather than fear of a rule-based morality that held people to chaste standards. Robinson (1970, p. 30) wrote that he believed 'the nexus between bed and board, between sex and the sharing of life at every level must be pressed as strongly as ever by those who really care for persons as persons' and that, while everyone needs rules, when these were questioned it was important that people not be driven back to the law, but should refer instead to the principle of love. Robinson was aware that his 'new morality' probably appeared individualistic: 'The "paradigms of love" do indeed frequently strip the individual down to the bare relationship between him and God and the single neighbour', but moral decisions, he insisted, are always social. James Hemming (1969), a psychologist and humanist whose writings on morality achieved a wide audience in the 1960s, stressed the importance of personal fulfilment, but emphasised too that the road to it was not via egocentricity but rather through reciprocal, sensitive, creative relationships and self-management. Probably the new moralists of the 1960s, most of whom wrote within an explicitly Christian framework, expected too much of their fellow human beings in hoping for such a high standard of other-regarding personal morality.

Certainly there were some Christian writers who doubted their arguments. Demant's (1963, p. 113) analysis stressed the importance of an increase in what he termed 'emotional insecurity': 'The family is held together for purely individual needs, without much loyalty to it as an institution, and seems unable to bear the weight of meeting all the psychic needs which the wider community used to cater for.' It followed that what was needed was a firm, external moral code, the insecurity which bred the search for 'sexual union at almost any price' (ibid., p. 117) could only be exacerbated by easier divorce. A 1966 Report to the British Council of Churches by an advisory group on sex and morality, which was advised by Sherwin Bailey, reviewed the various positions adopted in the debate and concluded that for the most part a modified conservative position was best. The advisory group could not support the view that moral rules possessed permanent and absolute validity. But it was in favour of having rules, while acknowledging that rules alone were an inadequate basis for morality. Only a minority felt that moral rules could serve only an educational purpose.

The Archbishop of Canterbury (1967, p. 2) was convinced that '[A]t the present time, as is very evident, the stability and harmony of this country is grievously at risk for lack of any prevalent standard of morality, social, political or economic, strong enough to check or restrain or educate the present riot of individual and group choices and decisions.' He believed that the Church had to give authoritative guidance and agreed with the British Council of Churches' Report that while rules might need to be changed, rules were necessary. Furthermore: 'If the whole country has a strong, generally accepted "character", it can safely carry a great variety of groups and enclaves, some of which are subversive of good citizenship without harm' (ibid., pp. 12–13). This went to the heart of the debate about the possibility of imposing an external moral code: was any such thing possible in an increasingly plural and secular society? Alasdair MacIntyre (1967) argued that it was moral change that had caused secularisation rather than vice versa. Values had become increasingly private and Britain was already morally pluralistic, which made it difficult to impose moral authority. Theologians could only try to interpret Christianity in ways that made it more acceptable to modern society, or retreat into orthodoxy. MacIntyre, however, dismissed the effort to make love the supreme value as 'vacuous', because it divorced the morality of intention from the prescription of action. Nevertheless, increasingly both religious and legal opinion was of the view that pluralism, like situation ethics and ideas about a higher morality based on love, led to the conclusion that moral questions about marriage and the family had to be answered in private rather than in public.

Defenders of an external moral code were much more thin on the ground by the 1960s, but the intervention of Patrick Devlin in his second Maccabean Lecture, delivered in 1958 and published in 1965, proved particularly influential. Devlin had given evidence to the Wolfenden Committee in favour of reform of the law on homosexuality, arguing that there was an area of private morality that was none of the law's business. But he had changed his mind soon thereafter.

In 1958, he put forward the view that there should be a commonly accepted moral standard that in Britain would inevitably be based on Christian values. In other words, marriage and the family could not be simply private matters: 'A common morality is part of the bondage. The bondage is part of the price of society, and mankind, which needs society, must pay the price' (Devlin, 1965, p. 10). No particular boundary between public and private could be set if the institution of marriage, which was fundamental to the moral order, was to be protected. Devlin faced the difficult issue as to what constituted a shared moral standard. He resorted to the idea of what was acceptable to the 'reasonable' man on the Clapham omnibus or in the jury box, which might well change over time. He felt that most people would agree with the toleration of maximum individual freedom consistent with the preservation of the integrity of society: 'Every moral judgement, unless it claims a divine source, is simply a feeling that no right-minded man could behave in any other way without admitting he was doing wrong' (ibid., p. 17). Thus Devlin fell back on an Orwellian notion of 'decency'. But as Mitchell (1967) pointed out, his concern was focused on the preservation of the institutions – such as marriage – that in his view secured social cohesion, the views of a particular couple were of lesser import.

However, Devlin's critics were not at all sure that a common morality could or should be identified in the manner he proposed. Dworkin (1971, p. 69) put it pithily: 'What is shocking and wrong is not his idea that the community's morality counts, but his idea of what counts as the community's morality.' Munby (1963, p. 22) concluded in a similar fashion in his Riddel Memorial Lectures of 1962: 'It is one thing to hold a high view of Christian morality; it is another to insist that this should be the law of the land.' There was in any case the irony that traditional Christian morality was undergoing substantial change even as Devlin wrote. The majority of critics felt that Devlin's views ran the risk of 'democratic authoritarianism'. While Devlin stopped short of James Fitzjames Stephen's (1873) notable late nineteenth-century attack on John Stuart Mill, in which he argued that the enforcement of morality was a good in and of itself,[3] his position was bound to result in a measure of coercion in respect of the private lives of some. H.L.A. Hart (1963) pointed out that Devlin had not produced any evidence to the effect that loosening moral bonds was the first stage of disintegration in a society. Even if there was a general 'intolerance, indignation and disgust' in respect of a particular behaviour, it did not justify imposing the view of the majority on a minority. Devlin's views offended a wide spectrum of liberal opinion (for example, Wollheim, 1959; Hughes, 1962; St John-Stevas, 1964; Dworkin 1971) and found relatively few defenders (Rostow, 1960). St John-Stevas (1964, p. 31) summed up the view of many when he said: 'where there is no consensus, the question must be left to be determined in the private sphere'. Like reforming churchmen, the drift in the commentary offered by lawyers and politicians was towards the impossibility of imposing any prescription for behaviour in the private sphere of marriage and the family. By 1969, Establishment opinion was ready to reform the fault-based law of divorce.

FIN DE SIÈCLE ANXIETIES REGARDING MORALITY

Acceptance of the idea that morality should come from within rather than be imposed from without had significant implications for the role of family law and social policy. The 1974 members of the Committee on One-Parent Families made it clear that they believed that in a liberal democratic society it was well-nigh impossible for government to seek directly to control marital and reproductive behaviour. They therefore recognised that the burden of supporting lone-mother families would inevitably fall on the state:

> Once it is conceded that the law cannot any longer impose a stricter standard of familial conduct and sexual morality upon the poor than it demands from others, it follows inexorably that part of the cost of breakdown of marriage, in terms of the increase of households and dependencies, must fall on public funds. (Committee on One-Parent Families, 1974, para. 4.49)

However, some 20 years later, in the midst of heated debates about the causes of the rapid increase in lone-mother families and anxieties about the growth of selfish individualism (see above, pp. 5–14), Lord Mackay, the Lord Chancellor, seemed to revert to the older desire to make morality a top-down exercise when he announced his intention of introducing measures to cut the rate of divorce. However, the shift that was signalled was more complicated than this. In a 1995 White Paper on mediation and the grounds for divorce, he proposed instead a collection of measures intended to make divorce less expensive and more amicable, while ensuring that the obligation of husband and wife as father and mother to take responsibility for, and to secure the position of, children was fulfilled. The Consultation Paper that preceded the White Paper by two years had in fact accepted that the basis for marriage was love and that a decision as to whether this was present or absent could only be made by the couple:

> [A]lthough the law can lay down the formalities for marriage, it cannot prescribe the expectations with which individuals enter marriage and so it cannot enforce them. Reality may fall far short of the ideal. This can lead to widespread disappointment and disillusionment and, ultimately, marital breakdown. No statute, no matter how carefully and cleverly drafted can make two people love each other. (Lord Chancellor's Department, 1993, para. 3.3–4)

The Consultation Paper cited the findings of an influential Church of England working group in the mid-1960s, to the effect that in a pluralist and secular society, many may respect family life but not subscribe to the Christian morality that had underpinned fault-based divorce (ibid., para. 6.13). Nevertheless, the document concluded that the objectives of the law must continue to be the support of marriage. To this end, the approach in the mid-1990s amounted to a new formulation. The abandonment of a fault-based law of divorce was confirmed, but alongside it government sought to make a space for reconciliation and to ensure that people took responsibility for settling their own affairs:

> If changing the law cannot save irretrievable marriages, it can slow down the divorce process and enable the parties to do as much as possible to prevent the marriage from finally ending ... it can make sure that people are made to realise the full consequences of divorce for themselves and their children ... In that way they can take personal responsibility for their decisions. (ibid., para. 1.5)

The optimism that morality would come from within and that people would behave in a caring fashion towards one another gave way to public effort to impose structures and conditions that would ensure that they did so.

In many respects, this approach was in line with the backlash against the perceived growth in selfish individualism. William Galston (1991), the American liberal philosopher, argued that the liberal state could not afford to remain neutral concerning different ways of life. A fellow American, Philip Selznik (1992, p. xi) suggested that 'a robust community, however pluralistic, must embrace the idea of a common good'. While accepting that the kind of absolutist morality espoused by Devlin had become impossible to impose, Selznik rejected the kind of moral relativism that does not admit objectivity. In other words, he argued that values are not reducible to subjective preferences. But how to define what is acceptable to 'the community', whether by appeal to past experience and institutions or to contemporary dialogue, is extremely problematic, especially in the field of adult intimate relationships.

In Britain, a vociferous minority continued to argue that 'people can be guided in the right direction through the introduction of legislation' (Lord Stallard, *House of Lords*, *Debates* 11 March 1996, vol. 570, c. 630), but a majority accepted that it was difficult to argue that the law could determine a particular kind of marital behaviour. According to *The Independent* (28 April 1995), with the 1995 White Paper, Lord Mackay had 'recognised an important truth – that the state has limited ability and little right to intervene in the personal relationships of private individuals'. However, while government was ready to allow the decisions about divorce and intimate relations in general to be private, it tried to make sure that selfish individualism did not prevail and that people were forced to face up to their responsibilities, especially in respect of their biological children. In fact, as the next chapter will show, in the Parliamentary debates over what was to become the 1996 Family Law Act, considerable effort was made to turn the legislation into a vehicle that also promoted marriage. It has been difficult for governments to allow intimate relationships to be governed by morality from within.

Of course, it has remained possible for government to regulate the relationship between parent and child. It did this directly in the early 1990s via the 1991 Child Support Act, which obliged parents to support all their biological children. It could also attempt to do so indirectly by trying to ensure that adults negotiate their parental responsibilities, even as the regulation of spousal relationships waned. Thus from the mid-1980s much more attention was paid to the possibility of conciliation, although government hung back from making it compulsory. The 1985 report on matrimonial causes procedure noted that '[i]t is of the essence of conciliation that responsibility remains at all times with the parties themselves to identify and seek agreement on the issues arising from the breakdown of their relationship' (Booth, 1985, para. 3. 10). It was hoped that conciliation in respect of divorce would permit the state to step back and to reduce the amount spent on legal aid in particular, while nevertheless enforcing private negotiation. Thus, while attempts to enforce an external moral code were progressively abandoned, regulation was not. Rather, the focus switched from the relationship between adults as husband and wife, which had become much more fluid, to their roles as fathers and mothers.

Changes in the thinking about marriage and the marriage system on the part of opinion makers played a major part in making it impossible to hold on to the old fault-based law of divorce, which was founded on a strict moral code. But the effects were wider than the law itself. The change in thinking was part of the erosion of the whole holding mechanism of family law, which had carried a clear message as to the 'ought' of intimate relationships. Once the idea of a common moral rule had been abandoned then prescription became extremely difficult. The next chapter examines what happened to the law in this respect. As important was the way in which ordinary people became very wary of imposing their views on others as to how intimate relationships should be conducted (see below Chapters 6 and 7). As Michael Keeling (1967, p. 60) put it in a pamphlet for the Student Christian Movement: 'it is one thing to accept a moral standard for ourselves, but it is quite another thing for us to say that it should be enforced on everybody by law'. However, popular understanding of morality remained complex. Alasdair MacIntyre (1963) captured this in his comments on *Honest to God*. He referred to a survey by *New Society* (a weekly magazine on social issues and problems) of its readers on religion and morals, which found that a majority felt that Christianity was moribund, that this was sad, and that divorce should be made easier. MacIntyre commented on the paradoxical wish on the part of this educated audience to hold on to a morality which conflicted with their own on matters of central importance: 'Behind this paradox one senses a belief that Christian theology is false and a wish that it were not, which at other levels appears as a kind of half-belief' (ibid., p. 224). The relationship between the 'is' and the 'ought' was not necessarily clear at the individual level. No wonder, as the chapters in Section III show, that people became reluctant to prescribe for others in terms of whether they should marry or not and in terms of how they should organise their domestic arrangements.

NOTES

1. Certainly he had a magnetic effect on the Fabian nursery, which was to result in two affairs (with Rosamund Bland and Amber Pember Reeves) that plunged relations in the Fabian Society into chaos between 1906 and 1908.
2. According the John Selwyn Gummer, later a member of Mrs Thatcher's Cabinet, the Profumo scandal, which mixed spying and sex, showed that Britain had indeed become less censorious: 'a great deal of energy was expended by public commentators in explaining that it was his [Profumo'sl lie to the House of Commons and the possible danger to national security because of his liaison with Christine Keeler that was being criticised – not in any way his adultery' (Gummer, 1971, p. 6).
3. Stephen used the term 'moral majority'.

5. The law of marriage and divorce: towards privatisation and deregulation?

Major changes in the law of marriage and divorce followed the debates about the degree to which the imposition of an external moral code was either desirable or possible. The first major reform of divorce law came in 1937 and the second in 1969. This is not to argue for the pre-eminent importance of the relationship between changing ideas about morality imposed from without or within on the one hand, and legal reform on the other. The causes of reform were many and various and certainly also included changes in economic behaviour, the use of birth control and changes in patterns of family building. Prior to the Second World War, many reformers saw liberalisation of the law as a way of putting a stop to demands for the privatisation of decisions about the ending of a marriage, even though the reforms themselves were influenced by the new ideas about intimate relationships discussed in the previous chapter. Certainly, legal reform in the twentieth century, up to and including the 1996 Family Law Act, has been characterised by a retreat from the attempt directly to impose an external moral code imbued with traditional assumptions regarding the roles of men and women in marriage. This in turn opened up the whole question as to the nature of the boundary between marriage and non-marriage. There has been considerable debate about the intentions behind the reforms and the precise nature of the changes. Some recent commentators believe that this has resulted in a legal 'vacuum', what Glendon (1981) termed the 'deregulation' of family law (see above, p. 24). It has been observed that it is now easier to divorce someone than to fire them (Sandel, 1996), and that it is easier to renounce a marriage than a mortgage (Wilson, 1993).

Many broadly agree that this has indeed been the pattern of change and that there is now something of a legal vacuum that must be addressed. Thus, from a perspective sympathetic to neo-classical economics, Posner (1992) has argued that the growing individualisation of women, in terms of fertility control and more especially the growing economic independence, created conditions which make it impossible for the state to impose duties (or confer rights) on couples. He favoured an outright move towards 'contractual cohabitation', the terms of which would be determined by the couple. Some feminists, particularly in the US, have also argued that the law should take account of women's increased autonomy, and that explicit pre-nuptial, marital and cohabitation contracts are the best way of so doing (for example, Schultz, 1982; Scott, 1990; Kingdom, 1988, 1990). In this interpretation, the logic of increasing individualism in the private sphere is accepted and has led not just to new thinking about intimate relationships, but to a call for new legal forms.

However, the nature of change in respect of family law over time is open to conflicting interpretation. Interestingly, A.V. Dicey's enormously influential lectures on the relationship between law and opinion, delivered at the end of the nineteenth century, also suggested that individualism in the sense of democratic opinion involved marriage being seen as a contract, which in turn would make divorce easier (Dicey, 1948). But Dicey believed that this had already taken effect with the passing of the 1857 Divorce Act, which created a court for divorce and established the grounds for procedure. For Dicey, the 1857 legislation was a triumph of liberal individualism and he believed that this was being increasingly threatened by socialist or collectivist opinion, which was inclined to see marriage as a benefit to the state. While Dicey's view shows that the idea of a relationship between individualism and the relaxation of the law of marriage and divorce is far from new, it also serves to indicate long-standing confusion about the precise nature of the law of marriage and divorce and of legal change.

Legal commentators have long argued about the extent to which marriage can be conceptualised as a contract or a status, and about the extent to which it remains sacramental. O'Donovan (1993, p. 76) has suggested that marriage has a 'sacred, magical status'. It may have contractual and institutional elements, but it is difficult neatly to categorise it. The whole idea of fault-based divorce implied an idea of contractual obligations (Atkins and Hoggett, 1984), but it is the state rather than the parties to this implied contract that controls both entry to it and its ending. Henry Maine (1861, p. 170) had argued that the progress of the law was from status, derived from 'the powers and privileges anciently residing in the Family', to contract, which emerged from private transactions between individuals. The irony was that the law appeared to be slow to change precisely in respect of intimate relationships in the family. In other areas, as Dicey perceived, the state began, from the late nineteenth century, to limit the freedom of contract and to offer alternative forms of collective welfare provision in recognition of the fact that the parties to the contract between capital and labour were profoundly unequal in terms of economic strength. It is noteworthy that in the case of marriage, many, including some feminists, have argued *against* the recognition of increasing individualisation by the more explicit adoption of contract, calling attention to the fact that women remain unequal in terms of their access to income, wealth and resources of all kinds (notwithstanding their increased economic independence), and to the concomitant obligation of the state to continue to regulate the marital relation in the interests of the weaker party (Okin, 1989; Wax, 1998; Baier, 1986).

The fact that private contract continues to be proposed as a solution to the problems of the private law of the family shows that deregulation in the sense of the complete withdrawal of the state is actually far from complete. Indeed, most legal commentators have recognised that marriage defies simple characterisation in terms of status or contract. Cohen (1933) pointed out that while contractarians held that obligation should ideally arise only out of the will of the individual who freely entered into contract,[1] with minimalist intervention by the state, feelings of security depended on the protection of government. Thus in the case of marriage, while the act of getting married was voluntary, the legal consequences were not contractual but were rather imposed 'from without' by the state in the public interest. Later arguments also stressed the extent to which the voluntary agreement to marry established a status that in the case of women was subordinate (Rehbinder, 1971). The so-called marriage contract was, as Weitzman (1981) was to point out later still, an implicit contract, involving sexual services and care on the part of the woman and financial support on the part of the man.

However, the debate among legal commentators as to the nature of the law governing marriage and divorce may not be as important as the shift in the understanding of marriage that is signified by legal reform. Historically the law of marriage and divorce sought to uphold the idea of the 'unity' of husband and wife and the 'permanence' of marriage (Wolfram, 1987). In the nineteenth century, married women had no legal personality and hence no capacity to enter into contracts in the market place. The legal doctrine of *couverture*, which stated that husband and wife were as one and that one was the husband, was described clearly in Sir William Blackstone's (1771, p. 442) famous eighteenth-century *Commentaries on the Laws of England*: 'The very being or legal existence of the wife is suspended during the marriage or at least incorporated and consolidated into that of the husband under whose wing, protection and cover she performs everything.' This was the legal embodiment of Thèry's (1998) formulation of the couple as '2 make 1'. The shift towards women's individualisation in law took place gradually, beginning with the married women's property laws at the end of the nineteenth century, the equalisation of grounds for divorce in 1923, and continuing into the 1990s with the introduction of separate taxation and the recognition of possibility of rape in marriage. But it is still far from complete, the 1 + 1 that now make 2 are not fully individualised in the eyes of the law any more than they are fully independent in respect of income. The determination of social security benefits in particular continues to rest on the concept of household rather than individual income.

The substantial inroads into the doctrine of 'unity' that took place in the early part of the century did so without any explicit outright rejection of the traditional conception of marriage. Indeed, all legal reform was carried out with the express aim of upholding and strengthening marriage, with the sole exception of the

1984 legislation. Nevertheless, the need to improve the quality of marriage was widely admitted and often used to justify reform. Similarly, a shift away from the ideal of 'permanence' was never openly acknowledged. Rheinstein (1972) pointed out that changing ideas and practices in respect of marriage were managed by operating a 'dual law' of divorce, whereby the law on the statute book differed profoundly from what happened in practice. The law of divorce prior to 1969 relied on some idea of breach of contract, embodied in the effort to determine 'fault' and to apportion blame and just deserts. However, in many respects fault-based divorce had already been converted into consensual divorce early in the twentieth century (see Figure 4.1 above, p. 75), often via the practice of 'collusion' (a legal bar to divorce if discovered by the courts) between husband and wife to agree to provide whatever evidence was necessary, for example, of adultery. In other words, private action was employed to undermine the imposition of a strict moral code by the public authorities.[2] It was when changing ideas about marriage reached a crescendo first in the inter-war period and again in the 1960s that the dual law of divorce became impossible to sustain. Once morality was acknowledged to arise from within rather than without, then it became very difficult to apply any external judgements to intimate relationships of any kind, but the results were particularly significant in respect of divorce. Major reforms of the law in 1937 and 1969 were undertaken with the explicit aim of making family law more fit for the purpose of upholding marriage by acknowledging changes in behaviour and in the ideas about marriage. The movement towards no-fault divorce in the 1960s in Britain and the US explicitly recognised the changing ideas about marriage, in particular the possibility that it might not be permanent, and tried to codify the new understanding of marriage as 'partnership' rather than 'unity' (Weitzman, 1981; Kay, 1990), an understanding that reflected the post-war effort to 'update' the male breadwinner model in the form of the companionate family (see Chapter 3).

The fear about divorce law reform throughout the twentieth century has been that, in the absence of law based on a firm moral code, individuals would increasingly be able to decide for themselves how to arrange their intimate relationships and whether and when to leave a marriage. Reform was usually justified in terms of modernisation, which would permit the state to preserve the institution of marriage that was in turn fundamental to social order. For many at the end of the century, the issue was whether reform had gone so far as to tip the balance in favour of the indiscipline and selfish behaviour that it was intended to protect against. Rowthorn (1999) has argued strongly that no-fault divorce has undermined marriage as a 'contractual partnership',[3] thereby reducing the security enjoyed by women, and increasing male opportunism and the number of divorces. However, he has acknowledged that the results of quantitative work on the last of these has produced very conflicting results in the UK and the US. Any attempt of this kind to make a causal connection between law and behaviour is bound to be very difficult to substantiate because the nature of the relationship is far from clear. It has already been argued that it is more likely that law follows behavioural change and then facilitates and legitimises certain kinds of behaviour (see above, pp. 2–5). Just as changing ideas about the nature of marriage have had an effect on the law, so Weitzman (1981) has suggested that the obligations imposed by the law of divorce will affect ideas about marriage. This in turn may be what serves to legitimate certain kinds of behaviour. The fear of many policy makers at the end of the century is that the steady march of legal reform away from the imposition of external rules has encouraged the growth of selfish individualism, in the sense, first, that the parties to a marriage have increasingly been allowed to make the decision as to whether it should continue; second, in the sense of legitimising the kind of opportunistic behaviour that may cause breakdown; and third, in undermining the assumptions regarding the obligations attaching to the male breadwinner model that were written into the law of divorce. This in turn makes for reluctance to do anything about major outstanding issues such as how to treat cohabitation, for fear that it might further weaken the distinction between marriage and non-marriage and give additional reinforcement to the changes in ideas and behaviour that have already taken place.[4]

The reform of family law in the twentieth century has been characterised by a movement towards what might be termed 'self-regulation' (by the couple), in other words the privatisation of decision making about the ending of a marriage, which is in line with changing ideas about the source of sexual morality. But this movement is not necessarily equivalent to deregulation. After the major reform of 1969, it was found that partnerships that were conceptualised as equal-but-different proved no more easy to treat on divorce than the fundamentally unequal relationships that were assumed to exist under the legal regime of no-fault (Carbone and Brinig, 1991; Fineman, 1993). Fault-based divorce was perceived as securing the gendered obligations of the male breadwinner model family. Changes in the law of divorce spoke volumes about changes in ideas about marriage. By the late twentieth century, couples were increasingly treated as equal individuals, regardless of their actual position, and encouraged to take responsibility for sorting out their own affairs on divorce. Figure 5.1 attempts to illustrate what happened with the shift away from a strict external moral code. The idea that true morality could only come from within the individual meant that individuals were left much freer to make decisions about their intimate relationships. However, law did not go into full retreat, rather it began to try to enforce private responsibility.

The shift away from the direct public regulation of intimate relationships has been profound, but rarely explicitly acknowledged. Towards the end of the twentieth century, several observers have noted that the law has had less and less to say about the adult partners to an intimate relationship, but that it continues to regulate their relations as parents (for example, Dewar and Parker, 1992; Lewis and Maclean, 1997). To tell couples wishing to part that they must seek to reach accommodation about their children is a form of regulation. Freedom of husbands and wives to part so long as they continue to carry out their responsibilities as mothers and fathers is also the kind of change that was demanded by Bertrand Russell as long ago as 1929.

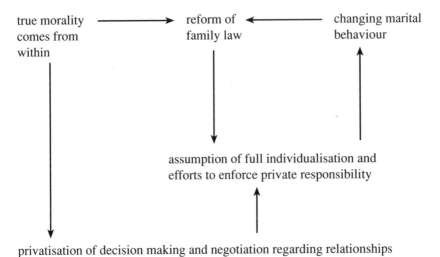

Figure 5.1   The implications of the shift away from an external moral code

REFORM AS CONTAINMENT: 1912–1937

Substantial reform of the divorce laws was proposed by the Majority Report of the Royal Commission on Divorce and Matrimonial Causes in 1912 and finally enacted in 1937, when the grounds for divorce were expanded to include desertion, cruelty and insanity. The framework of fault was expanded in an effort to close the widening gap between law and behaviour, although the concern in 1912 – over the amount of separation and cohabitation – was very different from the anxiety in the 1930s over the degree to which the law was being abused by couples seeking divorce. The nature of the reform may also be read as a reflection of the new understanding of what constituted marriage. After all, desertion, cruelty and insanity were not compatible with an idea of marriage as a loving, 'higher' relationship. *The Times* had referred in apocalyptic terms to the 'abolition of marriage' after the court's judgment in the 1891 Jackson case, which ruled that a man was not entitled to keep his wife in confinement in order to enforce the restitution of conjugal rights. But increasingly it was recognised that the legal framework governing marriage and divorce had to be reformed if it was not to be bypassed.

The 1912 Report of the Royal Commission sought to expand the grounds for divorce and access to it in order to put an end to what it saw as the 'evil' of judicial separation (Royal Commission on Divorce, 1912a, para. 234). Working people who lacked both the money and grounds necessary to obtain a divorce sought judicial separation from the magistrates' courts (Behlmer, 1994) and often then went on to 'live in sin'. It was the hope of the majority of the members of the Commission that easier divorce would allow them to remarry. Thus liberalisation was proposed in order to draw a firmer line between the married and unmarried, and to promote marriage:

> So far from such reforms as we recommend tending to lower the standard of morality and regard for the sanctity of the marriage-tie, we consider that reform is necessary in the interests of morality, as well as in the interest of justice, and in the general interests of society and the state. (ibid., para. 50)

Reform was thus justified as the means of imposing an external moral code more effectively and of stopping the poor making informal living arrangements. Hensley Henson (1910), then a canon of Westminster Abbey, argued that marriage was degraded if it was possible to be separated and yet still married. Separation and cohabitation often made eminently good sense to the poor, as the evidence presented to the 1912 Royal Commission by a Poor Law visitor showed. She told the story of a poor woman who insisted that the importance of securing an effective male breadwinner justified leaving a 'hopelessly out of work' husband and cohabiting with another man (Royal Commission on Divorce ..., 1912b, Q. 20120).

Some divorce law reformers also drew on the kind of arguments used by those who insisted on marriage as a 'higher relationship' (see above, pp. 76–7). Part of the case for extending the grounds for divorce rested on the idea that if the grounds were confined to adultery, this undermined the notion of marriage as a spiritual as well as a sexual relationship (Hamilton, 1909). As the Earl of Birkenhead (1927, pp. 154–5), who was President of the Divorce Law Reform Union from 1922 to 1930, put it: 'to limit the causes of divorce is to ignore the fact that the spiritual and moral aspects of marriage are incomparably more important than the physical side'. More pragmatically, the Marquess of Queensberry (n.d.) had insisted at the turn of the century that an inflexible divorce law was inevitably accompanied by high levels of prostitution.

The argument of the Majority Report of the Royal Commission for reform that would promote marriage encompassed a measure of individualisation. It was argued that the grounds of divorce for men and for women should be the same: 'In principle there can be no adequate reason why two persons who enter into matrimonial relationship should have a different standard of morality applied to them' (Royal Commission on Divorce ..., 1912a, para. 210). There was some degree of support for this, and not only from those who wanted liberalisation. Feminists had argued strongly that inequality in this respect degraded marriage when women were expected to take the lead in cultivating moral feeling (Bremner, 1912). This position was increasingly hard to refute, especially when Millicent Garrett Fawcett, the suffragist leader, told the Commission that she did not want the grounds of divorce extended. She wanted to see equality for men and women in respect of divorce on grounds of adultery (prior to 1923 only men could petition on grounds of simple adultery alone), but she insisted that moral standards be levelled up rather than down, which meant making divorce harder for men (Royal Commission on Divorce ..., 1912a, Q. 21732).

However, the perceived threat of reform to permanence was a different matter. The Church of England believed in indissolubility and several witnesses before the 1912 Royal Commission were prepared to testify as to the general benefits to society of their position. There could be no question of leaving the decision about ending a marriage to the parties concerned. As Bishop Weldon (1912) put it, people could not be allowed to contract and dissolve their marriages at will. Nothing could be further from the interests of public morals and order. The Lambeth Conference of 1920 reiterated this position: 'No comparison for present hardships in particular cases can justify the lowering for all of the standards of Christ, which alone ensures the welfare of society and of the race' (cited by Holmes, 1986, p. 213). The Minority Report of the 1912 Royal Commission (written by the Archbishop of York, an ecclesiastical lawyer and the Warden of All Souls College, Oxford) regarded any expansion of the grounds for divorce as 'the thin end of the wedge'. They wrote that the family was being threatened by socialism and by the 'assertion of individual liberty' (Royal Commission on Divorce ..., 1912a, para. 187). Similarly, the Mothers' Union told the Commission that 'the national character is quite as much benefited and raised by the patient endurance of hardships as by loosening the responsibilities of marriage' (Royal Commissio on Divorce ..., 1912b, Q. 16925).

The rationale for reform put forward by the Majority Report of the 1912 Royal Commission was not strong enough to withstand this kind of strong opposition, especially when it was argued in addition that the poor, at whom reform was aimed, had little desire for it. Stephen Reynolds, a journalist campaigning on behalf of the poor, maintained that easier divorce did not concern poor people. He pointed out that divorce (as it stood) was essentially a punishment for what had occurred rather than a dissolution of marriage for the benefits that would ensue. Only in respect of property was the law oriented towards the future, but that had no meaning for the poor. A reform of the divorce law would only be helpful to the poor if it were to be on the basis of mutual consent. As it was:

> It would be better for the poor to continue seeking the solution of matrimonial diffi-
> culties in desertion, or in relations not legally recognised, than that they should for
> the sake of legal divorce, submit themselves to conventions which are neither theirs
> nor applicable to their conditions of life. (Reynolds, 1910, p. 496)

Reynolds' view was not necessarily representative, and may have more accurately captured the opinion of working men than of women. Certainly, the Women's Co-operative Guild, an organisation of respectable working-class women, offered moving evidence to the Commission and asked for easier access to divorce and equal grounds between men and women.

Reynolds' arguments were very different from the more usual defence of a strict law of marriage and divorce as crucial for social and moral order. But his point about the general character of divorce law was important. Not only did it endeavour to enforce a strict moral code, but it was also designed to be both a difficult experience (elaborated painfully in Arnold Bennett's 1906 novel, *Whom God Hath Joined*), and to apportion blame. Divorce was heavily stigmatised until after the major reform of the late 1960s. Reynolds' argument that divorce was in any case irrelevant to the needs and concerns of the poor, about whose behaviour the Commission was most concerned, was also prescient. The growth of cohabitation among the very poor in the late twentieth century – in a Britain that had become more socially polarised than at any time since the period before the Second World War – has been explained in terms of the relative lack of meaning of marriage for those with few possessions (McRae, 1993), and as a rational response by women in particular to the risk posed by a long-term commitment to a man in a precarious job or with no employment at all (Smart and Stevens, 2000).The Church may have been successful in marshalling a majority of establishment opinion behind its views about the imposition of a strict moral code via the divorce law in the early part of the century, but the fact remained that a substantial proportion of the population did not subscribe to, or live by, its conventions. Ironically, in Reynolds' view this was also a reason for not extending access to divorce to the poor.

By 1937, when the recommendations of the 1912 Majority Report were finally implemented, the case for reform was very different. The grounds for divorce in respect of adultery were equalised between men and women in 1923, partly in response to pressure from the organised feminist movement after the partial granting of the suffrage, and partly as a means of stemming the demand for more radical reform. As a result, the number of petitions for divorce rose and, furthermore, petitions from women overtook those from men for the first time. The importance of sex and of fidelity in marriage emphasised so often by the moderate reformers during the inter-war years was recognised in the 1923 legislation, but those rethinking the whole idea of marriage were anxious that it should not be thought to rest on sexual fidelity alone. In 1927, the Earl of Birkenhead wrote in terms that foreshadowed the Law Commission's reference to 'empty shell marriages' almost 40 years later that:

> [t]o insist upon the divine origin and nature of marriage in order to keep in existence unions which have ceased to have anything in common with real marriage but the shadow, and in the name of God to refuse redress to society and the individual, is to fall into the error of those who had to be reminded that the Sabbath was made for man. (Birkenhead, 1927, p. 156)

Furthermore, there was increasing evidence of cynical exploitation of the law.

While Mary Ward's polemical novel against divorce, published in 1909, had stressed the importance of self-sacrifice, especially on the part of women, in order to make the supreme test of marriage work, almost 20 years later Somerset Maugham's novel, *The Constant Wife*, painted a picture of a relatively civilised but rather cynical marriage of convenience, underpinned (at least initially) by the woman's economic dependence. During the 1930s there was growing evidence of collusion between better-off husbands and wives to conceal evidence from the court. A.P. Herbert, who was responsible for piloting the 1937 legislation through Parliament, in his novel *Holy Deadlock* (1934) exposed the hypocrisy of carefully staged hotel scenes, designed to provide the evidence for divorce on the grounds of adultery. The solicitor explains to a couple willing to part amicably that one of them must commit adultery:

> The Judge would say: 'Pardon me Mr Adam, but have either of you committed adultery? We are not here, Mr Adam, to secure your happiness, but to preserve the institution of marriage and the purity of the home. And therefore one of you must commit adultery.' ... 'The position is that someone has to commit intimacy for the general good; someone has to behave impurely in order to uphold the Christian ideal of purity, someone has to confess in public to a sinful breach of the marriage vows, in order that the happily married may point at him or her and feel themselves secure and virtuous.' (Herbert, 1934, pp. 23 and 29)

According to Herbert's own account of the passing of the 1937 Act, this kind of behaviour was widely felt to be bringing the law into disrepute (Herbert, 1937). Under a fault-based system, the fault had to be genuine if the law was to be respected. Herbert recognised that, notwithstanding his own sympathies clearly expressed in his novel, he could not concede the principle of mutual consent. In a sense, private decision making regarding the ending of a marriage was manifest in collusion. Herbert argued that widening the grounds of divorce would remove the temptation to collude. Reform could thus be seen as a means of shoring up the imposition of an external, fault-based moral code, albeit one that was much more in tune with new ideas about marriage, because it permitted divorce for causes – insanity, cruelty and desertion – that were patently at odds with a loving relationship. As Cordelia Moyse (1996, p. 372) has convincingly argued: 'the thinking which underpinned the concept of matrimonial offence had changed'.

Those wishing to exercise continued caution in respect of divorce law reform, including Lord Merrivale, who presided over the divorce court for more than a decade, began to sound as though they were siding with hypocrisy in their defence of marriage as an institution over and above its relational aspects, albeit that Merrivale (1936, p. 10) dismissed these as 'a clamour of individuals'. Warnings from Christian organisations and leaders about the possible effects, of collusion on the morality of homelife and in particular on the sensibilities of children (COPEC, 1924), and about the need to 'inculcate a higher view of marriage' (Inge [the Dean of St Paul's], 1930, pp. 363–4) were more common. Herbert called his legislation a 'Marriage Bill'. The long title of the 1937 legislation referred to an Act to amend the law relating to divorce 'for the true support of marriage, the protection of children, the removal of hardship, the reduction of illicit unions and unseemly litigation, the relief of conscience among the clergy [by giving them the right to decide whether to allow divorced people to remarry], and the restoration of due respect for the law'. Divorce was no longer viewed as a *punishment* for fault. It remained fault-based and the law continued to impose an external framework on intimate relationships. However, its aim was now more in line with changes in ideas about the importance of the quality of the marital relationship and of companionship between husband and wife.

'BREAKDOWN BY PROOF' REFORM IN THE 1960s: A COMPROMISE BETWEEN THE PUBLIC AND PRIVATE INTEREST

As in the vast majority of western countries in the late 1960s and early 1970s, Britain undertook a radical reform of the divorce law. The shift everywhere was towards 'no-fault' divorce. In its pure form, this meant that the courts had little interest in the reasons for divorce, which became a private matter for the couple. Instead, the courts focused their attention on what had hitherto been the 'ancillary matters' of division of property and provision for children. However, the shift in Britain was far from complete. Partial no-fault divorce was enacted in 1969 and represented a compromise between the legal and religious establishments. In practice and with the advantage of hindsight, what happened can be seen as another effort to reduce the gap between law on the one hand, and changes in ideas and behaviour on the other, without abandoning the external framework of control. It should perhaps come as no surprise that right at the end of the century, the President of the Family Division, Dame Elizabeth Butler-Sloss, was reported as describing the system of divorce once more as a 'hypocritical charade' (*The Guardian*, 16 October 1999, p. 2).

After the passing of the 1937 legislation, the Church of England exhibited increasing unhappiness about the way in which marriage was being treated. The Joint Committee appointed by the Convocations of Canterbury and York to consider the problem of what the teaching of the Church should be on marriage and divorce reported in 1935 that there 'is in many quarters a revolt against any view of marriage which emphasizes its social aspects and obligations and an increasing tendency to regard it as a purely individual affair' (Convocations of Canterbury and York, 1935, p. 3). The worry was that the increasing recognition being given to the importance of the marital relationship threatened the idea of marriage as permanent (Macmillan, 1944). In the view of the Canon of Worcester the 'indissolubility of marriage is for most people their best protection against their own indiscipline and selfishness' (Lacey, 1947, p. 209). Despite being granted the freedom to decide whether to solemnise a second marriage by the 1937 Act, the Church saw fit to pass a resolution in 1938 (reaffirmed by a 1957 Act of Convocation) to the effect that remarriage always involved a departure from the true principles of marriage. During the course of a 1947 House of Lords Debate on the funding of marriage guidance, the Archbishop of Canterbury described each divorce as creating 'an area of poison and a centre of infection in the national life' (*House of Lords, Debates*, 27 March 1947, c. 887). He referred to the need to convince general opinion' that 'marriage is an obligation with binding duties and sanctions ... [and] that divorce is always the final record of human disaster' (ibid., c. 888).

The Church's defence of its traditional view of marriage was part of the conservative backlash produced by the widespread disruption of families during the Second World War and the significant jump in the divorce rate in the mid-1940s. However, the rethinking of the meaning of marriage and divorce which had taken place in the inter-war years could not be driven underground for long (see above, pp. 81–5). Attempts at legal reform were also renewed. In 1951, Mrs Eirene White MP attempted to add a new matrimonial cause in the form of seven years' separation to the existing grounds for divorce. Her main aim was to enable people who had been separated for a number of years to remarry. This had nothing to do with fault and would have made it possible for one of the parties to the marriage to divorce the other against his or her will, which to some commentators made it even worse than divorce by mutual consent. In return for securing the withdrawal of White's Bill, the government promised to set up another Royal Commission on marriage and divorce.

The Commission was asked to inquire into the law on divorce and matrimonial causes and the powers of the courts, keeping in mind 'the need to promote and maintain healthy and happy married life and to safeguard the interests and well-being of children'. The chairman, Lord Morton, made it clear that he saw it as his responsibility to defend the institution of marriage. Professor O.R. McGregor (1957), who was extremely critical of the Commission for failing to carry out any empirical social research, called those on the Commission who opposed any further reform (the majority), the 'institution-alists'. The Majority Report of the Commission was dominated by the overriding fear that marriage was being taken too lightly:

> There is a further factor in the problem of marriage breakdown, which is more dangerous, because more insidious in its effects, than any of the others. In fact, we believe it lies at the root of the problem. There is a tendency to take the duties and responsibilities of marriage less seriously than formerly. (Royal Commission on Marriage and Divorce, 1956b, para. 46)

The emphasis on marriage as a relationship, and particularly the importance attached to a satisfactory sexual relationship, was blamed for this, alongside 'modern psychology' that stressed the importance of 'self-expression'. Female emancipation in particular meant that some women did not realise that their 'new rights do not release them from the obligations arising out of marriage itself, and indeed, bring in their train certain new responsibilities' (ibid., para. 45). The Commission did not put nearly as much emphasis on the importance of marriage for the welfare of children, probably because the balance of the evidence it heard, including that from the British Medical Association, took the view that divorce was not as harmful to children as a bad marriage. Indeed, there was rather more evidence expressing concern about the fate of older wives, who, in the view of many, were likely to be divorced and left badly off.

The Commission heard evidence from Professor L.C.B. Gower that 'collusion' took place in as many as 50 per cent of undefended divorce cases in the upper income groups, resulting in the continued degradation of the law. Gower insisted that it was not that marriage was no longer respected, but merely that it was no longer necessarily life-long and that the law should be changed to take account of this (Royal Commission on Marriage and Divorce, 1956a). However, the Commission was inclined to attach considerably less importance to the hypocrisy that continued to surround divorce than it was to the possibility that any further reform would exacerbate the tendency to see marriage as impermanent. When Mrs White MP gave evidence to the Commission, the chairman pointed out the dangers inherent in recognising the concept of marital breakdown. Young couples might marry thinking that they could just 'try it for a while' (ibid., n.p.).

The Majority Report turned its face firmly against the recognition of marriage breakdown, which did not rely on fault, as grounds for divorce. To do so would involve some recognition of divorce by consent, which would undermine, and 'ultimately destroy, the concept of life-long marriage' (Royal Commission on Marriage and Divorce, 1956b, para. 69). The Majority Report explained that marriage was a status arising out of contract, and as a status it concerned the community as well as the parties: 'If husband and wife were free to terminate their marriage at pleasure, then marriage would become a *purely contractual relationship* and the interests of the community would receive no recognition' (ibid., para. 69 (vii), my italics). In the words of A.T. Macmillan, a barrister and a writer on Christian issues, marriage would become merely a 'tenancy at will' (Royal Commission on Marriage and Divorce, 1956a).

The Archbishop of Canterbury accepted that the 'purposes' of marriage, which he listed as 'the procreation of children, natural relations and the comfort one ought to have of the other', were thwarted by adultery, desertion or cruelty. Thus he accepted the case for fault-based divorce. But, given that life-long marriage was in the public interest, it was not possible to argue for an extension of the grounds for divorce to include the subjective judgement of the parties concerned. The President of the Probate, Divorce and Admiralty Division, Lord Merriman, was also prepared to accept divorce as a 'relief' for a proven injury, but not at the will of the parties concerned. Most of the evidence received by the Commission was conservative. Even Helena Normanton, a feminist solicitor, who had supported both the recommendations of the Majority Report of the 1912 Royal Commission and the 1937 legislation on divorce, opposed further relaxation of the law mainly because of the alarming rise in juvenile crime and the link that was being made between this and broken homes (for example, by Mullins, 1954). But she also felt, as did other feminists throughout the 1950s and 1960s, that further divorce law reform would do nothing to reform marriage as an institution and in particular women's dependent economic position within it. Indeed, given women's economic dependence in the male breadwinner family, easier divorce posed a threat to their welfare.

Most witnesses appearing before the Commission were asked whether they thought that there was more 'divorce-mindedness' in the population, and many, including the General Council of the Bar of England and Wales, thought that there was. In other words, divorce bred divorce. The majority of the members of the Commission were determined to recommend nothing that might increase the tendency to divorce. Indeed, they felt that unless the tendency was checked it might be better to abandon divorce rights altogether (Royal Commission on Marriage and Divorce, 1956c, para. 54). In short they were not at all ready for the argument of the Marriage Law Reform Society that marital breakdown should be permitted as a ground for divorce because it was impossible to make people love one another. There was little recognition of, or sympathy for, the rethinking of the basis of marriage that had gone on during the inter-war years and that was continuing among some Christian writers during the 1950s (see above, p. 85).

However, only six years after the Royal Commission's Report, Leo Abse, Labour MP for Pontypool, introduced his Matrimonial Causes and Reconciliation Bill, which revived the demand for divorce after seven years' separation. The Church immediately mounted an organised campaign against the Bill, marshalling the Bishops to speak and vote against it in the House of Lords; organising a joint statement condemning it by the Archbishop of Canterbury, the Catholic Archbishop of Westminster and the Procurator of the Free Church, and mounting a letter campaign through the Mothers' Union. The change in ideas about the basis for sexual morality in the 1960s strengthened the reformers, but the battle over legal reform revolved around the extent to which marriage could be privatised to the couple.

The Church saw marriage as a vocation. The couple plighted their troth before God and a marriage came into being when the parties exchanged vows. This could be viewed as the making of a contract, but in the Church's view the exchange of vows was merely a means of bringing the marriage into existence. As a vocation, marriage had no other properties of contract and could therefore not be dissolved by the parties themselves. Limited civil divorce had been reluctantly accepted, but anything resembling mutual consent could not be countenanced because it would effectively undermine the Church's understanding of the whole nature of marriage. If it was accepted that marriage was no longer life-long, it would be difficult for the Church to marry 'just any parishioner' or to recognise the validity of state marriages. As Archbishop Ramsey wrote later in 1966: 'If civil marriage were to become terminable by mutual consent it might be difficult for the church to recognise civil marriage in its present matter' (cited in Lewis and Wallis, 2000).

However, the Church's opposition to the separation clause in Abse's Bill resulted in considerable anti-clerical feeling. As the Bishop of Leicester admitted to the House of Lords, it was worrying that the Church was seen to be 'wrongly attempting to dictate to the community as a whole how it should react to these possibilities' (*House of Lords, Debates*, 22 May 1963, c. 394). Simple opposition to further reform was increasingly difficult not least because of the difficulty of imposing Christian morality on the whole population. In 1963, the Archbishop of Canterbury announced in the House of Lords that he had asked 'some fellow churchmen' to attempt 'to find a principle at law of breakdown of marriage which was free from any trace of the idea of consent, which conserved the point that offences and not only wishes are the basis of breakdown, and which was protected by a far more thorough insistence on reconciliation procedure' (ibid., 21 June 1963, c. 1547). This group produced the report *Putting Asunder* in 1966, which seemingly reversed the whole position of the Church in respect of marital breakdown as ground for divorce. It recommended that 'the doctrine of the breakdown of marriage should be comprehensively substituted for the doctrine of matrimonial offence as the basis of all divorce'. Faced with the choice of maintaining fault or replacing it entirely with breakdown, the group agreed that breakdown was a preferable principle, because it accorded 'better with social realities' and showed divorce 'for what it essentially is ... a defeat for both' (Archbishop's Group, 1966, p. 18). However, the group had been asked to come up with a principle of breakdown free from any idea of mutual consent. It therefore had to address how breakdown was to be judged, and eventually settled on a process of judicial inquest. The courts would investigate the current state of the marriage to discover whether or not it was still viable, rather than seeking evidence of individual fault.

Both the Labour Government and the Law Commission (established in 1965) were committed to reforming the divorce law. The latter produced a response to *Putting Asunder*, which ostensibly restricted itself to 'a consideration of what appears from a lawyer's point of view to be practicable', specifically avoiding 'such controversial social issues as the advisability of extending the present grounds of divorce' (Law Commission, 1966, paras 2, 3). However, in practice the document represented the viewpoint of the reformers in the Law Commission (Cretney, 1998). They urged that the aim of the law should be to enable dissolution of a marriage with 'the maximum fairness and minimum bitterness, distress and humiliation' (Law Commission, 1966, para. 15). The Law Commission opposed breakdown-by-inquest as presenting practical difficulties of time and costs, both human and financial. In its place the Commission wanted a straightforward objective test. However, the Church could not allow divorce by consent of the parties alone. The result was a famous compromise between Church and state. The overarching principle of breakdown was secured, but proof was required. The Act created a single ground for divorce – irretrievable breakdown of marriage – which had to be demonstrated by the petitioner proving one or more of five 'facts'. These consisted of the old 'fault' grounds of cruelty, adultery, insanity and desertion, with the addition of two new separation-based facts: separation for two years if the respondent agreed or deserted, and separation for five years irrespective of the respondent's preference. These two controversial clauses were similar to Abse's proposal to add seven years' separation as a ground for divorce.

The Church had fought for a minimum of three years' separation to count as desertion, for the court to be required to refuse any divorce it believed to be against the public interest, and for stronger economic defences for the weaker party. It was also concerned that reconciliation should be encouraged. All these, like the compromise at the centre of the new Act, were fudged. Those wanting a quick divorce (the vast majority) chose adultery or 'unreasonable behaviour' as a cause of breakdown, and these grounds continued to mask the consensual nature of late twentieth-century divorce. As Cretney (1996) has pointed out, if MPs, let alone the Church, had known that investigation by the courts into the affairs of the divorcing couple would be but a formality and disappear altogether from undefended cases in 1977, when the so-called Special Procedure was introduced by regulation rather than Act of Parliament, the legislation would probably not have passed.

On the last point raised by the Church, it was decided that the new legislation would not be implemented until further provision was made to cover financial arrangements. The divorce reform legislation was not implemented until 1971, by which time the 1970 Matrimonial Proceedings and Property Act had put in place the recommendations of the Law Commission regarding the division of material resources on divorce. The court was asked to 'place the parties, so far as is practicable and having regard to their conduct ... in the financial position in which they would have been if the marriage had not broken down' (Law Commission, 1969). In all probability the Law Commissioners were aware of the threat that no-fault divorce posed to wives who had made their marriage bargains in the 1950s on the assumption that their husbands would act as the breadwinners. This had been raised by many of those giving evidence to the 1956 Royal Commission and formed the basis for substantial attacks on the new divorce legislation in Parliament. Edith Summerskill feared the effects of the legislation on the wife who was 'cast off after many years' service [as a housewife/carer]' (*House of Lords, Debates*, 30 June 1969, c. 310). However, the Law Commissioners may also have seen the effort to enforce the obligations of the male breadwinner to provide financial support as a deterrent to divorce. The reference to an assessment of 'conduct', which had been part of fault-based divorce, supports this view. But, like investigation by the courts, this provision was rapidly eroded. In 1973 the Court of Appeal ruled that conduct should be relevant only if 'obvious and gross' (*Wachtel* v. *Wachtel* [1973] Fam. 72). More important still, the injunction to make sure that the parties to the marriage did not suffer financially as a result of divorce amounted to mere exhortation. In practice, it proved impossible to perpetuate the male breadwinner model beyond the life of the marriage. Finally, while the provision requiring solicitors to say whether they had discussed reconciliation with their clients helped to secure support for the reform (Dingwall and Eekelaar, 1988), it too remained something of a dead letter.

The major reform of divorce legislation in 1969 represented a further substantial shift away from the idea of divorce as a test by the courts of fault. Instead, the parties to a marriage were invited to state how their marriage had broken down. It remained the case that 76 per cent of them (as late as 1986) continued to use adultery or unreasonable behaviour as proof of breakdown (Law Commission, 1988) and, just as in the period between 1937 and 1969, a large number of these couples had probably agreed to present their cases in this way. However, substantially more turned on the decisions of the couple themselves. The principle of breakdown-by-proof was confused and was the price of gaining the Church's support. For the Church, the main issue was marriage, not the technicalities of divorce, and the crucial concern was to preserve marriage as a vocation. The Church could not accept divorce by consent, which would assume marriage to be a (private) contract pure and simple and would give the parties complete control over it. However, it accepted that marriage was being thought of less in terms of what it was *for* (as *per* the Archbishop of Canterbury's evidence to the Royal Commission in 1952) and more in terms of what it actually *was*. In other words, the quality of the relationship had become paramount (Church of England, 1971). The very value of the new principle of breakdown lay in its ambiguities and it continued to be defended by the Church during the 1970s.

CHANGING THE NATURE OF STATE REGULATION AT THE END OF THE TWENTIETH CENTURY

Increasingly it was assumed that the decision by the parties to a marriage about divorce would be accepted. The major government documents on the family during the 1970s – the Report of the Commission on One-parent Families in 1974 and the Home Office and Department of Social Security's report on marriage and marriage counselling in 1979 – subscribed fully to this idea. As Murch (1980, p. 13) put it, the interest of the courts in the reasons for ending a marriage dwindled to 'vanishing point'. Indeed, in 1980, Clive was prompted to suggest that marriage was an unnecessary legal concept. But, as part of the process of change, husbands and wives were increasingly treated as if they were indeed equal individuals in decision making about divorce. The kind of concerns about women's economic dependence that were so much to the fore prior to divorce reform in 1969 were singularly absent afterwards. The focus of law makers switched from men and women as husbands and wives to men and women as parents, and, until 1996, away from marriage as a public institution. But in so doing, family law tended to run ahead of a social reality in which women and men were not fully individualised in the sense of being self-sufficient.

The principle of alimony had enforced the responsibilities of the male breadwinner and punished fault. Coincidentally, it had also provided an element of compensation to the wife for her unpaid care work, but historically this had not been recognised by the courts, as Lord Denning's efforts in the 1960s to secure the right of a woman on divorce to occupy a marital home owned by the husband showed. When fault was abandoned (at least in principle) alimony was difficult to sustain. However it was difficult to separate the needs of women as wives from those of women as mothers. Given that women tended to take responsibility for the day-to-day care of children, this affected their capacity to earn and had knock-on effects for their financial welfare. As Cretney (1985) commented, it proved difficult 'to articulate modern principles' to govern what should happen in respect of maintenance after 1969. The 1969 legislation tried to give voice to the principle of an 'equal-but-different' partnership between husbands and wives. The effort to put the parties in the financial position they would have been in had the marriage not ended signalled an effort to compensate women for their unpaid work. However, the courts had great difficulty in deciding how to value that work.

The 1984 Matrimonial and Family Proceedings Act showed the extent to which the assumptions about men's and women's roles within marriage had changed since 1969. The legislation abandoned the idea of compensation for women's care work and favoured a 'clean break' approach to divorce, the rationale, according to the Attorney General, being the need to make divorce 'a more respectable and cleaner operation' (*House of Commons*, *Debates*, 16 February 1984, c. 405). The aim in promoting a clean break for adults was in large measure to facilitate remarriage (Alcock, 1984). Men and women were assumed to be fully individualised, which meant that women were assumed to be free-standing, employed individuals (Maclean, 1991; Eekelaar, 1991). However, the prescription followed by most of the women seeking divorce had been that they should give most of their attention to their homes and families. The 1984 legislation did state that primary consideration should be given to children. However, as Maclean and Eekelaar (1986) have commented, the debate about the legislation proceeded without much reference to children. Indeed, the kind of approach taken in the 1984 legislation was only made possible by the open acceptance that a large number of divorcees and their children would have to become dependent on state benefits. In *Delaney* v. *Delaney* ([1990] 2 FLR 457), the court held that the fact that the wife could claim benefits in the absence of maintenance payments would allow the husband to establish a home in which he could see the children and justified only a nominal maintenance order. In practice, it seems that the courts followed the principle of need, pragmatically assessing the resources available and trying to deploy them such that housing was settled first and traded off against financial support (Jackson *et al.*, 1993).

While the strong male breadwinner model of the 1950s was being eroded in terms of both fact and normative expectations (see above, Chapter 3), it was premature to assume that women were fully individualised within marriage. Later research findings confirmed the financial difficulties experienced by women and children after divorce (Committee on One-Parent Families, 1974; Bradshaw and Millar, 1991). In this regard, the startling figures reported by

Leonore Weitzman (1985) for California, where no-fault divorce had been implemented in the early 1960s, were influential. She suggested that women's income decreased by 70 per cent on divorce, while that of men's increased by 40 per cent. Her calculation as to the degree of inequality between men and women was subjected to vigorous criticism (Duncan and Hoffman, 1985), but this did not affect the general policy impact of the research. It became increasingly apparent that in privatising decision making about divorce to the couple, arrangements in respect of their roles as parents were insufficiently addressed. Successive governments exhibited concern throughout the 1980s and 1990s about the heavy reliance of lone mothers on state benefits and the relatively small amount contributed by 'absent fathers', notwithstanding the passing of the Child Support Act in 1991, which attempted to force fathers to pay for their biological children (Kiernan *et al.*, 1998). Increasingly the attention of policy makers was focused on the rights of fathers, divorced and unmarried, to contact with their children, largely in the hope that more maintenance would be paid as a result. The 1987 Family Law Reform Act abolished the status of illegitimacy and allowed unmarried fathers to apply for a parental rights order, while the 1989 Children Act allowed them to share parental functions by private agreement with the mother. Having effectively permitted adults to decide whether to stay together, it was not possible to ensure the workings of the male breadwinner model through the law. Thus new initiatives focused, albeit with little success, on securing the male breadwinner role of all fathers, no matter what their marital status.

The Family Law Act of 1996 sought to embody both the idea that the decision to divorce should rest with the couple *and* the notion that men and women should take responsibility for sorting out their affairs, particularly in respect of their children. To the latter end, couples were required to settle their affairs before seeking divorce, a complete reversal of the procedure required prior to the 1969 legislation. Prior to reform in 1963, any couple making their own arrangements about property, for example, ran the risk of being accused of collusion. In 1996, it was assumed that both parties would participate in rational discussion and negotiation, making use of mediation. As Lord Mackay put it in a speech to a consultation meeting: 'I believe that mediation, with the accent on couples meeting face to face to resolve the difficult issues surrounding the breakdown of their marriages, is often the best way to resolve these problems' (Walker and Hornick, 1996, p. 61). Husbands and wives were assumed to be able to communicate and negotiate as equals.

The final acceptance of full no-fault divorce was justified mainly by the effects of adversarial divorce procedures on children. The Law Commission (1988, 1990) referred to the concern that the present divorce process might be making matters worse for children. In particular the reliance on the old fault-based grounds to prove irretrievable breakdown was feared to be resulting in

unnecessary bitterness and recrimination (Booth Report, 1985). The Law
Commission (1988, para. 5.2) dismissed any lingering notion that a more
restrictive law of divorce could buttress the stability of marriage or reduce the
rate of marital separation and breakdown: 'Such a reduction is far more likely
to stem from a change in individual attitudes and expectations than from a
change in the law.' A return to fault-based divorce was not appropriate because
the law could not and should not allocate blame in marriage matters (Law
Commission, 1990; Lord Chancellor's Department, 1993). The Lord
Chancellor, Lord Mackay, asked:

> How can it be said that a requirement to make allegations of fault provides the law
> with an underlying moral base when in fact to commit a wrong – such as adultery –
> actually means that you can be divorced in less than six months and so be free to
> marry again? (*House of Lords, Debates*, 30 November 1995, c. 701)

Thus the arguments in favour of a full and final move to 'pure' no-fault divorce
rested mainly on what was best for children, together with the much older
concern about the hypocrisy inherent in the use of partial no-fault legislation.

But reformers also accepted the more modern idea of marriage as a 'relationship' and agreed that the judicial allocation of fault in personal
relationships was impossible. The large and complicated debate about the
legislation revolved around the status of marriage. Opposition to the complete
abolition of fault came from MPs who felt that it would, as John Patten put
it, 'empty the marriage contract of any meaning' and 'turn a contract for life
into a probationary matter' (*Daily Telegraph*, 9 September 1995). The term
contract was used here to signal the importance of permanence and stability
rather than in any strict legal sense. The underlying fear was that marriage
would become indistinguishable from cohabitation, the 'tenancy at will' feared
at the time of the 1956 Royal Commission on Marriage and Divorce (see
above, pp. 108–110). Lord Coleraine argued that 'to make of marriage a
licence to cohabit, terminable at one year's notice by either husband or wife,
is likely so to destroy the significance of marriage in the eyes of the young
unmarried as to make them ask – even more than now – why they should
marry rather than cohabit' (*House of Lords, Debates*, 30 November 1995, c.
724). The Family Homes and Domestic Violence (FHDV) Bill had already
been lost in 1995 as a result of a rebellion by MPs determined that cohabitants
should not have an equal legal status to married people. Part III of the Family
Law Act, which sought to cover the same ground as the lost FHDV Bill, called
upon the courts to have regard when making an occupation order for a
cohabitant to the fact that they had not given the commitment of marriage.
This, together with other clauses that rendered cohabitation 'less eligible' than
marriage, were, according to the Lord Chancellor, intended to 'emphasise the

important general message that marriage is special in a way that no other relationship is' (*House of Lords*, *Debates*, 30 November 1996, c. 705).

The sole proof of irretrievable breakdown in the new legislation was to be a waiting period of one year, which was to apply to couples without children as well in order that marriage should not be devalued (Lord Chancellor's Department, 1993, para. 6.36). This signalled a preoccupation that became much more pronounced as the Bill made its way through Parliament: saving marriage. As Phillips (1991) has noted, no-fault divorce is not necessarily permissive. The imposition of a long waiting or 'cooling off' period together with measures to enforce that the couple take responsibility for sorting out their affairs can make divorce difficult. Some MPs showed more concern about the fate of marriage as an institution than had been evident at any time since the 1956 Royal Commission. The one-year waiting period was intended to encourage reconciliation. In the Foreword to the government's consultation paper, Lord Mackay wrote:

> I believe that a good divorce law will support the institution of marriage by seeking to lay out for parties a process by which they receive help to prevent a marriage being dissolved ... It is important that the process leading to divorce should enable the parties to do as much as possible to prevent their marriage from finally ending if that sad event can be avoided. (Lord Chancellor's Department, 1993)

Theresa Gorman was something of a lone voice in her insistence during the Parliamentary debates of 1996 that the law was about divorce and not marriage (*House of Commons*, *Debates*, 25 April 1996, c. 27).

In the event, the part of the Family Law Act dealing with these issues was abandoned in 1999. As well as the grave difficulties in implementing the detailed provision of the legislation, there were tensions between the aims of marriage saving and divorce, and between the promotion of reconciliation and conciliation (McCarthy *et al.*, 2000). Divorce remains regulated by a regime of partial no-fault.

CONCLUSION

Even when government seemed at last to have accepted that the decision to end a marriage should be left in the hands of the couple concerned, there was an attempt in 1996 to turn the new arrangements for no-fault divorce to serve the purpose of saving marriage and of preserving a boundary between marriage and non-marriage. In large measure, the struggle throughout the twentieth century has been to modernise the law of marriage and divorce without ceding the principle of state regulation completely. If in 1996 government had accepted the twin logics of private control over divorce and state regulation of the parent–child relationship, in the manner advocated by Bertrand Russell in 1929, the Family Law Act would have been less subject to internal contradiction. However, just as the family has always been perceived as bedrock and yet fragile, so governments have always been reluctant to facilitate divorce, while the Church has viewed relaxation of the divorce law as a threat to the whole conception of marriage as life-long. The preoccupation of the 1956 Royal Commission on Marriage and Divorce with 'divorce-mindedness' seems quaint, and yet divorce has become an intrinsic part of the marriage system (Phillips, 1988; Furstenberg and Cherlin, 1991). Given the concern of governments throughout the century about the family, it is not surprising that relaxation of the law of marriage and divorce has always been hedged, equivocal or, in the last part of the century, balanced by a determined attempt effectively to impose traditional obligations on post-divorce and never-married mothers and fathers (Smart and Neale, 1999).

The erosion of the prescriptive framework in the form of a body of family law underpinned by a strict moral code, like the erosion of the male breadwinner model family, opened a space for negotiation. In the absence of both firm, codified rules and normative expectations regarding male and female roles in the family, more responsibility for negotiation has been passed to family members. In the case of family law, governments reached the logical conclusion at the end of the century that people should be prepared to negotiate their own affairs. However, in so doing, it assumed that adult family members were fully individualised in the sense of being economically self-sufficient (and able openly to communicate), which, as Chapter 3 showed, is far from the case. The problems inherent in requiring couples to negotiate their parental roles are closely related to the unequal division of work, paid and unpaid, between husbands and wives, as the qualitative research reported in Chapter 6 shows.

The way forward is far from clear. Some, right-wing economists as well as feminists, would like to continue down the individualist road and make marriage a matter of private contract, which would recognise in legal terms a full and final shift from institution to relationship. At the other extreme, commentators such as Rowthorn (1999) would like to put the clock back and return to a strict moral code and fault-based divorce. As political parties found to their cost during the 1990s, the politics of the family arouses great passions, while any attempt at definitive action all too often pleases no one. I return to these issues in the final chapter, after an exploration of what has actually gone on inside families.

NOTES

1. This was the position of the late nineteenth-century feminist, Mona Caird (see above, p. 79).
2. Olive Anderson (1999) has discovered something comparable in the operation of a 'dual regime' of state and civil society in the nineteenth century that resulted in significant numbers of private separation contracts.
3. The term is not very satisfactory in view of the complex relationship between contract and status in respect of marriage.
4. Nevertheless, the slowness of the UK to legislate for 'cohabitation partnerships' compared to many of the continental European countries is of course a much more complicated issue than this. For example, it may also be argued that having abandoned the direct regulation of marriage, the state is reluctant to enter the new field of cohabitation.

PART III

6.   Inside relationships: the decision to marry or cohabit and the nature of commitment

There has been little research as to what has actually happens within intimate relationships. Neither surveys of attitudes nor aggregate demographic statistics reveal anything about changes in the meanings of relationships. In the UK, there has been only one major in-depth qualitative study of intact marital relationships in the last two decades of the century (Askham, 1984). Interestingly, this drew attention to the importance of the tension between 'identity and stability', that is, between the creation of the sense of self and the importance of a 'habitualising' relationship. The research reported in this chapter and the next aims to explore the nature of 'commitment' (to the other and to the relationship) and the extent to which there has been a growth in the pursuit of individualism (in the sense of prioritisation of self), focusing on differences between married and cohabiting relationships among younger respondents and on differences between these respondents and their parents.

The research consists of a qualitative study of intact relationships of married and cohabiting couples with children under 11 and of the, again, intact relationships of their parents. It is supplemented by a limited quantitative survey. This research makes a start on the task of investigating what the ideas and everyday practices of people in intact relationships look like: are they more selfish, merely more independent, or more consciously committed? The data show that there has been real change. However, the simple reading of greater individualism from the statistics of family change is not accurate. The changes do not amount to the individualistic hell of the pessimists or to the new egalitarian, democratic commitment of the optimists. The data clearly demonstrate the effects of the erosion of prescriptive frameworks and changing norms. Indeed, the whole idea of commitment is articulated in terms of something that comes from within rather than being imposed from without. Intimate relationships have become more subject to choice and more open to negotiation. This has its positive side, but the absence of firm rules also often makes family life for today's young adults more difficult than it was for their parents.

THE IDEA OF COMMITMENT

Considerably more has been written about the idea of individualism, which is thought to be increasingly characteristic of intimate relationships, than commitment. However, a study that sets out to investigate change over time among couples in relationships that are still intact must look for commitment as well as the possibility of growing individualism and must also be alive to the possibility that the nature of commitment may undergo change.

Social scientists have experienced difficulty in defining commitment. Early social-psychological studies tended to conflate it with satisfaction, but partners in a relationship can be happy without being committed and vice versa. Brickman (1987) pointed out that commitment might indeed be greatest in times of trouble. Commitment obviously bears some relationship to Askham's (1984) notion of stability and is also often tied in the minds of policy makers to permanence. Most writers on the subject agree that commitment involves behaving in ways that support the maintenance and continuation of a relationship. Rusbult (1987, 1991) has further proposed that commitment can produce other behaviours that extend the longevity of a relationship. Adapting Hirschman's (1970) categories of exit, voice and loyalty (applied originally to behaviour in the public sphere), Rusbult has suggested that commitment results in the exercise of voice and loyalty, rather than neglect and exit.

However, stability in the sense of permanence is the outcome of those behaviours, while commitment is a motivational state. Johnson's (1991) work has been important for breaking down the concept of commitment. He suggested that commitment has three dimensions: personal commitment to the person or to the relationship, summed up as 'wanting' the relationship to continue; moral commitment, summed up as feeling the relationship 'ought' to continue; and structural commitment, summed up as feeling that the relationship 'has' to continue because of the kind of investments (for example, in the form of property, children or more intangible things such as reputation and regard) that have been made. The major new element in Johnson's conceptualisation was, as his critics acknowledged, the moral dimension. As Smart and Neale (1999) have noted, morality also re-entered the work of sociologists in the 1990s, and has increasingly peppered the public debate on policy issues, whether in respect of 'welfare dependency' or family law. Johnson argued that the moral commitment to stick to the relationship might originate in prescription external to the couple, but this obligation had to be internalised. Adams and Jones (1997) have refined Johnson's three dimensions of marital commitment and have succeeded in comparing them empirically:

- an attraction component, based on devotion, satisfaction and love (= commitment to spouse);

- a moral-normative component, based on a sense of personal responsibility for maintaining the marriage and a belief in marriage as an important institution (= commitment to the marriage);
- a constraining component, based on the fear of the social, financial and emotional costs of ending the relationship (= feelings of entrapment).

In this analysis, commitment to the relationship is located in the second, moral-normative component, which fits better with sociological analysis. The separation between commitment to the other person and to the marriage is similar to Mansfield's (1999) idea that there are two forms of commitment: to what she terms the relationship, which is personal and now-oriented; and to what she terms the partnership. The partnership consists of a 'structure of understanding' which serves to link purposes to expectations and is future-oriented, thus amounting to an elaborated notion of commitment to the 'institutional aspects' of the relationship that encompasses a shared understanding of the kind of investments that will be made in it. Mansfield deliberately does not confine her analysis to marriage: because commitment may also characterise cohabiting relationships, it is an empirical question as to how far it does so. However, it may not always be easy to separate personal commitment from commitment to the relationship, as both Adams and Jones and Mansfield do. Quinn's (1982) idea of the 'promise, dedication and attachment' aspects of commitment crosses these two dimensions. Similarly, Scanzoni *et al.* (1989) have suggested that it is not easy to separate personal gratification from investment, and that commitment is probably a complex amalgam of 'want to' and 'have to'. If we add some idea of 'ought to' (continue), then we arrive back at the three dimensions identified by Johnson (1991). Smart and Stevens (2000) have argued that commitment should be viewed as a continuum, with 'mutual' commitment (to the other person and the relationships) at one end, and 'contingent' commitment (dependent on any number of issues to do with the behaviour of the other person) at the other.

It is thus far from easy to identify the dimensions of commitment. Furthermore, having differentiated them, it is necessary both to understand the way in which they interact and to consider which dimension is of particular importance under which circumstances. Mansfield (1999) has argued that the more future-oriented commitment to the 'partnership' is crucial to long-term stability. Her idea that this is defined in terms of a 'structure of understanding' is important because it raises the issue of what it is that structures the understanding. It is likely that Johnson's and Adam and Jones' moral-normative dimension – the belief in the idea that the relationship ought to continue – is central to the answer. Historically this belief in the 'ought' has been derived from the prescriptive frameworks that carried a clear notion of how relationships should be ordered economically and morally in accordance with the male breadwinner model and family law. The erosion of these has meant that the responsibility for working out relationship behaviour has passed increasingly to the individual couple. This does not mean that there will be no consciousness of an 'ought', but it is no longer imposed and has to be negotiated. As Smart and Stevens (2000) argue, it may be rational for those who are poor and unemployed to cohabit and effectively to 'hedge their bets', making their commitment 'contingent'. Most recent sociological studies of commitment have stressed the importance only of the first and third of Adams and Jones' dimensions of commitment (for example, Stanley and Markman, 1992; Nock, 1995a), but this is to miss what is probably the most crucial site of developing commitments in intact relationships. The interviews carried out for this study also show that changes in moral-normative frameworks for thinking about obligations in marriage affected the ways in which the older and younger respondents approached the issue of investment.

Johnson (1991) has pointed out that the structural commitments entailed in the investments that are part and parcel of the third of both his and Adams and Jones' (1997) dimensions do not become relevant until personal and moral commitments (the first two dimensions) begin to fade. Given that the sample for this study contains people in intact relationships, all of whom also expressed satisfaction with their relationships (albeit in different degrees), evidence of 'commitment constraints' would not be expected. However, the study sought to explore 'the pattern of investment' by each party to the relationship (Rusbult and Buunk, 1993; Brewer, 1993), through attitudes, feelings and perceptions, as well as the actual contributions made, for example, to the work of the household and to the expenses of the household. These issues are explored in the next chapter. This chapter examines the first two aspects of commitment identified by Adams and Jones through what the respondents said about the meaning of their decision to marry or cohabit and about the nature of their commitment to each other. Are those who choose to cohabit more individualistic and less committed? And are younger couples more individualistic and less committed than older couples?

Interviews for the study have tried to explore the nature and meaning of commitment in marital and cohabiting relationships, as well as looking at the same time for evidence of more individualistic behaviour (for example, in respect of careers, leisure time and money), and at whether and how the pursuit of commitment and individualism are reconciled. Burke and Reitzes (1991) have suggested that commitment connects an individual to an identity and a stable set of self-meanings, which in turn suggests that the relationship between the two may not necessarily be one of tension. The evidence from this research supports this view, but also indicates that 'balance' is certainly hard to achieve. This is what the negotiation that comes in the wake of the erosion of the old normative prescriptions is chiefly about.

THE SAMPLE[1]

For the qualitative study, the final sample consisted of 17 married and 12 cohabiting couples and 72 of their parents, consisting of 32 married couples and eight widows. These will be referred to as younger married people, cohabitants and older married people. Cohabitants were given more proportional weight in the sample than their position in the general population warrants (cohabitants with children account for only 4 per cent of families, compared to the 42 per cent that are married couples with children), because of the upward trend in rates of cohabitation and extra-marital births, the lack of qualitative studies of cohabitation, and the argument that cohabitants are more individualistic than married people.

For a small, qualitative sample, purposive sampling is recognised to be appropriate, 'partly because the initial definition of the universe is more limited, and partly because social processes have a logic and a coherence that random sampling can reduce to uninterpretable sawdust' (Miles and Huberman, 1994, p. 27). Reducing the differences between the couples by limiting the parameters of the sampling frame makes the sample more homogeneous in terms of life experiences and circumstances, which then helps to confirm or deny research hypotheses. This was particularly important in view of the fact that the sample frame already included both married and cohabiting individuals, men and women, and two generations.

The target sample was a group of mothers working either full- or part-time, with children of primary school age or younger. Advertisements were placed in the nursing, teaching, housing and social work press, the rationale being, first, that women in these occupations could be expected to show a similar commitment to their work and, second, that the bulk of the post-war expansion in married women's work has been in the employment of 'the welfare state'. Potential respondents were asked to contact the interviewers. All these women had qualifications beyond A levels (one-quarter of the women in the BHPS first wave survey beginning in 1991 were so qualified, Corti *et al.*, 1995).

Other boundaries set to ensure that respondents in the sample were not too diverse were that both partners in each couple should not have been married before. Couples with children from other partners were also screened out. Couples were included if their parents' marriage was still intact, or if their mothers were widowed and had not separated before the death of their (first) husbands. To ensure that the experiences of the two generations were not overwhelmingly disparate, younger generation female respondents were only included if their mothers had worked when they were children. The older generation female respondents had for the most part not been engaged in work that demanded training or could be considered a 'career'. Indeed, the labour market participation of women with young children for this generation of women was very low. As late as 1973, only 25 per cent of women with children 0–4 years old were working; by 1995 this figure had risen to 49 per cent (ONS, 1997a, table 4.7, p. 52). To further aid comparability, particularly in respect of the experiences of the older generation, ethnic minority respondents were screened out. Those involved in minority religious sects were also excluded. Respondents all lived in England and Wales.[2]

The younger generation respondents were asked to establish if their parents were able and willing to be interviewed. In seven cases it became clear that, despite the assurances of their children, the parents were not willing to participate; 17 parents were either too ill to be interviewed or were deceased; in addition, it emerged that the parents of one cohabiting woman and one married man were either separated or divorced.

Men and women were interviewed separately and simultaneously by two researchers in the couples' homes. The accounts of men and women differed in emphasis, but were remarkably consistent. Interviews were semi-structured and organised to explore various dimensions of commitment in terms of both behaviour and mentalities. The schedule was divided into a series of questions that invited respondents to tell the story of their relationships and their decision to marry or cohabit, followed by a section that explored particular topics likely to reveal the balance between attention to self, as opposed to attention to other and to the relationship. Older married people were asked to talk about the period during which they brought up their children. They were asked about feelings and meanings, as well as activities, although the study did not explicitly explore the area of what Duncomb and Marsden (1993) have called 'emotional work'. Finally, all respondents were asked about their views on particular aspects of contemporary family law and social policy.

The age of the younger respondents ranged between 27 and 50. Just under two-thirds (38) were aged 35–45. The sample of cohabitants was drawn to match the married, the whole idea being to get two groups of married and cohabiting couples who were as alike as they could be in terms of their basic characteristics. However, this means that the cohabitants were significantly older than the general population of cohabitants with children. They were also much better-off: 15 couples (nine married and six cohabiting) had a joint income of £30–40 000 (a further three were very close to this income range), usually achieved by one partner working full-time and one part-time. In nine cases, both partners worked as teachers or nurses. Incomes at the top of the range were achieved where both worked full-time (three married couples and four cohabiting couples). Three much higher than average incomes were reported by two married and one cohabiting couples where the men were doctors (two) and a computer analyst. The lower than average incomes belonged to couples (three married and one cohabiting) where both were working part-time, where the man was unemployed (albeit with a substantial redundancy payment), and where the man was self-employed as a builder and earning very little.

Most (25 couples) had been together for at least 10 years, and nearly half (13 couples) for 15 or more years. Most of the married and cohabiting couples had waited 5 years before having their children. All the cohabitants waited at least 3 years and all but one of the married couples. Ten cohabiting and 14 married couples had waited five or more years. A majority of couples (21) had two or more children, but a larger proportion of cohabitants had only one child.

The older respondents were for the most part retired, but were not as homogeneous a sample in respect of previous occupations. Eight of the men had been professionals; five of these had been teachers. The vast majority were almost equally divided between white-collar and skilled manual occupations. Two had been unskilled workers and two had been in the armed forces. While paid work had not been part of the sample frame specified for the mothers of the younger male respondents, 39 of the 40 older women had worked, eight in professional occupations (four as teachers), 22 in white-collar occupations, two in skilled manual jobs and seven in unskilled manual work, mainly as cleaners. Thus only 12 worked in jobs requiring training beyond the secondary school level. In addition, many had worked but a very few hours per week and only for a few years.

The ages of the older respondents ranged between 52 and 87. More than half were in their sixties and the vast majority were in their sixties and seventies. However, the youngest was only three years older than the oldest of the younger respondents. Twenty-eight older couples had their children within two years of marriage. Indeed, the youngest of the older respondents had been pre-maritally pregnant, while the oldest of the younger respondents had waited 12 years before having children. It is therefore necessary to be cautious about characterising differences between the parents and their children in terms of generational change, both because of the age overlap between the parents and children in the sample, and because what is observed may be the effect of ageing rather than generation. However, all but five older couples married between 1948 and 1959, when cohabitation was not socially acceptable, and they began to bring up their children when it was still expected that white married women would primarily be housewives and carers (Lewis, 1992a; Giles, 1995; Webster, 1999). Lesthaeghe and Surkyn (1988) have suggested that there is support for a model of ideational change regarding the 'ought' that is cohort- and education-driven.

The earliest marriage among the younger generation couples took place in 1978, and the majority (10 couples) married between 1980 and 1990. It was not until the early 1970s that the first (overly optimistic) observations were made regarding the emergence of the 'symmetrical' dual-earner family (Young and Willmott, 1973). The vast majority of the older and younger generation couples are thus separated in terms of getting married and having children by the 1960s, when a major change in attitudes regarding sexual morality and the basis for intimate relationships took place, accounting in part for the relaxation of the law on divorce, homosexuality and abortion at the end of the decade. Given that the interviews endeavoured to elicit information from the older generation respondents about the time when they were bringing up primary school children,[3] it is possible to be reasonably sure of tapping into two different sets of post-war experiences. Interestingly, Scott *et al.*'s, (1999) work for the fifteenth British Social Attitudes Survey, reported that differences between old and young, in attitudes towards cohabitation for example, were more pronounced in the UK than in West Germany, The Netherlands or Sweden, but they also cautioned as to whether this was a generational or life-cycle effect.

One of the main aims of the study was to look at the changing nature of intact intimate relationships over time. All the younger couples and all but two of the older couples expressed considerable satisfaction with their relationships. Thus the sample had a built-in conservative bias. The way in which the sample was drawn worked to minimise the amount of difference that might be found between the experiences of parents and children, which makes the fact that more similarities between the cohabiting and married younger respondents were found than between the younger and older married people all the more significant.

In addition to the qualitative sample, a module of questions was included as part of the Omnibus Survey in September 1997 and again in March 1998.[4] The questions were asked of all married and cohabiting people with dependent children, and of cohabitants without children, in both sweeps – 777 people in all. Both married and cohabiting respondents included never-married and once-married people (Table 6.1). There were almost twice as many women as men in couples where one partner had been married before (71 women to 36 men) but in other groups the numbers more or less matched. General Household Survey data for 1995 showed that divorced people are most likely to cohabit and that cohabiting is more common among divorced men than divorced women.

Table 6.1   Omnibus sample: sex of respondents

	Both first married + children	One married before + children	Both never-married, cohab +	One never-married, cohab +	Both never-married, cohab.no	One never-married, cohab.no	Total
Men	240	36	23	12	36	19	366
Women	245	71	25	18	36	16	411
Base	485	107	48	30	72	35	777[a]

Note: [a] Of the 777, two were not asked the questions in the module and have therefore been left out of any analysis.

The vast majority of the Omnibus sample was aged 25–44, 85 per cent of married people and 91 per cent of cohabitants with children, while 83 per cent of married parents and just over half the cohabitants fell into the 30–49 year old age group (the groups containing the majority of the younger respondents in the qualitative sample). In contrast with the qualitative sample, but in line with the general population, the never-married cohabitants were more likely to be under 25 than people in other groups and this is especially true for the childless cohabitants; nearly a third of this group are in the youngest age group. The never-married cohabitants were also much more likely to have a child under 5 than any of the other groups in the Omnibus sample. Less than half of the married respondents had a child under 5 compared with nearly 80 per cent of the never-married cohabitants.

Again, in contrast with the qualitative sample, over half the cohabitants with children had an income of less than £10 000, as did 49 per cent of the married respondents. Only 10.5 per cent of the cohabiting parents received more than £20 000 compared to 22.4 per cent of the married parents, although cohabitants with children were only marginally less likely to have education beyond A level than married parents. The Omnibus sample is more representative of the general population of cohabitants with children than the qualitative sample in respect of income. Nevertheless, it does indicate that the population of cohabitants with children is polarised; the qualitative sample for this study was drawn from the (as yet) small group of better-off cohabitants with children.

THE MEANING OF THE DECISION TO MARRY OR COHABIT

In the 1960s, marriage was virtually universal. With the emergence of cohabitation, this is no longer the case, even though most cohabitants marry eventually. Mansfield and Collard's (1988) study of newly-weds in the early 1980s stressed the way in which marriage was the most obvious and natural means of validating adulthood. According to the 1981 Census, four out of five single men and seven out of ten women lived with their families of origin, thus 'getting a place of their own' was a matter of considerable importance and marriage a means of achieving it (see also Leonard, 1980). This was not true for any of the younger couples in the qualitative sample drawn for this study, the vast majority of whom left home to undertake further training before marrying or cohabiting. Indeed, this is something that differentiated their experience from that of their parents. The young married couples in the sample had actively to make a decision to get married; it was not necessarily the most natural way of achieving adult status.

We know relatively little about the way in which cohabitants enter their relationships, and whether or how they actually make a decision not to marry before living together and having children. Nor do we know much about how cohabitants with children think about themselves: as essentially married, or as having a quite different status. Conclusions as to their lesser degree of commitment and greater degree of individualism cannot be reached without knowing more about the meaning of cohabitation. The views of academics are divided on meanings, but as Manting (1996) has pointed out, cohabitation probably has very different meanings for different sub-groups. This signals the danger not only of looking at cohabitants with and without children together, but of ignoring the rapid changes in marriage when coming to conclusions about the nature of cohabitation. The interest of this study was not so much to establish why people marry, as to consider what marriage and cohabitation signify in terms of differences in commitment to the other person and to the relationship, and whether this has any implications for children. It was also concerned to investigate the changing nature of the expression of commitment over time, and whether the younger married couples had more in common with their married parents or with their cohabiting peers in this respect.

The Decision to Marry

The 17 younger married couples in the qualitative sample ranged in age from 27 to 50 and had been married for between 5 and 20 years. Five couples had cohabited for a period of 18 months or more and six had lived together for a few weeks or months before marrying, usually because house purchase was completed. Two couples who moved into the marital home for about a month before marriage said that they did not consider that they had lived together before marriage. Both came from religious backgrounds and were strongly committed to the institution of marriage. All but four couples got engaged and announced the engagement well before cohabiting. The engagement was referred to in practical terms as allowing a period of planning for the wedding, as well as being a means of making their commitment to each other public.

A range of practical reasons for marriage was given by those who did not cohabit long term or who did not cohabit at all. Five of the women referred to parental pressure to marry. Of the 42 parents of the young married respondents in the sample, six disapproved of all forms of cohabitation, 13 disapproved of cohabitants having children, 12 were in favour of cohabitation, and 11 expressed a preference for marriage rather than cohabitation, but were reluctant to prescribe for others. Mr D's rather convoluted reply to the interviewer on this topic was not untypical:

Well, yeah, I mean, from a religious point of view, from that angle and upbringing, I don't see that [cohabitation] as the ideal circumstance that I would like to see. No. But OK, where I stand on that is, it happens, and like who am I to throw the stone. So I'd prefer it if it wasn't the case. But I, you know, I don't find anything sort of [*sharp intake of breath*] about it.

Two of the 12 parents who favoured cohabitation had other children who were cohabitants.

Two couples did not cohabit before marriage, but the woman became pregnant, which prompted marriage. Five of the married couples came from religious backgrounds that ruled out long-term cohabitation, although not sex before marriage. Two women referred to their desire for companionship and fear of living alone, and one of these also felt that the status of a married woman was still higher than that of her single sister. A further two women and a man described their relationships as reaching a stage when either they took the decision to marry or broke up: 'I think we'd probably reached a stage, you know, you either get married or you split up ... .' This may also be what five other male respondents meant when they talked about it 'being time to marry', although it seems that in these cases they were also making reference to their own biographies as well as to the state of the relationship. Nordstrom (1986) reported from his qualitative study of 71 men that many spoke of being 'ready' to marry, by which they meant 'settle down'. Two-thirds of the married respondents had had a previous 'serious relationship' (defined by them as having some combination of the following: lasting a long time; involving sex and/or caring deeply about the other person; living together). While many reasons were given for ending these previous relationships, one of the more common ones was that the respondent did not feel 'ready to settle down'.

Married women were more likely to refer to precise reasons, practical and principled, for marrying. Men tended to talk in a more generalised way of making a commitment. Mr F. said that he married mainly because his wife wished it, but that he was conscious of making a commitment:

I thought marriage was an outmoded institution and wasn't necessary. And I think I actually surprised myself when I actually asked her but I think ... J's [his wife's] expectations were more down that way, and her family. Whereas I would have been quite happy to just carry on. So it seemed interesting at the time to feel as if you were saying: 'Yes I'm making this commitment to you.'

Four of the five long-term cohabiting couples married largely because they wanted to have children. The Cs cohabited for 5 years, in part because they could not afford to marry (meaning that they could not afford a big white wedding), a reason that was the most popular among the Omnibus sample of cohabitants with and without children, but which was not mentioned by any other respondents in the qualitative sample. Mrs C. obviously wanted the additional 'security' of marriage before having children; her partner was prepared to agree without seeing the necessity for it. Mrs E. also mentioned children as a reason for marrying, but said that this was not the whole reason, although she was unable to articulate what exactly the reasons had been:

> I think maybe we'd said that if we ever had children it would be nice to be married. That maybe it cuts down on names and complications, things like that, but nothing other than that really. Can't really tell you why we did it.

The only married woman to keep her maiden name, Ms G. said:

> I sat down and thought to myself one day, I knew I would never be pregnant by mistake. I knew that I would control it and that I wouldn't allow it to happen unless I was married and I had to face up to that really.

She also said that she only 'felt' married when she had children. Mrs R. made a similar point:

> I knew I wanted to have children, so I wanted to get married because I knew that one day I'd have children. I think it's a public thing as well getting married isn't it? ... The marriage in a way becomes like a piece of paper once you have the children. That's the commitment, that's what I mean. The children are the commitment really.

Those who had been long-term cohabitants before marrying tended to make much more definite statements regarding the commitment they felt that they were making by getting married. Both Mr and Mrs P. spoke of the importance of making a public commitment. In the words of Mr P.:

> It's all the relationship with the families ... it was about really saying to L., yes, I am sort of committed to this. And also saying to her family that, yes, I am committed to your daughter.

Such expressions of commitment do not bring us any further forward in understanding why some long-term cohabitants feel the need to make a *public commitment* and others do not, but it does point to the fact that when couples cohabit for relatively long periods of time, as increasing numbers do, the nature of the decision to marry is rather different and is more likely to focus on the nature of commitment, whether to the children as in the case of Mrs R., or the relationship and allied to this the kin group, as in the case of Mr P. Expressions of commitment by the young married people in the sample were mixed. Commitment to the spouse, to the relationship, to children and to wider kin were all mentioned. The public expression of commitment embodied in the promise to marry seemed to be important for the wider kin group which then knew 'where it stood' *vis-à-vis* the relationship. A cohabiting relationship was not a cause for family celebration in the same way, although the advent of children often resulted in a significant change in the inter-generational relationships. All the long-term cohabitants were clear that they were making a *public* commitment by getting married. So, are long-term cohabitants who do not make a public commitment less committed, or is the nature of their commitment and the way they express it merely different?

The 'Decision' Not to Marry

The Omnibus sample of 185 cohabitants was asked their main reason for living together rather than marrying. These cohabitants included both those with children under the school leaving age (78) and those without children (107); 71 per cent were aged between 25 and 44. The most popular reason for not getting married was that they could not afford it (21.6 per cent); however, these people were much more likely to be young (aged between 16 and 24). Only 9.7 per cent said that they would not consider getting married and 11. 9 per cent said that cohabitation was 'what most people do nowadays', which may indicate that they saw cohabitation as a stage in a relationship which could eventually be legalised by marriage. Nevertheless, for some 22.7 per cent, marriage appeared to be unimportant. These data are suggestive, but leave unanswered the process of decision making over the life of the relationship.

The 12 cohabiting, never-married couples in the qualitative sample had been together for between 6 and 25 years, the youngest was 28 and the oldest 49. The vast majority can be said to have '*drifted*' into cohabitation. There was usually no very explicit rejection of marriage; rather, no decision was made. Later, there was a sense from many respondents of having reached a point of no return. It seemed 'pointless' to marry when they had been together so long, and even the arrival of children did not affect this view. However, by the time they had children, there is evidence that the cohabitants had thought about the meaning of their relationship and the nature of their commitment.

Housing arrangements were key in explaining how the cohabitants started to live together. Housing was also an important variable explaining why McRae's (1993) sample of cohabiting mothers started to cohabit. Five couples described very similar pathways through shared student accommodation, followed by the search for a house or flat together, which was also often shared with another couple in the early stages, and finally to living alone as a couple. Meuleman (1994) and de Singly (1996) have suggested that cohabitation is a way of dealing with sexual activity that starts early, education that ends late, and late entry into the workplace.

Ms R. said that in their first shared house where they met, they had separate bedrooms because 'that was the arrangement'. In the second house 'there was no reason to not live together'. Ms T. described how eventually renting a cheap house together seemed the 'sensible' thing to do; the turning point came when they decided to buy it together. When another couple who rented space from them moved out the realisation dawned that they 'couldn't move out when it didn't work'. Sharing costs was a major part of deciding to share accommodation in the first instance and few seemed to have thought about the future in any detail or to have taken a long-term view. In the case of one couple, the woman had quite wanted to marry when they began to cohabit as students, but the man had refused out of fear of his parents' wrath. In this case, it would have been considered more problematic to marry than to cohabit because his parents considered him too young to make a decision that seemed to them to involve a more lasting commitment. Housing decisions were also identified as key by those who did not meet as students. One couple said that their cohabitation only felt permanent in the eighth year, when they made a commitment jointly to own a house. In three cases one or both parties owned their own properties and it was a major sign of commitment to invite the other person to take a share of the house, or to decide to sell one of the properties. The decision to live as a couple and usually to invest jointly in housing was a major sign of commitment and signalled some degree of permanence to all the couples.

Two of the male cohabitants insisted that they had continued to 'drift', raising the issue of marriage from time to time, but 'never getting around to it':

Q: Have you ever talked about getting married?
A: Yes. It is on the list of things to do ... I jokingly say it's under getting the gutters fixed.
Q: And why is it still on the list and you didn't do it ten years ago?
A: I couldn't be bothered ... I don't know. I didn't get round to it. I don't know.

Interestingly, both these men belonged to couples who were the least committed to the status of cohabitant and were most likely to marry at some point in the future. Other couples eventually arrived at a more principled defence of their position as cohabitants, although it is doubtful whether they ever took a single decision not to marry. Rather, marriage was something that had been brought up for discussion and rejected on a number of occasions.

Given the main reason for marrying among those in the sample who had cohabited for a long period and then married, it is reasonable to suppose that having children would have caused these cohabitants to think seriously about marriage. However, eight of the couples said that marriage had not been an issue. All had waited at least three years before having children, and ten more than six years. Two women had had abortions because they felt that they were not ready for children earlier in the relationship. One talked of waiting until the relationship was 'strong enough' for children. They were therefore all well established as cohabiting couples before children arrived. One woman considered marrying because of the expectations of others, particularly at the school where she worked, but in the end could not see that it was necessary. Marriage had become irrelevant to their commitment to each other and therefore to the child, although, as will be seen, they were more prepared to make their commitment to their children public than they were their commitment to each other.

Five couples experienced considerable pressure from at least one set of parents, although even in the most extreme case the parents stopped making a fuss when the grandchild arrived. Only two (of the 30) parents of cohabitants said flatly that they did not approve, but about a third said that they would prefer it if the young couple would marry. It seems that a combination of pleasure at being grandparents, together with a decision to treat their children 'as if they were married', was powerful for about half the parents. Almost one-third said explicitly that they drew a firm line between stable and 'promiscuous' cohabitation, and a clear majority inferred as much. The comment of Mrs R. was typical:

> I found it very difficult with both [my daughters] when they started cohabiting with their partners. I took a long time to come to terms with it. D. [her husband] didn't. But the short answer is that I have no strong feelings about cohabiting. My bottom line is that if a relationship is sincere and committed, no matter how much I value marriage, I think the important thing is the commitment and the couple concerned.

Axinn and Thornton (1993) found in their study of mothers and their cohabiting children (using US panel data) that while parental attitudes affected the behaviour of the children (especially between mothers and daughters), children's cohabiting behaviour also affected parents. Mothers whose children cohabited between 1980 and 1985 had a more positive view of cohabitation in 1985 than in 1980.

Only three couples reported reaching or reaffirming a principled decision regarding cohabitation as a direct result of childbirth. The issue of marriage only occurred to one woman when the couple visited her partner's parents to tell them about the pregnancy:

> I'd not thought of it and, when we were there, I sort of realised that there it was, it was now back on the agenda and I was shocked at myself because I'd not – I'd not predicted it and I'd just not thought it through.

Her partner explained that she had reached the view that she wanted to be in a relationship 'where I'm here because I want to be here not because I'm feeling under a moral or legal obligation'. Taking the moral high ground on commitment, another man said that he would not have wanted it to be thought that he was getting married only because of the child. His views were similar to the 18 per cent of those in McRae's (1993) study who had married after the birth of a child and who stated explicitly that they had not wanted to marry while pregnant. This respondent and one other man felt that from their observation of married couples, their own common law relationships had more to recommend them in terms of stability and quality.

Most cohabiting couples knew few other unmarried parents and most reported that many of their cohabiting friends had decided to marry. Two couples knew of no other cohabiting parents among friends, colleagues or in their community. Of the remainder, half knew 'one or two' others, and half 'quite a number'. There was therefore no evidence of strong peer group pressure to reject marriage, but nor did any of the respondents seem to feel that their status as unmarried parents was very unusual.

All couples reported discussions over the babies' surnames. Naming the children raised issues regarding the couples' commitment as parents, which the majority seem to have regarded as more an issue than their relationship to each other. Married couples also felt this, as the comments of Mrs R. about children 'being the commitment' (see above, p. 134) showed, but the cohabitants were different in their greater propensity to acknowledge and articulate that their public commitment tended to come from parenthood rather than from living together. Eight of 24 cohabitants identified only as parents, another 10 put parent co-equal with partner or worker. None identified only as a partner and only one as a worker. Eight of 34 married respondents identified as parents, another eight as a parent and a spouse, two as a parent and a worker and three equally as all three. These findings are in line with Oliver's (1982) small qualitative study, which concluded that cohabitants were more preoccupied with their status as parents than with marriage and their status as a couple.

Seven cohabiting couples chose the father's name, two the mother's and three both names for their children. Two women wanted their children to have the father's name in order to tie him into the family in an explicit way:

> I certainly had partly the feeling that it makes T. [her son] more something to do with P. [her partner], rather than just to do with me, if he has his name.

Two more women and one man felt that giving the child the father's name symbolically redressed the legal disadvantages faced by unmarried fathers. One said that the choice of name 'was very deliberate and it was where the law actually did come into it in that N. [the father] again felt that he had no rights in relation to J. [the son]'. Two couples felt that it was in the children's interests to have the father's name. The couples choosing both names were rather more concerned about equality in their own relationship. One of the three described how they:

spent hours deciding what to do for a second name because I wanted my name and he wanted his, which is perfectly reasonable. And people kept saying, 'but if you got married then it wouldn't be a problem' – and you're saying, well yes, it would. So he's got both names.

While cohabitants started off life together in a more explicitly pragmatic fashion than most of those who got married, they reached a point, certainly by the time they had children, when they felt comfortable with cohabitation and were also prepared to articulate their commitment to the different status it represented. Respondents in all but the two couples who often called themselves married articulated a clear *private commitment* to the interviewers. The commitment they spoke of was private in two senses: it was theirs alone and did not involve Church, state, kin or community, and it eschewed any public ceremony. Mr S. said:

We see our commitment as being a very personal one and nothing to do with signing a bit of paper or a service or anything like that.

His partner said of the marriage ceremony:

I just hate that ... I'm very very self conscious ... and I actually think its farcical really.

Ms L., the youngest respondent, said:

I believe that my commitment to A. is totally personal and I only want to make promises to him in private and I don't really want to make promises to him in public and stuff. The other thing is that I really don't fancy getting married. I don't fancy the idea of getting all dolled up and having lots of people come and see me ... .

Three of the men expressed strong feelings about not wanting the state to become involved – one said that the more the government made the family an issue the more he was determined not to commit publicly – but for the most part respondents insisted that they did not want or need to make a public commitment. As Ms A. put it:

I know you can go off and get married very quietly ... but marriages – weddings tend to be very public affairs ... We don't need to make a public statement about our love for each other. We can do that between ourselves and end of story, we don't need to publicise that.

Expressions of commitment by the cohabitants to each other were more likely to be personal and above all private, with a separate, strong and more public commitment being made to children.

However, marriage had not disappeared from the cohabitants' agenda entirely. Six respondents did not rule out the possibility of marrying at some point in the future chiefly for financial reasons. Ms S. said:

> If we were thinking of getting married, I'd probably wait 'til another baby was out of the way. Because the marriage would be very much sorting the finances and stuff out and the right to pensions.

Five couples mentioned the issue of lack of entitlement to each other's occupational pension as a reason for marrying in the end, even if it was just before the age of 65. Two said that they were 'aggrieved' at having to consider this, and three said that they were 'irritated'.

Public and Private Expressions of Commitment Among Younger Couples

The data from the Omnibus survey supports the idea that both married and cohabiting couples feel that making a long-term commitment to each other is central to what a relationship is. In every category of respondent, the scores of those agreeing with the statement were 90 per cent or over. However, the qualitative evidence suggests that the nature of the commitment is different. It seems that the cohabitants in the qualitative sample interpreted decisions about marriage primarily in terms of their relationship to each other (the first dimension of commitment identified by Adams and Jones, 1997); it was not something that they saw as a central issue in their decision to become parents. And while the cohabitants declared themselves to be as committed parents and as committed to the relationship (Adams and Jones' second dimension) as the married couples, their perceptions of their adult relationships were significantly different in some respects. The dislike of making a public commitment to each other was usually accompanied by expressions of a desire to keep a more independent identity, especially on the part of the women. Ms G. articulated this strongly when she said:

> He's my partner is a different statement, I still sort of keep the coupleness out of it in a way and I'm actually proud of that ... .

All had to make a decision about how to refer to each other, just as they had to make a decision about their children's surnames. Different lines were drawn on this issue. The two couples who expressed least commitment to a separate cohabitant status were prepared to refer to themselves as married and call themselves husband and wife if it was socially easier so to do, with clients, for example, as in the case of the couple who ran a complementary health care practice. The rest would not refer to themselves as husband or wife, and drew different lines as to whether they would correct others. One woman teacher would not correct the parents of the children at her school, but would always make the point that she was a cohabitant and not married to any representative of officialdom. Indeed, this was the most common kind of distinction made. Cohabitants were forced to think about their identity in a way that married couples were not. Most found the choice of term to describe the person they lived with problematic. When asked whether they called the person they lived with 'partner', five responded in the affirmative, but others found the choice of term very difficult:

> I hesitate to use any term. I grope for a term. Partners is in any sense like two solicitors ... I mean there's not a good term is there? (Male respondent)

> Oh God, yes, this really irritates me. I used to say he was my partner, but it's like being called Ms at work ... people always assume that you are some sort of rampant ballbreaking feminist, you know ... And it is the same with partner, you sort of think that it is like you are trying to make a statement or something and I'm not ... (Female respondent)

> That's a tough one. I never know which word to use at all. I try and lend some circumlocution to avoid it ... (Male respondent)

Official forms presented particular problems in terms of whether to write in 'cohabiting' on a form that gave the option to be single, married or divorced/separated. All the couples had some sense, more developed in some than others, of occupying a separate status. According to Ms H., it was akin to 'smoking roll-ups rather than cigarettes'. Ms O'C. said:

> I don't think it has [got a status of its own], but I think it ought to ... Not legally, because then you'd have to go to the registry office say ... But like on forms, I wish they'd put it as an option. You know, it's 'married, single or divorced'. Well excuse me, I'm none of that you know.

Recognition of a separate status for cohabitation was intimately linked to the private commitment the couples felt that they had made to each other and their strongly felt commitment as parents, which made them want some form of separate recognition as people with responsibilities.

Unlike the married couples, cohabitants rarely referred to themselves as 'a partnership' or 'a team', although one man who rejected such a description of himself and his partner referred to the whole family (of three children) as 'a team'. Four respondents, three women and a man, went further and talked about the importance of choosing not to be legally tied to another person:

> Every day you made this decision – and if you wanted to stay, you stayed ... it can
> be a daily decision.

This woman admitted that she had held this view fiercely only in the early days
of her cohabitation, but she continued to feel the absence of promises for 'long-
term fidelity or dependency' to be important. Mr C. also insisted that the
'freedom to leave' was important, even if in practice there was no such freedom
because of the self-imposed commitment of parenthood. Ms L. said:

> No it's more that I feel that we are two individuals with clear goals in life and it's
> fortunate that they happen to coincide in a lot of ways with things that we are
> interested in ... .

This picture of cohabitation as two people choosing to live together for so
long as it suits their personal agendas seems closely to match the individualism
of the 'pure relationship' identified by Giddens.[5] However, Ms L. also provided
one of the clearest statements of private commitment to her partner (see above,
p. 139). The desire to establish an individual, independent identity is not
necessarily in conflict with commitment, and only a small minority of younger
married couples in the sample said that their commitment was entirely uncon-
ditional. There is a sense in which cohabitants make only a personal private
commitment (which is consolidated by the arrival of children), while the married
couples have from the beginning a more public sense of their relationships in
the context of the wider kinship network. However, for the most part, the
cohabitants were as much in touch with their parents as were the married
couples. It is possible for the absence of promises regarding permanence and
the perceived freedom to leave a cohabiting relationship to result in a need to
reaffirm commitment that makes the relationship stronger, even if only in a
minority of cases. Certainly many of the cohabitants felt that in fact it was they
who occupied the moral high ground, having thought hard about the nature of
their relationships and their commitment. However, it may be that for a majority
of cohabitants with children in the *general* population, who are younger, poorer
and who often have step-children, the sense of 'drift' that characterised the
experience of these cohabitants in the early stages of their relationship does not
get transformed into the kind of 'private cohabitation commitment' that was
observed in our sample. This might be part of the explanation of the high levels
of breakdown among cohabitants with children. However, as Smart and Stevens
(2000) have argued, the majority of the general population of cohabitants with
children who are poorly educated with little by way of employment prospects
may be rational risk-takers and be making the best bargain possible under the
circumstances.

It would be wrong to assume that, in contradistinction to the cohabitants, the young married couples were entirely 'we-centred' and without concern for their independent, individual identities. However, the desire for a separate identity, on the part of the married women in particular, was expressed more in terms of behaviour (see Chapter 7) than in reflection about the nature of their status and their commitment. All, even those in relatively traditional partnerships and in part-time jobs, very much wanted to assert their identity as paid workers and were committed to developing a career. A few also spoke of the importance of securing enough time for themselves in order to develop interests they did not share with their husbands. But just as they had made a public commitment to a partnership, so they more often spoke in terms of a joint identity.

The Older Respondents

This was even more true of the parents of both the married and cohabiting couples. Their accounts of why they married combined the pragmatic reasons favoured by cohabitants and the broader range of feelings about attachment that were given more attention by the younger married couples. The older generation had married when it was impossible for women to get mortgages on their own account and at a time of housing shortage; the majority (47 of 72) had lived with their parents before marriage and 18 couples had continued to do so for a period after marriage. It made no difference that all the mothers of the younger women in the sample had been employed before and after marriage. It was also the case that unmarried people tended to be regarded as 'odd' in the 1950s and early 1960s, as indeed they were at a time of near universal marriage.

The most common expression used by the older respondents (in 11 cases) in regard to getting married was that it was 'a natural progression', or a 'natural evolution'. Two men elaborated on the term in the following way:

> You find somebody you fancy and you like and you love them and all that sort of thing. And you then have to have a steady job ... And er, and that was the, then you ... became part of the community.

> You started going out with one girl and then you, you kept going out with them unless there was some big reason why you shouldn't.

Interestingly, the idea of a 'natural progression' was also used by two of the younger respondents, but to describe their drift into cohabitation rather than marriage. Many older respondents made the point that they had no option other than marriage if they were to achieve independent adult status, because of the housing conditions and because 'living in sin' was virtually unheard of and was certainly socially unacceptable. Mrs A said:

you either got married, or you weren't together really ... the option of living together
without getting married really didn't exist.

Thus the decision made by the older couples to marry was significantly different
from that of the younger married couples because there was no other option
available. Once marriage became a choice rather than a necessity, a much more
conscious decision had to be made to enter it.

The difference between the older and younger respondents (both cohabiting
and married) was extremely clear when they were asked about their commitment
to each other. A third of the older couples spoke about the importance of being
a 'partnership', 'a little team' and, most commonly, of 'pulling together'.
Commitment was 'just something you expected'. Four spoke strongly about
the expectation that marriage would be for life and that they would stick to each
other. Commitment was seen as very much part of the 'natural progression'
into marriage. Respondents did not reflect on the nature of it. Similarly, when
the older respondents were asked about their obligations to one another, all but
one answered easily, often referring to the marriage vows and what was
expected to follow from them. The men stressed protection and 'looking after',
the women most often spoke of the need to keep their husbands 'comfortable'.
Five of the women went further and talked about their sense of duty. One, who
had experienced considerable difficulties in her marriage, had considered
leaving her husband:

but what would he have done? ... I think I was brought up to be so completely unselfish
that I have always had this give, give, give ... .

Three of the men also spoke of a strong duty to provide. One whose wife had
suffered a very long nervous breakdown said:

I haven't been totally happy with the situation, but that is the situation I took on and
it was up to me to maintain that situation.

Younger respondents, both married and cohabiting, were much more likely
to qualify or reject the idea of obligation. Half the cohabitants and just under a
quarter of the married respondents either said that they had no obligations or
had not thought about them. Most of these questioned the term because they felt
that it was incompatible with a 'freely given', 'voluntary' commitment. A
married woman practising a very traditional division of household labour said:

I don't particularly feel we have any obligations. I don't think that's a word that I
would consider.

Of those younger respondents recognising obligations, more men did so than
women, but only a small minority mentioned the marriage vows. Faithfulness,

'being there' and sharing were the most commonly identified obligations. On the whole, the younger respondents felt a sense of obligation similar to that expressed by their parents towards children, but not to each other.

It may be that a sense of obligation grows with the investment that is made in a relationship and thus has something to do with age rather than generation. However, commitment was understood by the younger respondents as voluntary and as something that comes from within in the manner described by Johnson (1991) in his discussion of moral commitment. The older respondents usually associated obligation to some degree with the marriage vows and thus with external prescription. The timing of the shift from the more publicly understood concept of obligation to the more privately negotiated, but often (in the case of married couples) publicly stated, idea of commitment has not been investigated. It would seem reasonable to associate it with the major shift in thinking about sexual morality that took place in the 1960s, which resulted in the notion that the basis for a true morality had to come from within – from love for the other person – rather than from an externally prescribed moral code. This shift highlights the importance of considering the extent to which marriage has changed, as well as the differences between marriage and cohabitation, and helps to explain why the differences between the older and younger respondents were more apparent than those between the younger married and cohabiting couples. In the case of the younger couples, all acknowledged the importance of the fact that they had made a commitment. The cohabitants preferred that it remain private, but this made no difference to the nature of their commitment to their children. The younger couples (and to a large extent their parents) were united in believing that the kind of commitment a couple makes – public or private – is *their own affair*. While many older respondents wanted to see young people marry, very few were prepared to tell them that they should do so. To this extent, they too had been affected by the changed understanding as to what constitutes sexual morality. The crucial thing for the majority of all respondents was seen to be the existence of commitment rather than its manifestation. Given this, and the choice that now exists between marriage and cohabitation whenever a new intimate relationship is initiated, it is not surprising that most people in the sample also felt that it was proper to treat married and cohabiting parents the same (see below, Chapter 8).

NOTES

1. Full details of the sample and of the interview schedules for the study are available in the detailed report published by the Lord Chancellor's Department (Lewis with Datta and Sarre, 1999).
2. It was decided not to include people living in Scotland because of the differences in Scottish family law and the implications of this for that part of the interview schedule that is discussed in Chapter 8.

3. This means that the interviews with the older generation respondents were largely retrospective, which is recognised to involve methodological issues of a different kind, especially in
respect of the nature of memory (Thompson, 1988). The data from these interviews were considerably less rich than from the younger respondents, but as will be seen, this may also have
been a function of the fact that the questions had less resonance for the older respondents. For
the younger respondents, it seemed that the questions touched on issues that they were actively
considering and discussing.

4. The Omnibus Survey is a multi-purpose survey conducted by the Office of National Statistics.
It carries out face-to-face interviews with a nationally representative sample of adults throughout
Britain in most months of the year. Approximately 1900 interviews are carried out every month
and respondents are asked core questions about themselves and their circumstances, to which
can be added modules of questions from researchers. The Omnibus sample is representative of
the whole of England, Wales and Scotland (8 per cent of those answering the module of
questions for this study came from Scotland).

5. Drew (1984) reported exactly this approach to cohabitation among her sample of American
college cohabitants in the mid-1980s.

7.   Inside relationships: individualism and commitment and the investment of time and money

The interviews conducted for the study also explored the extent to which men and women were determined to pursue their own agendas in respect of the allocation of time and money, as against the extent to which their behaviour was oriented more towards investing in each other and the family. Thus, the material discussed in this chapter refers to what the couples did with their time and money, although they were also asked to comment on whether they *thought* the way in which they divided and spent their time and money was fair, and the extent to which they *felt* independent or dependent. That is, they were asked about mentalities as well as about behaviour.

There is no easy way of assessing this qualitative data. Eichler's (1981) early critique of the literature on power in marital relationships noted that it was impossible to assess power structures by totting up decisions about money and tasks, the usual approach to the study of the division of work in the household. Doucet (1995) made a valuable point when she stressed the importance of examining as many aspects of intimate relationships as possible as part of the attempt to see the 'whole picture'. Her study of gender equality and difference in respect of paid and unpaid work in households failed to find the kind of 'traditional, equalitarian, and transitional' models that are so often differentiated in the sociological literature. For example, a couple might look equal in regard to the division of household tasks, but be conventional in terms of the division of paid employment. Bielby and Bielby (1992) have also stressed the need to look at commitment to both work and family; many have assumed the latter to be an unproblematic, 'natural' commitment.

In regard to the balance between individualism and commitment, it is important to look across the spectrum of behaviours of each respondent, and also at both the behaviour and its meaning. For example, many of the older men may be categorised broadly as 'traditional breadwinners'. Their jobs were extremely important to them, they did little or no unpaid work at home, and often spent little time with their young children. However, they may also have given over the vast majority of the money that they earned and have felt that they 'worked for the family'. A pattern of activity that might appear relatively selfish nevertheless only had meaning in relation to the family. An assessment of behaviour alone is unlikely to reveal the 'whole picture'. Many aspects of behaviour among the younger couples were relatively 'traditional', especially in respect of the division of the responsibility for unpaid work in the household. There was rather more change in terms of how parents and children behaved in respect of the division of money. However, there was a much greater change in terms of awareness among both younger men and younger women of the issues to do with the division of time and money in their households. These divisions were no longer assumed to be 'fixed', as they had tended to be for the older respondents when they were bringing up their children, but were recognised to be open to negotiation. This meant that there were substantial differences in orientation towards self and other between the younger and older respondents.

The bulk of the literature to date has in fact focused on the extent to which women have sought a more equal and independent role in the family. Blood and Wolfe's (1960) early study of the dynamics of marriage suggested that women's increased earnings would allow them to impose a more equal division of labour in the domestic sphere, an argument that has been repeated often (Scanzoni, 1972; Blumstein and Schwartz, 1983; Wheelock and Oughton, 1994). However, the sociological research of the 1980s revealed little support for the view that women have achieved more independent, equal, separate lives, stressing rather the extent to which they prioritise the needs of others and to which inequalities, especially in respect of domestic work, are a source of tension.

Differences in terms of orientation towards individualism or self-development on the one hand, and commitment in terms of 'jointness' or greater investment in family and home-related activities on the other has also been strongly predicted by the literature on cohabitation. South and Spitz (1994), for example, found that in a representative sample of American women, married women did more unpaid work than cohabiting women in similar circumstances. However, the research for this book revealed little by way of significant differences between younger married and cohabiting couples in terms of their ideas and less than might have been expected in regard to their practices regarding the division of time and money.

TIME: PAID WORK, UNPAID WORK AND LEISURE

The Omnibus survey asked respondents both about room for self-development, and how much they valued different sorts of time and money in the context of their relationships. At first sight, the results appear to be contradictory. Respondents overwhelmingly agreed that individual development was important. But when asked what they valued most in a relationship, 50 per cent of the married and cohabiting parents said 'time with each other' and another

31 per cent 'time with children'. Married people with children were somewhat more likely to choose time with partner or spouse than were cohabitants with children; there were no significant differences between men and women. Some 81 per cent of married parents and 88 per cent of cohabiting parents chose these two options, although they showed little interest in the kind of working conditions (generous holidays and flexible hours) that might make them more possible. Overall, these people seemed to be saying that they wanted *both* the chance to develop individually *and* to invest time in relationships with other family members. This was in fact confirmed by the qualitative data, which also made sense of the apparent paradox, illuminating the changes that have taken place over time and the ways in which the tensions around the complex allocations of time are played out.

The Division of Paid Work Among the Younger Couples

Blumstein and Schwartz (1983) have commented on the way in which paid work has become the medium by which adults achieve autonomy. Indeed, the independence provided by a wage has become the essential ingredient of modern citizenship (Pateman, 1988b). Men and women both engage in paid work to an increasingly equal degree in terms of simple employment rates, but their structural position in the labour market in terms of hours of work and rates of remuneration remains profoundly unequal. In addition, the division of unpaid work in the home has also remained unequal. Gershuny *et al.*'s (1994) longitudinal data showed an increase in men's participation over the period 1975–87 from a very low base, especially if their partners were in full-time employment, but Warde and Hetherington's (1993) conclusions from qualitative data were less optimistic about the change in men's behaviour in this respect.

The patterns of paid work among the cohabitants were considerably less traditional than those of the young married couples (Table 7.1). Five of the young married women and four cohabiting women earned more than their husbands, although in one case this was only a matter of one or two thousand pounds. Nevertheless, these were somewhat higher numbers than would be predicted from Arber and Ginn's (1995) analysis of General Household Survey data on male and female earnings. All the younger female respondents worked in one of the social services and 20 of the men did so as well. Five men were self-employed and only two were manual workers, both builders.

Most of the men working part-time had suffered redundancy or a change in the nature of their jobs that had made them much less attractive. Thus one took redundancy because he detested the introduction of the internal market in the NHS and two had found the deteriorating terms and conditions for teachers in further education impossible. The men working part-time tended to think of themselves first as parents – 'I think of myself as being home-based rather than work-based' – which was an identity that all had come to welcome, even when it had not been sought voluntarily. The behaviour of this group of men bore out the findings of Gerson's (1993) American research, which showed the importance of period effects in determining men's degree of involvement in their families.

*Table 7.1   Numbers of younger male and female respondents working part-
and full-time*

Paid work	Cohabitants		Marrieds		Total
	Men	Women	Men	Women	
Full-time	7	5	13	6	31
Part-time	4	7	4	11	26
Total	11[a]	12	17	17	57

Note: [a] One man was temporarily out of work and therefore not included.

The men working full-time expressed more ambivalence regarding their dedication to career as opposed to investment in family work. A majority of both cohabiting and young married men said that they would like more time at home, but their statements to this effect were frequently convoluted and it was often clear that they were extremely committed to their jobs. Mr C., a cohabitant working in a local authority social services department, spoke for some time before acknowledging a 'chronic prioritisation problem' regarding his mix of paid and unpaid work:

> They're not the same thing. [*Pause*] They're not the same thing and I'm not sure, I'm not sure that I could say that one's prioritised over the other. [*Pause*] I mean, I mean, you know, work is a very big part of my life, and I mean, [*Pause*] I wouldn't call it a calling, 'cause again that's a bit sort of, you know, sicky, but I mean, I feel highly committed to that. But it is work and it's over there ... it's an emotional conflict that's not straightforward about, you know, I would rather be *at home*, I would rather be *home on time*. I would rather not cause any sorts of difficulty and spend that time with W. [his partner] and spend that time with the boys, but I'm going to stay at work, because if I don't, you know, somebody will possibly die or be in danger, or what-have-you. (Italics added)

Mr R., who was married, was typical in the way in which he expressed his ambivalence. He said that work and personal independence were 'more important than I'd like to admit', and then went on:

> Sounds like I feel guilty about it. I see myself very much as a family man. You know, if somebody said to me, define, I would say I'm a family man. I spend time with my

family, I like my family, I don't want to go outside my family for things ... I'm just part of the family and I feel quite independent within that.

Despite his expressed preference for 'family time', he did not know what he would do if a better job with longer hours was offered to him. Another married man said:

I've obviously got to do what I have to with my job, but at the same time I've got to try and balance it with making sure I don't just live my job, as much for M. [his wife] as probably for my kids as well.

All the cohabitants and all but three of the young married men said that they would like more time at home and had no intrinsic objection to working fewer hours, but their responses were not wholly convincing on this score:

I see myself as sort of providing the bulk of the money, as the sort of principal wage-earner. Though her money's good as well. I mean, I mean, if it was the situation that she was the one that could earn lots of money, it would make more sense for me to work part-time, perhaps. (High-earning male cohabitant)

Mr W., who was married and who had had a short period of part-time work, said that he would prefer more time at home and then added:

Well, it's easy to say when you're working full-time isn't it? That time when I did work part-time wasn't very good – it's a complicated balance – I'd struggle if I had to spend a lot of time at home.

What distinguished all these men was the fact that they had thought about the issue, recognised that there was a problem of balance, and acknowledged that both their jobs and their families required an investment of time. There were only three unreflexive, traditional male breadwinners in the sample of young men, all of them married. These freely admitted their commitment to their careers, were content to leave family work to their wives, and saw no problem in so doing.

A majority of both the cohabiting and the married women followed what has become the normal pattern for British women with young children and worked part-time (see above, p. 62). A majority of the female respondents needed to work in order to pay the bills. However, the most striking aspect of these women's accounts was their commitment to their jobs. Mrs B., who was married to one of the three unreflexive, traditional male breadwinners, said that her job was 'an opportunity to sort of keep my individuality'. Another of the women married to a traditional man said that her job as a teacher was important for her 'self-esteem' and that the nature of the work gave her an opportunity to exercise authority. The wife of a self-employed man, who identified strongly with the role of breadwinner but who was aware that making assumptions as to a traditional division of labour would be problematic, said that despite her husband's doubts about her job she would 'just carry on and do it, because there are certain things in life that you've got to do and the other one's not going to like'. She felt that her job made her 'a better person because I've got an interest of my own' and that it was important to her 'as a person'. Much as her husband disliked the shifts she had to work as a nurse, he acknowledged that she was committed to her job and that he could not 'suppress' that commitment.

This commitment to paid work and an insistence on seeing it as important and often in terms of a career was common both to those women who wanted to work part-time and to the few (two married and two cohabiting) who would have preferred to work full-time. However, a majority also said that they had changed their priorities after having children. Mrs. E was typical:

> It used to be very important and now it's just fun and it pays the bills and it gives us a very comfortable lifestyle ... I think the children have shifted my priorities.

However, this did not mean that their jobs had become 'just a job' or that they had decided to forgo all notions of career progression. In terms of the determination to pursue a career, there was much less difference than might have been expected between the part-time and full-time women, whether cohabiting or married. The full-timers were very committed to their careers, but only one cohabitant and two married women identified solely as workers. Like the majority of the men, the women expressed ambivalence about their commitment to career and to unpaid work, but the order of their priorities was, in the main, reversed. Varying degrees of conflict and guilt were often voiced (somewhat more strongly in the accounts of the married women). On the whole, the women were mother-workers, whereas the men were mostly worker-fathers.

Unpaid Work: the Younger Couples

The fact that the younger female respondents were committed workers as well as committed mothers raised the possibility of the kind of tensions around the domestic division of labour discussed so eloquently by Hochschild (1990), because men do less unpaid housework and child care. Hochschild found that the unequal division of domestic labour was wished away, usually by women, who would often pretend that the relationship was more equal than it was in fact. The findings from this study showed evidence of an 'economy of gratitude', on the part of men as well as women, but little myth-making in respect of the domestic division of labour. In only one (married) couple was the division of labour grossly unfair (the man worked part-time and did virtually no unpaid work) and in this case the wife bent over backwards to make excuses for her husband in order to justify the situation and to make it appear 'fair'. Five of the younger married men did very little unpaid work (including the three traditional male breadwinners), but their wives openly accepted the situation.

The interviews revealed something rather different to be important. Again, the key issue was the degree to which there was *awareness* on the part of *both* men and women that there was a tension between desire for self-development (usually through paid work or leisure activities) on the one hand, and investment in family work and activities on the other. Awareness of having more time for self on the part of the men often led to 'compensation' behaviours, such as emotional support, or doing a specific task that the women particularly disliked (getting breakfast, in the case of three men). The point is that the issue of how time should be allocated was on the table for discussion. In the vast majority of cases it was not glossed over. Awareness did not always result in domestic harmony, but where it was accompanied by an openness to change, it resulted in a *flexible response* which was crucial to the performance of what were often very complicated household routines and in the achievement of balance in the relationship.

Five younger women, two cohabiting and three married, discussed at some length their expectations, indeed assumptions, that their partners/husbands would share domestic work. They made the point that their expectations in this regard were different from those of their mothers because the nature of their paid work and their commitment to it was very different. A female cohabitant said that she had completely different expectations' of her partner 'to what my mother had about my father'. Another said that she was very disappointed that the domestic division of labour was not more fair and was surprised at how difficult an issue it had proved to be. The vast majority of the men (the three traditional male breadwinners excepted), married and cohabiting, were aware that the performance of unpaid work was an issue, and divided into the following groups:

- those who agonised about it;
- those who knew that it was not fair, were grateful that their wives did more and showed it in word and deed;
- those who knew it was not fair and actively tried to do something about it;
- those who knew it was not fair but were not doing anything about it;
- those who knew it was not fair and felt resentful at having to confront it.

Most younger generation male respondents fell into one of the first three categories; three cohabiting and four married men fell into the last two. The most significant dividing characteristic was exposure to higher education. One of the married men referred at some length to the importance of his time at college in changing his ideas about the role of women and what men should do in the home. Ross (1987) also found that better educated husbands in the US were more likely to participate in household tasks. Men who worked part-time did not necessarily invest more in unpaid work. Three of the eight part-timers did less housework and child care than their partners/wives. The rest did rather more child care, but not more housework, which is in line with Coltrane's (1996) findings. Two of the men doing more child care were nevertheless less likely to take time off work to look after a sick child *because* they worked fewer days in the first place. Full-time men working in jobs with flexible hours (such as teachers in further education) were able to do more in this respect.

Mr C. (cohabiting) and Mr R. (married), who had both given rather tortuous responses to questions about whether they would be prepared to take jobs with fewer hours, were 'agonisers' when it came to their investment in unpaid work. In answer to a series of questions about who performed and took responsibility for a variety of domestic chores and childcare, Mr C. said: 'W. [his partner], W., W., God!'. Mr R. said:

> you end up being incredibly traditional ... You try and think you've worked it out rationally ... but ... you just take on the straightforward roles that everyone else did .... You can answer these [questions on domestic labour] by now.
>
> Traditional. I'm desperately hoping you're going to ask me something and then I can give you the wrong answer.

In the second group a married man recognised that his wife, who also worked full-time, was the 'driving force' in terms of family work and activities. He felt some guilt about this and said that he would hate to think that he made no contribution at all. Another married man was eager to point out that he was always prepared to do something extra on the family front if the circumstances demanded it. This was confirmed by his wife, who nevertheless wished 'that he could sometimes do my Tuesday', which required particularly complicated scheduling in respect of the children. The men in this group were for the most part dependent on their wives organisationally and on their families emotionally, most of their leisure time being spent in the family. Recognition of their dependency in these respects made them grateful.

In the third category, a married man recognised that he 'could do more housework to be honest with you', but felt that he had a 'moral responsibility' to share the child care. He was aware that it would destroy his relationship if he left the latter entirely to his wife. A male cohabitant said that he knew that it was important 'not to make assumptions about what she should be doing', and that he had 'responsibilities to S. [his partner] to do the shopping, cooking and all the other gender-defined roles'. However, the men in the last two categories felt that they could not do more. One married man was aware that he did not pull his weight – ' "Oh bugger, I've got to look after the kids" is selfish' – but still resented the expectation that he should do more. Another said that parent–teacher meetings, for example, did not interest him, and in any case, 'whatever I do will never be enough'. One cohabitant said on answering the questions on domestic labour that he felt 'scored' and resented feeling that way.

There were what one female married respondent termed 'running battles' over particular aspects of the domestic labour in the case of five cohabiting couples and 11 married couples. Relatively few couples (five) bought in help with housework; indeed, rather more of their parents had done this. It was in any case a solution that only worked to diffuse arguments so long as the couple already accepted the nature of their respective investments in household work (see also Gregson and Lowe, 1994). Fairness was an issue for all the younger couples and, as Thompson (1991) observed, fairness was measured by more than a simple division of tasks. Men's awareness that there were issues to be discussed was usually enough to mollify their partners, even if no substantial change in their behaviour followed.

Among the majority who actively debated the issues, three couples, one married and two cohabiting, had achieved a high degree of flexibility. Their contribution to unpaid work had changed significantly over time, the men having been prepared to take part-time work and do more household labour in response to their wives'/partners' growing involvement in their jobs. Furthermore, they were able to anticipate further changes in the way in which they organised things in the future. As one female cohabitant who earned more than her partner put it: 'I was more dependent on P., but that's shifted now, and no doubt it'll shift again.' In contrast, the couples at the other end of the spectrum were distinguished by their relative rigidity in respect of the primary importance accorded to the man's job, and in their division of household tasks, which was often regarded as unfair by the women and to which the men were unwilling to contribute more. On balance, more of the married couples tended towards the rigid end of the scale, but the degree of similarity between the younger married and cohabiting couples in terms both of the extent to which unpaid work was recognised as an issue for debate by men as well as women and of actual behaviour was more striking than any differences.

Leisure: the Younger Couples

This was also true of leisure behaviour. All respondents attributed consider-able importance to time spent with 'the family'. All but one of the younger couples spent most of their leisure time on family-related activities. The exceptional couple (cohabitants) managed to go out separately twice a week, despite having a nine-month-old baby. A significant number, particularly of married respondents, felt that they would have liked more 'couple-time'. The main point at issue for the vast majority of couples was time spent alone. A majority of cohabiting and married men engaged either passively or actively in sporting activities (usually football) on a regular basis and two put a lot of time into music. A small number said that they had no desire to go outside the family during their non-working time (it was these men who were also grateful to their wives for performing a disproportionate amount of household tasks). The women were much less involved in regular, organised leisure activities and this was a source of friction for two cohabiting and six married couples. A minority of women felt that they had virtually no time for themselves. One married woman said that she felt as though she was always working for someone else, in her job, for the children, or for her husband:

> My Mum especially will tell you how tired I get, and how little time I have had over the past five years really for myself, just for me. I've always been doing something either for work or for the children or for T. [her husband]. But, you know, it's always been for somebody else. And I have really felt like I belong to somebody else, all the time, and I never get the time to just think, well what would I like to do with this bit of time?

Both men and women in married and cohabiting couples attached considerable importance to respect for each other's personal time. One married woman referred to her 'me-days' as being of great importance. Another recognised that her husband's identity (he had suffered redundancy) was very bound up with sport and in planning independent holidays: 'That's the thing that's kept him going is being able to go out.'

Several men said that they were aware of the fact that their partners did not have as much time to themselves on a regular basis and that they would like them to claim more. The vast majority of men were also aware that there were limits to the amount of time they could claim. As one married man put it:

> Sometimes it is hard, like you know, I'd really just like to go off and do this, that and the other, but you know, it's selfish to do it.

Others also drew a clear line between legitimate amounts of personal time and 'selfish' behaviour. Their female partners seemed to find difficulty in claiming a regular 'slot' for themselves, even when they expressed a strong desire to maintain their independence within the relationship. Yet a majority of women felt that living with someone or getting married had made them value time to themselves more: 'I didn't value my independence then as much as I do now.'

The broad picture with regard to ideas about, and the use of, time for the younger couples was, first, one of similarity between the cohabiting and married people; second, one of patterns of behaviour that tended towards traditional gender divisions; but, third, a high level of awareness on the part of men as well as women as to the fact that these patterns were open to negotiation. It was this last point that made communication an important issue for many couples. Communication was not important in and of itself as an indicator of more equal, democratic and independent relationships. Fitzpatrick's (1988) intensive study of patterns of communication among couples showed that 'traditional' couples in male breadwinner model relationships were the most likely to be able to predict how the other was feeling. Rather, communication was the means of dealing with the tensions between self and other, individualism and commitment. Seven cohabiting couples and 14 married couples indicated that this sort of communication was important. This did not mean that they talked about everything, and for many non-verbal communication was as important an expression of commitment to one another. Rather, the importance of communication followed from the awareness of the tensions between investment in own time and in other-related activities. It was also this change in mentalities that most sharply differentiated the younger generation respondents from their parents, particularly the men from their fathers.

The Older Couples

All but three of the younger respondents were on good terms with their parents, and only one of these three was actively hostile. A majority acknowledged their parents' influence on the way they did things, especially the female respondents in respect of child care and paid work. However, they also felt that their own efforts to combine paid and unpaid work were different to those of their mothers:

> I think, in some way I think there's more strain in that, although women used to work, women now do very different kinds of work. I would never put down the kind of work that my Mum did, 'cause I think she worked very hard, but ...

Men on the whole tended to be more vague about their fathers' attitudes and practices, but respondents were most likely to reject the example of their parents in respect of the division of domestic work. However, Gershuny *et al.* (1994) have suggested that the main reason for the slow change in the domestic division of labour is explained by the fact that younger men copy their parents' ways of doing things, which may be true of the majority. The five male respondents expressing the strongest views about their fathers (two cohabitants and three marrieds) consciously rejected the way in which their fathers had behaved. As one male cohabitant put it:

> Theirs is not a partnership in the true sense of the word. It's a traditional marriage in as much as my mother cooks everything. My Dad doesn't know where the cooker is type of thing. He doesn't know where the iron is. He would never load the washing.

However, rejection of their fathers was stronger at the level of attitudes than of behaviour.

The younger male respondents' orientation to paid work was also often substantially different from that of their fathers, but they did not talk about this. All the fathers had worked full-time. Many of the 13 manual workers were made redundant in the 1950s and 1960s, but always found jobs immediately. Their accounts of their work, which were often long (and unsolicited by the interviewer), bore a strong resemblance to the world conjured up by the 'angry young men' novels of the period.' They had little or no involvement in their work, but the money was reasonable and there were always plenty of jobs available. One-third of the older men contrasted their job security with that of their sons and made the point that while they had earned a 'family wage', younger women had to work to pay the mortgage. One said that 'job stability, which isn't there today' was the foundation of marriage. Another, who had been a teacher, said:

> Their lifestyle is totally different from anything I think I would be able to cope with, which is this insecurity which those four [his two daughters and their partners] face.

There was, therefore, a lively appreciation among the older couples of the changes brought about by an increasingly flexible labour market.

Many older respondents had difficulty answering questions about competing work and family identities; all the women identified primarily as wives and/or mothers, and the vast majority of the men as workers. Fourteen of the 32 fathers were, by their own definition, 'family men', in a sense that was quite different from any understanding the younger male respondents may have had of the same term. These older men regarded work merely as a 'means to an end'. In the words of one: 'work was a bloody nuisance. I know that I'd rather not have gone to work.' He said that he was a 'family man', even though he did no unpaid work and spent very little time with his children. Another talked about his work and his family 'being one'. Despite their often wholehearted concentration on paid work, these men felt that they worked 'for the family', rather than for themselves.

The rest of the older male respondents were as committed to their jobs, but had also been more involved in their work. Two admitted that they had been 'workaholic' and that they now felt that they had been 'selfish' in this respect. Some had also been dependent on their wives for providing a smooth-running 'haven' from the world of work in much the same way as were some of the younger men. But whether, like the younger men, they had recognised this at the time was difficult to establish through a retrospective interview. From the tenor of their remarks, even if they had recognised it, it is unlikely that it had resulted in discussion or negotiation.

All but two of the older women had worked at some point while having dependent children, but the vast majority had worked very short part-time hours. Only six of the 40 had worked full-time and only seven had seen themselves as having careers. However, paid work was still often important to identity. One said that at work she:

> became Mrs H., I became myself Because so far I had been my parents' daughter ... And then it was the wife of Mr H., you know. And then there was P. and M.'s Mum, you know. When I was there, I was really Mrs H.

Two had husbands who had stopped them working. One had worked the 'twilight shift' at the local factory (which started at 4 p.m. and was designed for working mothers in the 1950s), but her husband got tired of putting their daughter to bed. Only one of the younger male respondents voiced objections to his wife going out to work (though not to the point of insisting that she stop), and all recognised the importance of their wives' contribution in terms of both its material importance for the household economy and/or as something the women wanted to do. However, a large number of the older women felt that they got no encouragement from their husbands to develop an identity outside the home: 'I felt ... I didn't get recognition from A. [her husband]. I had to fight to be noticed.' A quarter of the older women agreed with their husbands' assessment of their earnings as 'pin money', but this did not mean that they attached no significance to their work. 'Getting out of the house', 'learning to stand up for myself and not to blush', 'having a bit of money of my own' were all important. One woman who ran her own business and earned almost as much as her husband, a manual worker, organised her life much as she liked, but at the price of permitting her husband to keep his identity as 'breadwinner' intact and of doing all the unpaid work at home.

The expectation that the woman would take care of the home and family was clear for the older respondents. One man struggled to acknowledge that things had changed and to justify how it had been when he had young children:

> I know ideas are changing, my own ideas are changing, but if the husband is the breadwinner, then the job is an important feature of the marriage, isn't it?

There was very little awareness on the part of the men that the way in which they and their wives divided their time was an issue, although two acknowledged fulsomely that they had begun to think differently in middle age under the influence of their daughters and of women in their workplaces. Nor was it an issue for the vast majority of the women, who had accepted the situation and worked round it if they had wanted a more satisfying job that required greater personal investment. Only two women said that they had felt aggrieved by this state of affairs; one of these became addicted to tranquillisers in the late 1950s before managing to train as a nurse. Male jobs were secure, the male breadwinner model was internalised and the gender division of labour was expected, and there was little or no room for negotiation or flexibility between husbands and wives.

In this context, it is not surprising that relatively few women had any complaints about the division of unpaid work. Five had reached the point in old age where they recognised that their husbands had done very little at home:

> Now I'm older and I've looked back and thought about things and I think, he never does anything to help me.

> Well, I mean he never put his hand to any cooking until he was ill.

For the most part these women accepted that they had been expected to invest much more heavily in family work. The fact that the division of time was relatively non-negotiable meant that fairness was not an issue for these couples. Unlike the younger respondents, most had never thought about it. Like the question of work/family identities, it was a non-issue:

> I don't think fairness comes into it. It is really just a matter of getting things done isn't it?

> I mean it didn't occur to me that there was anything wrong ... he just wasn't required, it never occurred to me to think that he should be doing more in the family.

> I never even thought about it ... I think you start thinking like that and things are not successful.

> I didn't think about it ... Very unquestioning, yes.

These quotations are from the women, but the men also said that they had not thought about it and had not discussed it.

The apparently much larger commitment to family on the part of women in terms of the division of time was unproblematic chiefly because the men's investment in their paid work was not perceived as 'selfish'. It was very important to the vast majority of male and female respondents that the men were not 'lazy'. 'Pulling one's weight' was important to the idea of partnership (or a 'team') that characterised most of the older couples' idea of marriage (see above, p. 144). One man said: 'if your partner was having a hard time to do what she was doing, you simply got up and you pitched in with it.' Several men said that they would not 'sit around' while their wives did the housework. One of the women said that her husband 'helped, I mean he didn't go drinking ...'. Going to the pub for long hours would have been classed as selfish behaviour.

These couples had been together for many years and all but two declared themselves to be very satisfied with their marriages; the absence of behaviour that would have been considered selfish was an important source of contentment. Lack of selfish behaviour constituted commitment to the family project and was something that women felt grateful for.

There was therefore some continuity between the older and younger respondents in terms of the operation of an economy of gratitude. But its meaning changed considerably from the absence of negative behaviours in the case of the older men to much more evidence of positive attitudes and, to some extent, behaviours in the case of the younger men, particularly in terms of their awareness of and attempts to address the issues raised by the unequal division of unpaid work.

The findings on leisure time reinforced many of the same themes. A significant number of older couples (eight) had led remarkably separate lives in terms of their leisure activities. One man said that he and his wife had lived in 'parallel universes'. The men were able to claim personal space easily while their wives were not, something that was also true of the younger generation; but again, for the older couples there was little or no awareness of this as an issue. A minority of women acknowledged their dependence on their husband's willingness to permit them to do things by themselves:

He lets me be independent.

I have been heavily dependent on D. [her husband] to encourage me that I can do things alone, that I can be self-sufficient, that I can make decisions without him.

Any flexibility that was achieved in the household arrangements regarding the division of time, leisure included, tended to depend on women developing ways of manoeuvring within parameters that were regarded by both parties as fixed. The issue of time for self and time for family was not on the table for discussion and it is not surprising that a majority of older couples reported that communication was not so important to their marriages. The youngest woman in the sample of older couples remarked: 'I mean his generation of men didn't remotely express their feelings', something her husband, who was one of the two men who had begun to change his views on how time should be divided between him and his wife in middle age, agreed with. The young male cohabitant nearest to them in age had also experienced difficulty in engaging in debate as to how his partner was feeling about the division of time. The difference was that his partner's expectations were higher in this respect from an early stage in the relationship, and certainly well-established by the time they had children (12 years after starting to live together). Thus he had been forced to address the issue.

A quarter of the older women made explicit statements about their husbands inability and/or unwillingness to talk:

> If I think something's going to cause problems, yes, I don't discuss it ... so I have kept a lot to myself, yes.

Two more women described how in order to achieve a change in their household arrangements they needed:

> ... to make him feel that it was his idea.

> He thinks we have made decisions together, but it isn't always so – sometimes I make the decision and he thinks he has made it. That's the way it works and it works very well.

This is reminiscent of Komter's (1989) findings from a qualitative study of the interaction of 60 Dutch husbands and wives, which also showed, however, that women's strategies did not always work and that men were often able to stifle women's desire for change. The younger couples interviewed for this book operated much more openly in respect to disagreements and tensions. This did not necessarily make for an easier life. As the older woman who had to 'get round' her husband noted, her system worked well. Nor were behaviour patterns in the younger generation couples so different from those of their parents in respect of the investment of time. Young men were even more committed to the development of their careers and had a strongly developed notion of an entitlement to personal time. However, there was more awareness and more negotiation among the younger generation; their relationships were *relatively* more democratic.

The focus of this study was not the dynamics of interaction between the partners in a relationship; however, analysis as to how far partners looked out for themselves in respect of their time investments and how far they prioritised their families immediately highlighted gender differences as well as changes over time. It is likely that shifts in women's orientation and greater readiness to make claims to the right to self-development in terms of career and personal time has been the main driver of change. This is certainly what the bulk of the literature would predict. The younger women's commitment to paid work, even when only working part-time, was very different to that of their mothers. They wanted time for themselves *and* time for the family in respect of work and leisure. The female cohabitants were more consistent in their insistence on the importance of an independent existence within the relationship, which might have been predicted from what we know to date. The more surprising discovery was the change in men's mentalities. There were differences in behaviour between the older and younger men, but these had been produced mainly by changes in the market for labour and in the nature of jobs. A number of younger men had been either pushed into redundancy or felt constrained to take it. The younger men were doing somewhat more unpaid work, but, again as the literature would predict, the change was far from dramatic. However, the vast majority of these men no longer made ready assumptions about who would do what or who was entitled to what. It would be wrong to characterise this as a simple shift away from male privilege and devotion to self. While the older self-defined 'family men' often devoted most of their time to work and their own leisure pursuits, they did not necessarily enjoy their work and saw it as their duty as husbands and fathers (as we shall see, most gave over virtually all of their earnings to their wives). However, for the younger respondents, behaviour was no longer legitimised by a shared set of expectations about gender roles in accordance with the male breadwinner model, which entailed (relative) sacrifice of self in terms of career and own projects on the part of women.

Other studies have suggested that the removal of prescription does not mean an end to moral responsibility; rather, this becomes the subject of debate (Finch and Mason, 1993; Weeks *et al.*, 1999; Smart and Neale, 1999). With greater awareness on the part of men that the division of time is not fixed has come greater debate and negotiation. This, indeed, has made communication more important for the younger generation respondents. Refusal to communicate is a more serious issue when the division of time is no longer understood as fixed. It is not that communication in and of itself is some secret ingredient for successful relationships (as so much of the recent literature would seem to suggest: see Jamieson, 1998), but rather that it is necessary given the fact that the interests of self and other must be negotiated. Indeed, this may be why a survey of men and women living in European Union countries in the mid-1990s found that two out of three said that the most likely reason for getting divorced would be 'if there is no longer any communication between the partners': more than felt they would divorce if one partner was unfaithful (Eurostat, 1995, p. 56). Following Rusbult's (1987) adaptation of Hirschman's (1970) categories of 'exit, voice and loyalty', relationships of the older couples seemed to be characterised more by a passive 'loyalty' and those of the younger couples by an active, but not always constructive, use of 'voice'.

MONEY

One of the most serious measures of selfish behaviour would be the appropriation of financial resources by one partner. At the beginning of the twentieth century, there is evidence that working-class women whose husbands did not make proper provision for them and their children felt justified in walking away from their marriages (see above, p. 102). Selfish individualism in respect of the division of money (usually on the part of the man as the person with most control over resources) has serious implications for the welfare of other members of the household. When the division of household resources was rediscovered as a significant issue in the 1980s, the literature described a number of different types of financial management. Pahl (1989) and Vogler and Pahl (1993, 1994) identified five basic systems:

- the whole wage system, whereby either the man hands over his wage and the woman is responsible for all the finances of the household, or the husband has sole responsibility for managing all household finances;
- the allowance system, whereby the man gives the woman a housekeeping allowance and pays other bills himself;
- the shared management system (a common pool), whereby both have access to income, and expenditure comes from a shared pool (although the pool may be managed jointly or by one of the partners);
- the shared management system (a partial pool), whereby personal spending money comes from funds retained by each partner;
- the independent management system, whereby each partner has separate responsibilities and neither partner has access to all of the funds.

Over time, the importance of the whole wage and the allowance system, both characteristic of a male breadwinner family pattern, has faded. Changes in the banking system, with the much more widespread use of bank accounts and the introduction of direct debiting, together with changes in female labour market participation, has also affected systems of household management. Completely independent management is only possible in households with incomes from two full-time jobs.

None of the couples in the qualitative sample, older or younger, had any serious disagreements about money and the accounts of the men and the women were broadly congruent as to the nature of their financial systems. Respondents to the Omnibus survey did not prioritise high personal income for its own sake. Similarly, all the respondents in the qualitative sample were committed to sharing money in the household. Most operated a system that bore some resemblance to those listed above, but the vast majority of the younger couples operated what were actually rather mixed systems that often involved a number of different kinds of accounts and moving money around between them. This meant that it was frequently difficult to get a sense of the extent to which one partner was more in control than the other, for example, the person writing the cheques or organising the direct debits did not necessarily exercise the most control over the finances.

The Younger Couples

Among the younger respondents, two married couples ran a fairly traditional housekeeping allowance system, and the wives also kept their earnings, which they spent partly on household expenses and partly on themselves. Five couples, three married and two cohabiting, operated a common pool, and six (again a mixture of married and cohabiting) a partial pool, whereby a proportion of earnings was paid into a joint 'household' account. The rest of their money was kept in their own separate accounts. The remaining 16 couples each took responsibility for paying particular items of household expenditure. All of these had separate bank accounts. However, sometimes the money earmarked for particular bills was transferred into a joint household account and there was often a joint account for savings. Indeed, it cannot be inferred that the systems were *perceived* in terms of 'independent management'. One cohabiting couple operated separate accounts only because they had found that trying also to operate a joint account was 'very confusing', but they insisted that they saw all their money as joint. Some couples who pooled nevertheless drew on the pool without consultation. Others managed their outgoings from separate accounts, but made spending decisions together. There are therefore very real limitations on what can be inferred from the existence of joint or separate accounts (see also Wilson, 1987; Burgoyne, 1990). Singh (1997) has suggested on the basis of a qualitative Australian study that the joint account is effectively a ritual, a symbol of trust and fairness. Interestingly, a higher proportion of cohabitants saw all their money as basically joint (11 out of 12, compared with 12 out of 17 married couples). This is at odds with the finding that financial independence is a reason for cohabitation (Kiernan and Estaugh, 1993). All nine women who earned more than their partners saw money as joint, which may support Stamp's (1985) view that women who earn more than their partners are concerned to cede some power to the men they live with.

However, the real issue for debate among these couples was how personal spending money was to be defined and where the line was drawn between 'own' and 'joint' money. Schwartz's (1994, p. 136) qualitative study of 30 'peer marriages' in the US concluded that while all operated joint management systems for their money, autonomy was also important: 'having separate money is one way partners feel that they still have a separate identity'. Fourteen of the younger couples in this study (using both the pool and independent management systems) differentiated between 'joint' and 'separate' money when it came to spending decisions, feeling free to spend their 'own' money as they wished, but consulting on expenditures coming out of 'joint' money. Having access to 'separate' money was very important to the vast majority of respondents. As Mr H. put it: 'it is important to have something that's yours and not pooled'.

Some couples worked out a clear method of arriving at separate monies. Mr W., a married man, said:

> S.'s view has been the same as mine, that we wanted to have our own accounts, because S. didn't want to have to feel guilty about going out and buying something she wanted. And that's fine. But ... I tend to be, I don't know, more frugal in the way I spend money, and S. would admit that she always gets overdrawn ... And I mean, my view of that is that all we can do if we want to have that independence is agree that we'll proportion it out. And you know, if she decides to buy something or I decide to buy something, then we don't have to feel guilty about that. We have an agreement that our accounts are our responsibility. The joint account, that has to be maintained.

In fact their system guaranteed this couple equal independent spending money. This was achieved by the husband paying a sufficient sum into the joint account to permit his wife to have an absolutely rather than a proportionately equal amount of spending money (she earned only half as much as he did).

Again, fairness in respect of 'own' money was important to many couples. Not all had simple systems for ensuring this though. Many were rather messy in the way in which they managed to provide for separate spending money. One cohabiting couple operated separate accounts, a joint bill-paying account and a joint savings account. They both put the same amount of money into the bill-paying account, despite a large difference between their incomes (she worked part-time). The female partner played a greater role in controlling the system. According to her partner:

> it's a bit bizarre ... those accounts are completely separate ... it depends who needs to buy stuff. W. will put stuff into savings and then she'll say to me, I haven't got anything in my account, so I give her money.

This approach to moving money around in order to 'even things up' indicated a flexibility not dissimilar from that characterising the approach achieved by three of the younger generation couples in respect of the division of time. Such flexibility was much more common in respect of money among both married and cohabiting couples. Financial management systems were also changed over time, for example with the arrival of children (see also Burgoyne, 1990). Vogler and Pahl (1994) found that women had access to less personal spending money in both female- and male-managed systems. In this study, it was only possible clearly to identify who controlled the money in 13 couples, and in 10 of these it was a woman. There were only two couples in which the women (one married and one cohabiting) felt that they did not get enough personal spending money; in both the finances were controlled by the man.

The Older Couples

Many of the younger female respondents acknowledged the importance of their mother's influence in regard to wanting money to call their own; two mothers were remembered as also having given advice regarding joint versus separate bank accounts (in favour of the latter). However, the approach to joint and separate money on the part of the older couples was very different, being tied largely to the set of prescriptions that characterised the male breadwinner model. One woman who had inherited money of her own said that this had proved awkward because of the assumption that men should provide.

A large number of older respondents (21) referred to working some kind of allowance system, but there were differences in terms of whether the money came from a joint account or one in the husband's name, and, more importantly in regard to the welfare of the wives, in terms of who controlled the money. Some older couples had joint accounts, but the men controlled the finances. A further 23 couples had operated a partial or common pooling system. Fourteen couples had worked in cash when their children were young, often putting money in drawers or tins that were earmarked for particular kinds of expenditure and were freely accessible to both partners. There were no more complaints about the division of financial resources than about the division of time among these couples, but two women reported that they had experienced considerable difficulty managing on what had been allowed to them, which they did not think had been recognised by their husbands. There was no discussion as to 'joint' and 'separate' money. It was generally assumed that the husbands' earnings would be the means of meeting household expenditure. Blumstein and Schwartz (1991) have stressed the importance of this assumption in terms of its effect on how the wife's earnings are seen and on the relative power of husbands and wives. Often women also spent a considerable amount of their own earnings on the children, but any balance tended to be treated as their 'own' money, which was why own earnings were regarded as important by so many of them, even when they were only small and regarded as 'pin money' by them and their husbands. Many women did not know what their husbands earned, but nor did husbands necessarily know what their wives earned. The youngest male respondent from the older couples, a teacher, said that it was only recently that he had learned what his wife earned; it had been irrelevant to the financial management of the household.

Thus the younger respondents in general had a much more 'joint' approach to money, while also expecting to control 'own' money. The contribution that women's earnings made to household expenditure, especially to the payment of mortgages, was considerably greater in the younger generation, which meant that a decision had to be made about who paid for what. In the older generation, women's earnings were perceived by men and women as being primarily for 'extras'. 'Own' money was important to most of the older women, but it was not subject to negotiation in the same way, and mechanisms to achieve fairness in this respect were not put in place. The prevalence of the allowance system operated by so many of the older generation made a greater degree of selfishness possible in theory if rarely in practice, at least among this sample (a considerable amount was revealed by the investigations of the 1980s).

MENTALITIES, BEHAVIOUR, INDIVIDUALISM AND COMMITMENT

The previous chapter revealed differences between younger married and cohabiting couples in terms of the nature of the commitment they made to one another by deciding to marry or cohabit, but not in terms of the nature of the parental commitment they eventually made. This chapter has revealed few differences between them in terms of behaviour. Cohabitants spent rather more leisure time as a family, which may be in tune with the way in which they rethought their commitment with the advent of parenthood. More striking were the similarities between the younger married and cohabiting couples in terms of the change in mentalities, which meant a much greater awareness of the existence of issues to do with the allocation of time and money. The difference between the older and younger couples was particularly marked on this score, especially for men. This more explicit awareness of issues for negotiation among the younger couples is in tune with Morgan's (1996, 1999) characterisation of late twentieth-century family life in terms of 'family practices', implying that individuals are actively engaged in 'doing' family, rather than passively residing in a particular family structure. Both younger male and female respondents were particularly aware of the importance of fairness and were often anxious to give due credit to and to balance up different kind of contributions. This tallies with one of Fiske's (1992) four 'elementary' models of social relations: the model of proportionality that he termed 'market pricing'. The model allows for the comparison of qualitatively and quantitatively diverse factors. However, because the effort to achieve proportionality had a lot to do with the desire for 'communal sharing' (another of Fiske's elementary models) it had as much or more to do with a search for balance and a regard for the other as with any self-regarding motive.

The fact that mentalities would seem to have changed more than behaviour may be interpreted as a sign that behaviour will follow. However, sociologists writing in the 1970s were also convinced that they were studying a 'transitional' family form and that more 'symmetrical' patterns were just around the corner (Young and Willmott, 1973; Rapoport and Rapoport, 1971), which did not prove to be the case. Dysjuncture between mentalities and behaviour seems to be more common than correspondence.

However, the prescriptions that accompanied normative expectations regarding the male breadwinner model family have disappeared and there has been real change over time. Women's paid work was recognised as important by all the younger men and women, and the division of unpaid work was an issue for debate and, in the vast majority of couples, negotiation. Negotiation can be interpreted as a 'transaction cost' in families (Treas 1991, 1993) and hence something to be minimised. Certainly the amount of negotiation necessary in most of the younger respondents' households required considerable energy. But it also symbolised commitment in relationships where there were few fixed reference points. However, awareness of particular issues and debate over them did not mean an absence of resistance to change. Somewhat more resistance came from married than from cohabiting men; the only three traditional male breadwinners were married men. There was slightly more evidence of the increased flexibility that may result from a positive approach to negotiation among the cohabitants, with changes in the division of paid and unpaid work taking place between partners over time according to circumstances. This was possibly the result of the somewhat firmer sense of self among the cohabiting women, reflected in the nature of the more limited private commitments they were prepared to make. The younger couples, married and cohabiting, also showed considerable change in the way in which they handled money in their households. The commitment to sharing money was common among older and younger couples, but the issue of establishing a mechanism for deciding on 'own' money was apparent only among the younger respondents.

Many older respondents were aware that substantial change had taken place and talked about the absence of certainty regarding jobs and also the absence of an accepted set of rules governing behaviour. As one older female respondent put it: 'You haven't got those rules that we had ... we were expected to marry and we did.' Absence of prescription and constant debate and negotiation did not necessarily make for easier relationships. Many of the older couples seemed very settled in comparison with the younger couples. The words 'comfortable', 'calm' and 'pleasant' were often used to describe their marriages. Many had lived in the same house and followed the same routines year in, year out; they had never thought about many of the issues raised by the interviewers: 'you just go on from year to year ... I don't honestly know because I've never thought about these things.' A majority of older men and women were unreflexive and unable to answer questions about fairness and independence, but were ready with answers about the nature of their obligations one to the other. It was not uncommon for their answers to be bland and monsyllabic:

Q: And did you have to change?
A: Oh one had to be tolerant, yes.
Q: And do you think he had to change too?
A: I think so yes.
Q: In a similar way?
A: Yes.

In contrast, the younger respondents, male and female, were often extremely voluble. The most locquacious respondent was a cohabiting man whose answers to a single question often ran to a page of single spaced typescript. The issues that inspired this research were live ones for the younger couples, but were not and had not been for the older couples.

Thus, with the decline of the assumptions derived from the male breadwinner model, there seems to be a more explicit search for *balance* among the younger couples. Pahl (1995) identified a similar need for more balance in the life of the individual as a result of his interviews with successful men and women. The importance of balance for the health of marital relationships has been stressed by Gottman (1994). The interviews for this study have shown men and women striving *both* for commitment in terms of personal dedication and attachment, and investment in family in terms of time and money on the one hand, *and* for independence in the form of space for career development, personal time and own money on the other. It was not so much that they aimed for the 'interdependence' referred to by Cancian (1987), which is probably better understood as a defining characteristic of an intimate relationship (Johnson, 1991), but rather that they debated and often tried to negotiate a fair measure of space for self and for other. It was possible for older couples to have a considerable measure of independence in their relationships – to exist in 'parallel universes' – or to lead relatively joint lives, but in neither case was this usually the result of explicit debate and negotiation. However, as common to the younger couples as the older ones was the awareness that selfish behaviour, whether in the form of leisure time spent at the pub or lack of any interest in family activities, was dangerous. None of the respondents felt that they were 'unencumbered selves' (Sandel, 1996). This tends to confirm Pahl's (1996) suggestion that the pursuit of individuality must be distinguished from selfish individualism.

Above all, the younger couples were aware that, in the absence of prescription, balance in their relationships had to be achieved. As Mr R. put it:

We're very much into balances. I mean J. [his wife] has this concept of an energy pot, as a household, as a family, of which there is only a certain amount and one of us puts more in and the other takes more out at different times.

Negotiation and the communication involved in it were the means to achieving balance. Only a few couples had achieved the flexibility required to change their time allocations as circumstances demanded it and on a gender-neutral basis. Balance in relationships is of course multidimensional and there remain power imbalances between the sexes which this research has only hinted at. Both Safilios Rothschild (1970) and Gottman (1994) have stressed the emotional power that women may wield within the home, but they may lack confidence outside it and also lack control over material resources. Nevertheless, this research has revealed a more democratic *possibility* within the family, albeit that, *pace* Giddens (1992), we have not yet arrived at a democratic reality. Indeed, a more active attempt on the part of the state to provide collective support for 'reconciling' work and family via 'family friendly' measures that make the achievement of balance in respect of time easier would appear to be increasingly important.

NOTE

1. For example, Sillitoe (1994).

8. What is to be done: what should be the role of private law and family policy in respect of intimate relationships?

Government intervention in the private sphere of the family, whether through family law or family policy, is fraught with difficulty. Family law based on a strict moral code, together with the broad acceptance accorded the male breadwinner model, underpinned traditional ideas about obligation. Under the traditional marriage 'status contract', women were made responsible for domestic services, care and sexual services, and men were designated heads of families, responsible for the support of dependants (Delphi and Leonard, 1992; Weitzman, 1981). In Okin's (1989) view, it is because the terms of marriage were assumed at such a fundamental level that they were not actually enforced during the marriage. Olsen (1983) has suggested additionally that state respect for the privacy of the family has been grounded on the assumption that there are pre-existing obligations and roles. She cited as evidence (in the early 1980s) the fact that in the then rare cases where a US couple had drawn up an explicit contract governing their relationship, the courts ignored it. Yet, since the early part of the century, the state has been more than willing to enter the domestic sphere via the agency of social workers and health visitors in particular (Donzelot, 1980; Gordon, 1988; Lasch, 1977; Lewis, 1980, 1984). However, in Britain (and the US) family law and policy have tended to treat family arrangements as a private matter. The force of state regulation and intervention has been brought to bear only when things go wrong, and then in accordance with traditional assumptions about how families work.

The assumptions informing the traditional marriage contract constructed husbands and wives as equal-but-different partners. The idea of companionate marriage was based on the complementary nature of the contributions of the spouses. Sir William Beveridge's plan for post-war social arrangements was premised on this concept of marriage and the operation of the male breadwinner model (Wilson, 1977). Under post-war social insurance, women gave less by way of contributions and received less by way of benefits, which were also routed via their husbands. This model was founded on relationships of dependence that mitigated against equal citizenship and resulted in unequal social entitlements. Social policies have been used to support the traditional family form, through the tax as well as the benefit system, even though in the post-war period the availability of benefits to lone mothers also served to facilitate family change. After 1969, family law also tried to recognise the equal-but-different contributions made to a marriage in cases of breakdown, but with only limited success.

It was much easier for governments to underpin the traditional family model when only a minority explicitly questioned it and when expectations regarding the behaviour of men and women in families were largely in tune with it. After the 1960s, it got much harder for governments to make assumptions about either family form or the roles of adult family members. The 1974 Finer Report on one-parent families recognised the difficulties faced by the liberal democratic state in restricting the freedom of the individual regarding marriage, divorce and reproduction. This was why the Committee argued that:

> [t]he fact has to be faced that in a democratic society, which cannot legislate (even if it could enforce) different rules of familial and sexual behaviour depending on the ability to pay for the consequences, the community has to bear much of the cost of broken homes and unmarried motherhood. (Committee on One-parent Families, 1974, para. 4.224)

However, during the 1990s especially, there was increasing anxiety expressed inside and outside government about allowing the morality of intimate relationships to be determined privately.

In the view of William Galston (1991), the American liberal philosopher, the modern liberal state is committed to a distinctive conception of the human good and must therefore promote it: 'My guiding intention is that the US is in trouble because it has failed to attend to the dependence of sound politics on sound culture' (p. 6). Galston quoted Walter Mondale, failed Democrat contender for the Presidency, as saying in 1984: ' "The answer to lax morals is not legislated morals. It is deeper faith, greater discipline, and personal excellence" ', a classic statement in favour of morality from within. Galston was far from convinced that this would be sufficient. Both commentators from the political right and communitarians have deplored the reluctance to talk about morality (Wilson, 1993; Etzioni, 1994). But as we have seen (above, pp. 75, 101), the erosion of prescriptive frameworks in the form of family law based on a strict moral code and the male breadwinner model has been accompanied by a reluctance of people to express an opinion on the way in which others organise their private lives. A mid-1990s Eurobarometer survey showed 60 per cent of Europeans choosing the 'not for others to judge' option when asked about the desirability of cohabitation (Reynolds and Mansfield,

1999). Similarly, an *Observer*/ICM poll indicated late in 1998 that a majority of people believed government should steer clear of telling them how to conduct their private lives. However, while views tended towards the non-judgmental, they were not necessarily permissive: 47 per cent agreed that divorce should be made more difficult, as opposed to 44 per cent who disagreed (*The Observer*, 25 October 1998, p. 16). Politicians and some commentators may react to the erosion of prescriptive frameworks by seeking to promote a stricter morality, but whose morality?

Any attempt to dictate 'family values' by one person to another or by government to people is indeed fraught with problems. Feminists have long pointed out the impossibility of achieving a gender-neutral position, for example. Iris Marion Young (1995) argued in reply to Galston that leaving a marriage may not necessarily be selfish on the part of a woman, but rather a matter of escaping unjust subordination, and that the promotion of the traditional family requires women to be dependent on men for the sake of furthering the independence of their children. As Chapter 6 showed, commitment in intimate relationships was understood by younger married couples as voluntary. These couples would have agreed with Elizabeth Anderson's (1993) view that commitment to a shared life requires a dialogue on terms of mutual respect, and should not depend on economic dependence and lack of choice to exit.

A difficult balancing act has therefore been required of governments in respect of family law and family policy. Governments may regard the pace and nature of family change with anxiety, which was not so unreasonable in the last quarter of the twentieth century. In common with many academics they may worry about the extent to which self-interested individualism is overtaking a sense of obligation and/or commitment. But what is to be done about it? If people have become uneasy about the explicit prescription of norms and values, can governments seek to impose them? Is it feasible for governments to seek to 'put the clock back', or should they seek to recognise and work with the kinds of family change that have occurred? It has been suggested by some that a more decisive move towards treating intimate relationships – married and cohabiting – under the regime of contract would be more successful in addressing the changes that have taken place. Others would prefer to see steps taken to privilege marriage, or to reimpose a strict moral code via family law.

The major anxiety for governments is, or should be, the welfare of children. This also involves the welfare of their carers and brings any desire to treat men and women as similarly situated individuals into conflict with the realities of continuing inequality in the division of paid and unpaid work. Thus this part of the debate revolves around how far the issue of support for children should be met individually (by fathers and by breadwinning mothers) or collectively via the tax/benefit system and the provision of social services. It should be noted that family law and family policy are increasingly concerned about the same issues, most notably child maintenance in respect of the former and child poverty in respect of the latter, but the mechanisms involved are entirely different and have tended to be unco-ordinated.[1]

CONSERVATIVE AND LABOUR GOVERNMENTS AND THE FAMILY IN THE 1980s AND 1990s

Conservatives were divided between a more libertarian and a more authoritarian approach in the early 1980s (King, 1986). Ferdinand Mount (1983), Mrs Thatcher's family policy adviser in the early 1980s, defended the autonomy of the family and described it as being in 'permanent revolution' against the state. However, when families demonstrated manifest signs of failure, the state did not hesitate to step in. In the face of the cost of family change arising from the increasing number of lone-mother families drawing state benefits, the third Thatcher administration began to talk much more firmly about enforcing personal responsibility. As Jefferies (1996) has noted, for most Conservatives, the individual and individual freedom is underpinned by the stable moral order of the family. Personal responsibility was defined primarily in terms of the duties of parents towards their children. Mrs Thatcher (1995, p. 630) recalled in her memoirs that she 'was appalled by the way in which men fathered a child and then absconded, leaving the single mother – and the tax payer – to foot the bill for their irresponsibility and condemning the child to a lower standard of living'. The 1991 Child Support Act was the result of this thinking. It attempted to make unmarried and divorced fathers pay maintenance for all their biological children. In effect, this legislation tried to enforce the traditional responsibilities associated with marriage – of men to maintain and of women to care – where marriage had ended and where it had never taken place, but it did not seek explicitly to turn back the clock in respect of family change. The 1996 Family Law Act also sought to enforce the obligations of mothers and fathers, rather than husbands and wives, via its provisions for conciliation, but it also attempted to bolster marriage in its efforts to promote reconciliation and resuscitate 'marriage saving'. Both pieces of legislation demonstrated the Conservatives' deep regard for the traditional obligations that had been part of the male breadwinner model family, but in addition, the Family Law Act made it clear that the government was no longer content just to devise means of dealing with the results of family change. Rather, it wanted to try and reverse it by promoting marriage in the belief that marriage promotes stability.

The model underpinning developments in family law under the Conservatives, certainly since 1984, assumed that men and women could be treated in the same way and, with the 1996 legislation, that they are able and willing to engage in face-to-face communication and negotiation (Walker and Hornick, 1996; Lord Chancellor's Department, 1993). This model of marriage assumes that husbands and wives are able to take responsibility for sorting out their own difficulties. The affairs of divorcing couples in their capacity as husbands and wives have been substantially privatised to the couple, and the 1996 legislation anticipated that those who divorce will take responsibility for issues that arise from their position as parents, with the child support legislation acting as a backstop in respect of maintenance. Such privatisation militates against the achievement of social justice between men and women in the family, which feminists would argue to be a socially important goal (for example, Okin, 1989). The harsh consequences of failure to achieve it in the form of female and child poverty were documented by Weitzman (1985), albeit with a degree of exaggeration (see above pp. 115). While the extent of their poverty has been questioned, the fact that women and children do worse after separation than men has not (Jarvis and Jenkins, 1997). Some have attributed the raw deal that women and children get to the abandonment of no-fault divorce, but the levels of maintenance paid by absent fathers have always been extremely low (Eekelaar and Maclean, 1986). It is difficult to see how the adult relationships of men and women as husbands and wives, or 'partners', can be hived off from their position as parents in the manner assumed by family law in the 1980s and 1990s. What is certain is that because of the unequal gender division of labour, and particularly of unpaid work, it is not easy to address the position of children separately from that of their carers. As Cretney (1996) and Fineman (1993) have observed, there has been a complete absence of principles regarding the maintenance of spouses, and yet the care of children depends in large measure on the welfare and support of their carers. Honore (1982) pointed out some 20 years ago that to treat marriage as a gender-neutral contract is misleading because it is the husband who is usually the primary earner. Yet trying to enforce traditional patterns of gendered obligation where these have never existed, or have ceased to exist, as has often been the task of the Child Support Agency, also seems hopeless.

In the case of cohabitants, Eekelaar (1984) has argued that it is difficult to justify legal intervention in respect of their position as partners. However, this assumes that they have actively chosen not to marry and regard themselves as fundamentally different from married people, which is not true for many; cohabitation is sequential to marriage as well as an alternative to it. Indeed, it may be rather that marriage is outdated as a legal concept (Clive, 1980; Dewar and Parker, 1992; Burrows, 1995). In the case of married couples, traditionalists have favoured a return to fault-based divorce in an effort to secure the male obligation to maintain, even though there is no evidence that this was secured in practice. Some feminists have continued to favour the idea of treating the married couple as a partnership, but of expanding the concept of property to include, for example, the human capital represented by the degrees earned by the husband, which may have been made possible by wage-earning on the part of the wife (Weitzman, 1981). Others have favoured the equal sharing of income after divorce for a specified number of years (Singer, 1989). Still others have favoured a model by which a female spouse is compensated to the degree that her standard of living after caregiving falls short of what she might have expected had the marriage broken down without caregiving having taken place (Eekelaar and Maclean, 1986; Ellman, 1997). This links spousal support to child support (Eekelaar, 1991). The story of family law from 1969 to 1996 showed how difficult it is to square the desire to recognise the erosion of the male breadwinner model and to treat adult relationships as involving two equal individuals on the one hand, with the desire to provide properly for children on the other. This problem is almost certainly beyond the capacity of family law alone to solve, and a substantially more active family policy may therefore be necessary.

The Labour government, elected in 1997, has pursued a less coherent policy in respect of the family. This may be, as Baldock (1999) has suggested, because it is determined to take into account the often demonstrably contradictory state of public opinion on different issues to do with the family. The 1998 Consultative Paper, *Supporting Families*, stated firmly: 'Neither a "back to basics" fundamentalism, trying to turn back the clock, nor an "anything goes" liberalism which denies the fact that how families behave affects us all, is credible any more' (Home Office, 1998, p. 5, para. 11). As Fox Harding (1999) observed, the document repeatedly made the point that the government did not want to lecture, to preach or to nag, but it is nevertheless very different to the report on marriage prepared by the Home Office and Department of Social Security (1979) under the previous Labour government, which accepted the idea of marriage as a means to 'personal growth', as well as advocating a much larger role for relationship counselling. *Supporting Families* acknowledged family change and that many lone parents and 'unmarried couples' raise their children successfully, but also stated that 'marriage is still the surest foundation for raising children' (Home Office, 1998, p. 4, para. 8). While saying that marriage is best because more stable, the document promised no direct incentives. Indeed, the married couples' tax allowance was abolished in April 2000. However, the subsidies to those in work (in the form of tax credits), which have rapidly achieved a position of prominence in the social security system, assume, like income support benefits, familial dependency and entail a means test and payments directed towards the main earner, who is usually the man. The picture in respect of individualising the treatment of men and women under the tax and social security system remains, to say the least, confused.

The *Supporting Families* document focused rather more on the possibility of providing advice and guidance, for example in respect of the responsibilities and rights of those intending to marry or cohabit, and floated the possibility of pre-nuptial agreements. On the other hand, the state of the law regarding cohabitation was ignored in contrast to developments in many other Western European countries. In Barlow and Duncan's (2000, p. 141) view, 'basing a policy of supporting families almost entirely upon marriage as an institution seems to leave the government with its head rather deep in the sand'. In addition, in 1999, that part of the Family Law Act dealing with the final step towards no-fault divorce was abandoned. This was because of difficulties in imple-mentation, but also it seems that the government feared that it would smack of the 'nanny state', while not necessarily having the desired effect of promoting reconciliation. Certainly Paul Boateng, a minister in the Labour government, had spoken strongly while in Opposition in favour of saving marriage, urging that the new legislation 'should not be simply a vehicle for the dissolution of marriage, but a means by which marriage might be supported' (*House of Commons*, *Standing Committee E*, 25 April 1996, col. 4).

Like the Conservatives, the Labour government's main concern has been, not the unity of the couple nor even the permanence of relationships, but the need to secure stable arrangements for children. This has led to a continued emphasis on parenting beyond the bounds of marriage and on the importance of individual parental responsibility, which as Smart and Neale (1999) have commented, has not been accompanied by the same degree of attention to the quality of relationships. In keeping with the desire to enforce the obligations of biological fatherhood, in 1998 the Lord Chancellor proposed giving unmarried fathers automatic rights in respect of their children, something first raised by the Law Commission in 1979, but rejected in large measure because of the problem of the 'unmeritorious father'.

However, Labour also put considerable stress on the importance of family policies to support parents. This was a new departure in Britain, where histor-ically parents have been left to work out their own salvation, most obviously in respect of reconciling work and family responsibilities, unless there have been any gross manifestations of inadequate care. *Supporting Families* put better services and support for parents first, referring mainly to education and advice to be delivered via a National Family and Parenting Institute, a helpline and health visitors, but also through a funded initiative to provide child care, family support, primary health care, early learning and play for young children (the Sure Start programme.) The announcement of a National Child Care Strategy and a pledge to remove child poverty within 20 years have also signalled a much wider commitment to investment in children and support in the form of cash and services for families with children.

POSSIBLE STRATEGIES IN RESPECT OF THE LAW: THE VIEWS OF THE QUALITATIVE SAMPLE

The concerns of policy makers in the 1980s and 1990s have been focused primarily on the high levels of relationship breakdown. Broadly speaking, in regard to family law, two issues have been paramount: how to enforce obligations to children in case of breakdown, and whether to privilege marriage in an effort to promote those obligations.

The views of a qualitative sample of intact and mostly satisfied married and cohabiting couples on family law and policy are likely to be markedly different from those of couples who break up. The interesting point is that the nature of their commitment (as revealed in the last two chapters) is reflected in their views. They were asked about the desirability of pre-marital and cohabitation contracts, which have been promoted as a way of filling the vacuum in respect of the regulation of both marriage and cohabitation; whether marriage should be privileged over cohabitation, for example, in respect of tax; and a number of questions about divorce and continuing obligations to children. While their views on the last of these may be particularly remote from those who are involved in relationship breakdown, they make clear the extent to which there is a link between the nature of their commitment, expressed in their everyday principles and practices, and their notion of what constitutes fairness in legal arrangements and policies for the support children.

Contracts

During the 1980s, there was a burst of powerful criticism of the traditional assumptions underpinning the marriage 'status contract' from American feminist legal scholars, who observed that the male breadwinner model no longer matched either the social reality, as vastly increased numbers of married women entered the workforce, or women's aspirations. It seems that many of these critics assumed, in common with the sociologists of the 1970s, that future behaviour within marriage would become more egalitarian. Weitzman (1981, p. 183) wrote that 'new norms of sharing household responsibility are becoming widely accepted', and that while changes in men's behaviour had been slower than women's, greater equality in the labour market would in all likelihood be matched in future by greater equality in the home. Thus the views of this influential commentator on family law on the social context matched that of sociologists such as Young and Willmott (1973), with their predictions as to the emergence of 'symmetrical families'. From these observations, feminist legal commentators concluded that there should also be more egalitarian decision making in the home. While strictly patriarchal models of marriage had given way to a companionate ideal, the male breadwinner model continued to enshrine the husband as 'head' of the household. For example, in social security law this remained formally the case until the implementation of the 1979 European Commission's Directive on equal treatment. In respect of family law, the feminist answer was to advocate private ordering via contract (Weitzman, 1981) on the assumption that the marriage of the future would be sufficiently democratic to allow men and women to decide for themselves the precise nature of their commitment. This model had much in common with the beliefs of those who were inclined to be optimistic about increasing individualism in respect of the family. Schultz (1982) gave brief acknowledgement to the already extensive literature on the realities regarding inequalities of power in marriage (for example, Safilios Rothschild, 1970, 1976), but nevertheless argued that in an intimate relationship only those involved could determine what was right for them.

Thus a major strand in the argument for contract has been based on the idea that relationships are becoming increasingly egalitarian, individualistic and private. However, there was little evidence from the younger couples interviewed for this book to support the idea of gender equality in respect of either domestic or paid work (see also Jamieson, 1998), although there was a greater concern about perceptions of fairness. Indeed, McLelland (1996) attacked the idea of extending the realm of explicit contract to intimate relationships on the grounds that men and women are still manifestly unequal in many important respects. Models involving the idea of expanded partnership or compensation (see above, p. 177) are more realistic in terms of addressing the unequal economic position of women, although the old problem remains as to how to recognise and address inequality, whether in family law or social policy, without thereby reinforcing it. As for individualism, there was no evidence among the younger respondents that a greater concern with self-development had driven out commitment. Rather they co-exist in complicated ways. In the case of cohabitants, commitment to the partner is certainly conceptualised as private, but commitment to children is not. Contracts have of course the additional advantage that they can be applied to both cohabiting and married couples. Pragmatically, it has been suggested that they are more suited to relationships that may prove temporary (for example, Zelig, 1993). However, this view has been less strongly represented in the literature than has the assumption that men and women are now ready, able and willing to negotiate their relationships.

Proponents of a more contractual view of intimate relationships sought to recognise what they saw as the greater autonomy and growing equality of the parties involved and, by shifting the emphasis to private ordering, to provide a new means of securing obligations at a time when family law was perceived to be engaged in a process of deregulation. From the perspective of neo-classical economics, Posner (1992, pp. 264–5) suggested that given that no-fault divorce had effectively converted childless marriages into tenancies at will, thus '[t]oday spouses who want a really durable relationship must try to create one by contract or by informal commitments'. However, the notion of deregulation does not accurately capture the role of the state, which, while it has certainly changed, has not been in full retreat. In addition, the problem of obligation in personal relationships has in fact much more to do with the gap between the normative expectations of a new egalitarian model of marital relationships, which has increasingly informed state actions in respect of family law, and the social realities of marriage which have nevertheless continued to be characterised by various dimensions of inequality, particularly in respect of the division of unpaid work. This means that the problem of obligation is unlikely to be solved by contract and private ordering.

Weitzman (1981) and Schultz (1982) agreed with the view that family law had already proceeded some way along the path of deregulation and hoped that contract would fill the vacuum. However, it is equally possible to see contract as the logical end point of the trend in family law since the 1960s. And if the assumptions regarding adult behaviour in families that have underpinned reform of the divorce law have run ahead of behaviour, it means that private ordering via contract would only exacerbate this tendency. Schultz (1982) believed, contrary to the research evidence that has emerged since (Baker and Emry, 1993), that spouses entered marriage knowing the probability of breakdown and that, given this, drawing up a contract could only encourage communication between the parties and increase trust. Weitzman (1981) also argued that private ordering by contract was more egalitarian and therefore a better fit with the changing position of women, and that it would promote egalitarian relationships. There was therefore a sense in which the feminist literature in particular saw contract as both a means of recognising the more equal roles of men and women in society and as a way of promoting this development.

However, what is so striking is the capacity of even the well-informed, for example, law students, to separate their knowledge about marriage in general from their hopes for their own marriages (Baker and Emry, 1993); understandings of the law are cultural. Popular reaction to the idea of explicit marriage and cohabitation contracts is often negative.[2] The feeling that personal relationships are about more than rational calculation and negotiation translates into the view that their chemistry is too intimate to make it possible for the intentions of the parties to be known (for example, Dalton, 1985); that they threaten the trust on which intimate relations are built (Anderson, 1993); or that they run counter to the ethic of care that ideally pervades family relationships (Baier, 1986; Held, 1993). De Singly (1996) argued that love cannot be contractual because both partners must believe that they are motivated by feelings other than self-interest. Beck and Beck Gernsheim (1995) have also suggested that contracts would result in the secular religion of love losing its mythology and becoming a mixture of market forces and personal impulses. Certainly in the 1990s, acute difficulties were experienced in formalising the previously informal in the public sphere as contract was introduced into public sector services. In particular, it proved difficult to subsume the associational world of the voluntary sector to the rule of contract, which suggests that Karst (1980) and Bellah *et al.* (1985) may be right in questioning its effects on the world of intimate relationships. A private contract model for personal relations would in all probability serve to widen the gap between the social reality of those relationships and the legal assumptions.[3]

The data collected for this book, both quantitative and qualitative, showed little support for a more contractual approach to intimate relationships. Respondents to the Omnibus Survey were asked whether they agreed with the statement: 'People who are going to live together or get married should write down beforehand how they will divide their finances in case they split up.' Nearly half of all those questioned disagreed with the statement, just under a quarter agreed, and just over a quarter were undecided. The proportion of cohabitants with children agreeing with the statement was larger, but the numbers involved were small.

Seventy-three respondents in the qualitative sample answered a question about the desirability of pre-marital or cohabitation contracts, 26 of the younger couples and 47 of the older couples. Only five younger and 15 older respondents were in favour of contracts, the rest were opposed. Furthermore, there was little agreement as to what any proposed contract should contain among those who were in favour of them. A majority seemed to feel that the exercise of writing a contract would in and of itself be a useful educational tool. As one younger married woman put it:

> 'most people enter into it blindly without thinking about things. If they had something like this to think about, maybe an actual commitment which was legally binding – this is what we will do in the unlikely event of ... – It's a kind of insurance.'

Among those opposing the idea, 27 felt that contracts were inappropriate on the grounds that people and circumstances change over time and relationships require flexibility:

> I think it's a natural growing process and to write things down is fairly irrelevant anyway, because things develop. (Younger married man)

> Laid down rigid agreements are a recipe for disaster. Marriage is about flexibility. (Cohabiting man)

> You've no idea what's ahead, and you could set very false obligations and it could lead to a lot of friction. (Younger married woman)

I work in a job that always – it's always going back and saying, 'I know that we agreed this in writing three years ago, but ...' (Younger married man, working as a social worker)

Eleven people felt that contracts were 'too cold' a way of dealing with relationships. Twelve of those objecting were more favourably inclined towards something that set out in a general way the expectations for the relationship rather than what would happen on breakdown. A few, mainly older, respondents felt that contracts were 'defeatist' and a few, again older, respondents felt that they might be relevant for wealthy movie stars, but not for ordinary people.

Only one cohabitant was in favour of contracts, which might have been anticipated from the emphasis that these middle-class cohabitants placed on the private nature of their commitment to each other. Four of the cohabiting men were explicitly against any intrusion by the state into their personal relationships. As one put it: 'I consider myself as married as anybody else, it's just that I don't think it's any responsibility of the state or any religious organisation to deem what our relationships should be.' Thus the evidence from the qualitative research carried out for this study suggests that it is unlikely that cohabitation contracts would have any great appeal among those cohabitants who considered that they had made a strong commitment.

Elizabeth Kingdom (1988, 1990) has argued strongly in favour of cohabitation contracts from a feminist point of view as a means of providing an additional option and as recognition for cohabitation as a distinct status. However Michele Adams (1998) has suggested that cohabitation is 'psychologically friendly' to women because it is 'high on individuation and low on institutionalisation'. Any move to institutionalise it may therefore be to the detriment of women. Kingdom is correct in her assumption that cohabitants (at least, long-term better-off cohabitants with children) would like some recognition of their status, but there was nothing in the data from this study to suggest that they want a new legal status. Most wanted to be able to say for administrative purposes that they were cohabiting, but they did not wish formally to 'sign up' to a new status. Rather, they wanted some means of acknowledging that they were people with responsibilities.[4] Such a possibility might in and of itself encourage the development of private commitments in the general population of cohabitants, where the high rate of breakdown suggests that such commitments do not get made.

The Solicitors Family Law Association (Rodgers, 1999) recommended a new form of legal recognition for cohabitants that would protect the vulnerable without equating cohabitation to marriage. This necessarily involved the Association in defining cohabitation. The SFLA proposed 'registered partnerships' (a form already widely accepted in continental Europe) with a right to opt out. Cohabitation was defined as a relationship 'between two adults in which one provides personal or financial commitment and support of a domestic nature for the material benefit of the other'. Those applying to the court for financial relief on breakdown would need to have cohabited for two years. The Law Society's recommendations for cohabitation reform preferred to emphasise a definition of cohabitation that stressed 'public acknowledgement' of the existence of the relationship, in line with the Department of Social Security's longstanding definition (Gouriet, 2000). However, this would be somewhat at odds with the views taken by the cohabitants interviewed for this book as to the nature of their relationship. Cohabitation reform would provide for fairer treatment of cohabitants. It is not clear how popular such an arrangement would be and its precise form requires very careful consideration, but it may help to address the pressing issue of how to encourage private commitments in the first place by helping to create an environment in which commitment is expected.

Separate Treatment for Married and Cohabiting Couples?

Cohabitants are treated differently from married people when their relationships break down. Family law gives them no rights of occupation of the family home or entitlement to maintenance; these are issues that the idea of 'registered partnerships' is intended to address. However, in respect of the obligation to maintain children, public law has treated cohabitants and married people alike; the child support legislation obliges all fathers to support their biological children. Cohabitants drawing social assistance benefits (income support) are also treated as if they were married for the purposes of means-testing. Thus it appears that cohabitants lack many of the rights accorded to married people, but share significant obligations. Nevertheless, a number of commentators have been particularly concerned about what they perceive as the lack of explicit financial incentives given to marriage. For example, Patricia Morgan (1995) deplored the move to individual taxation in 1990 and the erosion of the married couple's tax allowance, which have served to raise the tax burden on couples with one main earner. The diminution of the traditional tax privileges accorded married people has also meant that the male breadwinner model has ceased to be privileged.

There was no overwhelming evidence from the data collected for this study that the desire for recognition of some kind of separate status for cohabitants was accompanied by a wish to differentiate between married and cohabiting people in these respects. The respondents to the Omnibus Survey were asked whether married or cohabiting people should receive more favourable treatment from the tax and benefits system. A majority of both married and cohabiting respondents felt that both should be treated equally, although 46 per cent of married people wanted to favour themselves.

In the qualitative sample, only one cohabitant (a man who was almost certainly going to marry) wanted to treat married people more favourably for tax and benefit purposes. More surprisingly, only five younger married respondents thought similarly. Indeed, only five younger respondents expressed any doubts about the wisdom of cohabitation with children. However, there was a considerable difference between the younger and older married respondents on these issues. A majority of the older ones, including a majority of the parents of cohabitants, wanted to see marriage favoured. This was in line with their more general preference for marriage over cohabitation, despite their reluctance to make any explicit prescription for individuals. These results may reflect the fact that the boundary between marriage and cohabitation has become increasingly blurred. The 1994 British Social Attitudes Survey reported that 58 per cent thought that it was a 'good idea' for a couple who intended to marry to live together first, even though virtually the same percentage still thought that couples intending to have children should marry before they did so (Newman and Smith, 1997). Nevertheless, for the younger generation marriage and cohabitation represent two equally viable options. Given this, it is not surprising that the younger respondents thought that they should be treated equally. After all, a majority of the married respondents had cohabited for a period of time. It may be that the older assumption that married and cohabiting people expect to be treated differently (for example, Deech, 1980) is breaking down, among married as well as cohabiting couples. In which case, the government's caution in taking explicit steps to privilege marriage is well founded.

Provision for Children (and their Carers)

All respondents in the qualitative sample, young and old, expressed grave reservations about ending a relationship where children were involved and showed considerable awareness of the difficulties in providing for children after relationship breakdown:

> If it's a family with children, I think it does have really far-reaching effects on the children and I think it's not a solution to necessarily split up, because actually to work together as meaningful parents after you've split up is real hard work. I mean you've got to get on with – your skills of communication have got to be even better and often you know if you could come to that level of agreement, you should work on it before you decide to split up! (Female cohabitant)

> There are other responsibilities beyond the responsibility to yourself. And I think, you know, I don't want to sound like I'm knocking the me-generation, whatever that might be, one of those phrases people bandy about, but there are other responsibilities and I think it's when people focus on 'I'm unhappy, I must sort it, I've got to feel happier. It's this that's making me unhappy, therefore I must leave this.' I think

it's unrealistic because it ignores all the dynamics about relationships. (Younger married man)

Nevertheless, only three younger respondents, two married men and one cohabiting woman, favoured staying in an unhappy relationship because of the children. The vast majority felt that while relationship breakdown was serious when children were present and that all possible avenues should be explored before deciding upon it, it would not be desirable for the law to try and make it more difficult. As one young married woman said of divorce: 'I don't think it's easy. It's very accessible. But then I don't think that's a bad thing.'

Only six older respondents felt that couples in unhappy relationships should stay together for the sake of the children, although 24 favoured some idea of fault-based divorce, and said that they thought that some 'reason' for wanting to end the relationship should be given to the courts. The parents of cohabiting children (who included the parents of two married respondents) were somewhat less likely than the parents of married children to think that it was too easy to leave a relationship.

In fact, despite the differences between the younger and older respondents in terms of the extent to which there was an awareness of issues to do with the organisation of everyday activities and a preparedness to negotiate them, there was little difference between their responses on issues to do with the law. A few of the older respondents, the least reflective, were unable to venture any opinions. As one older woman put it: 'I just think about this family, our family.' However, four of the older men volunteered particularly clear views on the difficulties involved in assessing the nature of the relationship between law and behaviour, for example:

> I think the law is simply an outward sign of a situation. The law is symbolic in that the real problems are much deeper, way away from the law.

> I think that because people's attitude to marriage has changed and that marriage break-up is now easier [socially], that that has put the demand on the law to have it changed. I don't think it's changed of its own volition. It's been changed by people's changing attitudes towards it, and they have wanted it to be made easier to divorce.

The broad similarities between the responses of older and younger people in the sample probably have to do with the fact that the questions asked about family law focused on the situation today and did not encourage retrospection. Older respondents were very much aware that the circumstances faced by their children were very different to the ones they had faced as the parents of young children. Given the changes in ideas and practices about marriage and parenting and the erosion of prescription, they were as reluctant as the younger respondents to say what other people should do. In addition, when it came to the legal specificities of support for children, and for parents with the care of a child after relationship breakdown, the vast majority of respondents, younger and older, had very little information, which meant that their answers were often vague and sometimes confused.

The qualitative evidence showed no difference in the degree of commitment of married and cohabiting respondents to their children. The issue of what surname to give to children (see above, p. 138) showed that the cohabitants were aware that unmarried fathers had fewer legal rights. Eight of the 12 cohabiting couples had made wills in each other's favour, yet only three had parental responsibility agreements (PRAs). None of the partners of McRae's (1993) sample of cohabiting mothers had PRAs. In 1996, of 232 663 births to unmarried parents, only 3000 applied for a PRA and a further 5587 obtained a parental responsibility order via the courts (Pickford, 1999). Seven of the nine cohabiting fathers in the qualitative sample for this study had never heard of PRAs, and yet the sample was drawn mainly from those working as teachers, nurses, social workers and housing officers. The three who did have them had direct knowledge of the relevant legislation as a result of their work. Those with agreements had found that it had been a 'hassle' to get them; indeed, one couple had an agreement in respect of their first child, but not the second. Government proposals to give unmarried fathers automatic rights would obviously resolve this problem, but making the process of obtaining a PRA more accessible and more straightforward might also serve.

The two main concerns of the younger men and women in respect of continued obligations to children after relationship breakdown were fairness and pragmatism. The former was resonant of similar concerns about practices in their adult relationships in regard to the division of time and money. Only two married men, neither of whom was inclined to change his domestic division of labour, thought that child support should be paid at a flat rate. The rest were all concerned that parents should contribute a 'fair' proportion of income, thus maximising the welfare of the child. Their responses stressed the difficulties of determining what was fair in the individual case. This is in line with research findings which have emphasised that even apparently straightforward cases may not be so (Davis, 1998), which in turn casts doubt on the capacity of an administrative child support formula to capture such complexity. Most respondents were aware of the Child Support Act and were concerned that it seemed not to operate 'fairly'. Opinions were much more divided on what should happen if the parent-with-care remarried: 13 felt that payments should either stop or be renegotiated. This signalled the importance that was attached to social rather than biological ties to children, which has also been emphasised by Maclean and Eekelaar (1997). However, there was no gender divide – with men emphasising social ties and women biological ties – of the kind found by Maclean and Eekelaar among their sample of unmarried and married parents.

A majority felt that there should be an element of maintenance for the parent-with-care, 11 attached some qualification to this, but 23 (11 women and 12 men) were unequivocal. Interestingly, cohabitants were more inclined to press for a continuation of child support payments if the parent-with-care remarried, and fewer cohabitants than married respondents expressed opposition to maintenance for the parent-with-care. This may reflect the greater commitment of this sample of cohabitants to negotiating and honouring their own arrangements. These cohabitants had reached a firm 'private commitment' to each other, which was part of the decision to become parents, and they were as committed also to debating and negotiating the division of time and money in their relationships to make them fair.

It seems that commitment to fairness on the part of a majority of the younger couples extended to their ideas about what should happen in cases of relationship breakdown and to legal arrangements for children and their carers. These couples did not make a dichotomous choice between the pursuit of individual self-fulfilment on the one hand, and the fulfilment of their obligations to other family members on the other. Rather, they sought conscientiously to juggle both. However, the concept of fairness is fraught with difficulty for policy makers because so much depends on 'the circumstances', which no simple administrative formula can adequately recognise. Nevertheless, the majority of these couples automatically took account of the gendered division of paid and unpaid work in a way that policy makers have conspicuously failed to do. Their approach signals the need to revisit the principles that underpin the law of maintenance and public policies affecting the way in which we provide for children.

CONCLUSION

Many conservatives argue that the solution to increased instability that has accompanied rapid family change is to promote marriage as an institution. Cohabitation is seen as a threat to marriage, delaying it and impeding it, and creating a cultural environment in which it is devalued (for example, Morgan, 2000). The logic of this position is that nothing should be done to recognise the alternatives to marriage. To use the language of the old nineteenth-century Poor Law, the alternatives, whether cohabitation or lone motherhood, have to be made 'less eligible'. Marriage has to be privileged in respect of the tax/benefit system and the alternatives to it treated less favourably. However, most conservative analyses stop short at the idea of making exit from marriage more difficult legally.

It seems odd that many of those seeking to promote marriage can only suggest ways of doing so that penalise alternative forms of intimate relationships. Institutions do matter, but one of the problems is that historically marriage has been far from just from women's point of view, both legally and (still) in respect of the gender division of labour. It is in any case far from clear that marriage *per se* would increase family stability. The group of cohabitants interviewed for this book were people of 'the middling sort' who had made a private commitment. But for the majority of female cohabitants who are poor, it is likely, as Smart and Stevens (2000) have argued, that cohabitation is a more rational option than shot-gun marriage to men who may be judged unreliable or than lone motherhood.

Commitment is key, but it is not the exclusive property of married people. It is therefore not very useful to treat marriage as some kind of zero-sum game, arguing, as Morgan (2000) does, that anything that strengthens the alternatives to marriage can only weaken marriage. The UK government has tended to put its head in the sand over cohabitation when it is possible that some form of legal recognition might serve to promote commitment. The pace of change has been very rapid and it is unlikely that solutions that rely merely on promoting traditional forms will be successful.

Perhaps the most striking theme emerging from this and other studies of what adults actually do in respect of their intimate relationships, and what they think they ought to do, is one of convergence despite the diversity of family forms. Thus Weeks *et al.*'s (1999, p. 85) study of non-heterosexual relationships suggested that 'alongside the discourse of difference which marks the non-heterosexual experience, we can also see the emergence of a certain logic of congruence' (p. 85). Just as for the married and cohabiting couples in this study, the cultural priority accorded individual choice by those in non-heterosexual relationships meant that commitment became increasingly a matter of negotiation rather than ascription. This finding is in line with that of Finch and Mason (1993), whose study of family obligations led them to use the concept of 'developing commitments' and to refer to the sense of responsibility worked out over time. Similarly, Smart and Neale (1999) have argued that parents who are divorcing have to make difficult moral decisions regarding the care of their children, and while some take more care over their decisions than others, they operate within a moral framework and do not simply act selfishly or egotistically. As prescriptive frameworks regarding the 'ought' of intimate relationships have eroded, so there has been much more to negotiate. There is evidence from attitudinal surveys that family issues and events matter most in most people's lives, especially for women and older people (Scott, 1997). Furthermore, a majority of people make an effort to negotiate their family lives in line with their 'moral sense' of how things should be (the term is Wilson's, 1993). They are nevertheless reluctant to prescribe for others, whose circumstances and beliefs might be different. Thus it seems that the idea of 'situation ethics' (see above, p. 87) does capture the way in which the majority of people think about intimate relationships. When the sense of social obligations is so fluid, it is undoubtedly difficult to find principles to underpin legal obligations,[5] but this does not excuse the tendency to impose principles that politicians feel to be right, regardless of the way in which people conceptualise their obligations and commitments.

It is important that the privacy of intimate relationships be respected. In respect of the family generally, historical evidence suggests that people are not necessarily opposed to state intervention, but that they do not want it to be either stigmatising or intrusive (Thane, 1984). Ulrich Beck's (1992) idea that in future governments should concentrate on providing stronger supports for families, while allowing individuals more choice as to how to organise their private lives, might be 'vague' (Dingwall, 1999), but it is not so far from what we know about how people are thinking about these things. To this extent, an approach such as New Labour's may look like post-modernist 'pick-and-mix', but probably accurately reflects the often contradictory feelings and beliefs about this fraught area of human life, and furthermore, may be the only politically feasible approach. Finch (1989) has warned that people's sense of obligation within families is often strongly held and easily offended by assumptions on the part of government that run counter to it.

But the problem remains of those who seemingly do behave opportunisti-cally and selfishly. Bradshaw *et al.*'s (1999) study of non-resident fathers included two men who supported their biological children from their first marriages, but not the children from their second marriages, because they did not get on with their second wives. Support for parents' responsibility to maintain their children was widespread before the passing of the child support legislation, and yet opposition to it since 1991 has been immense. In large measure, as comparison with the experience of other countries shows (for example, Millar and Whiteford, 1993), this was due to a process of imple-mentation that flew in the face of strongly held ideas as to fairness and what conditions the obligation to maintain entails. Maclean and Eekelaar (1997) found that while mothers were more likely to agree with the principle of support on the basis of biology, because of the financial problems they faced in taking responsibility for the day-to-day care of children, fathers were more likely to link support to social parenthood and contact with the child. The point is that it is a difficult and delicate task, and in all likelihood has become more so, to translate social obligations in the family into legal ones, even where a broad principle is accepted. Part of the problem in Britain during the 1980s and early 1990s was the willingness of government to ride roughshod over the niceties of people's finely honed ideas as to the justice of particular measures.

When it comes to the question of whether to defend marriage, particularly against the increasing propensity to cohabit, the answer is more difficult still, because views are even less clear cut. Most of the literature on the subject concentrates on specific aspects, such as the problem of the man who leaves his wife and children, often in order to live with a younger woman, or on the high break-up rates of cohabitants with children, many of whom are poor and have never been married. However, the broader issues of cultural change are often not addressed. A man in his late fifties who responded to Mass Observation's 1990 'directive'[6] on 'close relationships' exemplifies the point. This man was able to retire very comfortably from a job in the City in his mid-fifties. During his training – as a solicitor – he had minimal contact with women, having had little money to spend and fearing above all a 'shot-gun marriage' that would have ruined his career. When he graduated at 23, he was anxious to marry as a 'normal progression' and as the only respectable way to achieve a sex life. His wife quit a university course to marry him and stayed at home to raise their five children. After eight years of marriage, he began a series of affairs, the last being serious. In the end he chose to stay with his family, feeling unable to leave five children. He felt that he had been 'a conscientious husband and father' and insisted on the happiness of his family life. However, at the end of his response, he said that if he were starting again in 1990 he would not marry at all. He added that this must seem ungrateful and that he had never confessed it to anyone before. However, if he had his life over again, he would choose to spend his money on the pursuits he enjoys, take more business risks and have a lot of girlfriends. While he wrote that he would be distraught if anything happened to his family, if he had not had them he believes that he would not have missed them. He stated that he feels strongly that people should fulfil their obligations to their children. In his view, the men of his generation had little choice in respect of marital and family building behaviour. He has advised his own children to cohabit (Mass Observation Archives, 1990, Directive 32, C110).

It is impossible to know how many male middle-class pillars of the community might share this man's views, which he has divulged only to Mass Observation as an anonymous respondent. Deverson and Lindsay's (1975, p. 167) interview data from two middle-class London suburbs collected at the beginning of the 1970s also reported a significant number of men 'carrying on' for the sake of the children and keeping up appearances for the sake of neighbours and family. But more important is the way in which the Mass Observation respondent's account resonates with parts of the story told in this book, particularly the way in which marriage became a choice for young people in the late twentieth century. It also seems to lend support to those who fear not only that selfish individualism is increasing, but that the imposition of a strong external moral code via family law is the only way of reining it in. However, as the Mass Observation respondent recognises clearly, it is the very changed circumstances relating in part to greater female economic independence and to the erosion of an external moral code governing family behaviour that would make his expectations very different if he were starting out now.

What is of course unknown is whether he would in fact behave in the self-centred way he indicates. The majority of people do not. In any event, it is unlikely that any legislative framework would succeed in thwarting the kind of behaviour he has in mind. By his own lights, he would accede to regulation as a parent. Thus he would probably be in broad agreement with Ulrich Beck or the much earlier ideas of Bertrand Russell: that the state should only intervene in relationships where there are children. While there is reluctance to make rules for adult relationships, there is widespread agreement that the welfare of children must be ensured. Eekelaar (1991) has argued that if all childless relationships are to be unregulated, the meaning of marriage becomes unclear. However, many commentators have argued that while marriage has little purchase as a legal concept and many fewer economic advantages, this does not mean that it has no emotional (or sacramental) purchase. After all, the majority of cohabiting couples do go on to marry.

But as we have seen, it is easier said than done to separate men's and women's position as parents from that of partners in an intimate relationship. Even if there is a case for treating married and cohabiting adults the same in law, children require care as well money spent on them and it is therefore difficult to separate the needs of children from those of their carers, who are usually women. This brings us back to what can be expected from family law and family policy. Family law seeks solutions at the level of the individual, and while the obligations of individuals as parents and partners cannot be ignored, collectivist solutions to help ensure the care and support of children, and to address the fundamental problem of reconciling paid work and family responsibilities must also play a part. Creighton (1999) has suggested that shorter working hours is the only way to address the second of these; certainly it is the one major solution that has not been tried in the Northern and Western European countries that do offer collective child care provision and paid parental leaves. The logic of the problem of obligation in personal relationships demands both individual and collective support for children. But the implementation of British child support legislation has been a disaster, while the trebling in the number of children in poverty between 1979 and 1991 (Bradshaw, 1997) testifies to the general lack of collective support.

This does not mean that family law reform is irrelevant, but only that its limitations must be recognised. In the case of young and poor cohabitants with children, whose rate of breakdown is extremely high, it may be either that they drift into the relationship and parenthood without making any firm commitment, or that the women involved are making a rational decision that this arrangement is better than the alternatives: no father presence at all or a shot-gun marriage. In any event, it is difficult to see how more attention, first, to relationship and parenting education, and second, to the kind of investment in children that in the continental European countries plays a major part in raising expectations and delaying motherhood, whether married or unmarried (Kiernan, 1996), can fail to be both relevant and important.

Family law and family policy have tended increasingly to treat men and women as if they are fully individualised, in terms of assuming that they will be able to negotiate as equal individuals in case of breakdown and that both will be in the labour market. The legal and economic models of family behaviour that underpinned traditional patterns of dependency have largely disappeared, but the erosion of prescriptive frameworks has run ahead of the social reality. Most women do not want to be dependent on men, but the persistence of gendered inequalities in access to income cannot be ignored. If the problems that arise as a result of the needs of children for care are to be addressed alongside the desire of adults for self-fulfilment, then there must be a role for collective provision in the form of family policies. It is not possible to put the clock back and return to marriage based on the male breadwinner model and subject to the imposition of an external moral code. To that extent, individualisation is inevitable. But there is evidence that people want to make commitments as well as pursue their self-interest. Family policies offer a better hope of helping to reconcile these twin desires in this respect than the extension of more individualist mechanisms such as contract.

NOTES

1. I am grateful to Mavis Maclean for making this point.
2. One of the solicitors in the last (1997) run of BBC2's immensely popular sitcom, *This Life*, refused to contemplate the idea of a contract because he felt that it was unromantic and posed a question mark over his commitment.
3. Pateman (1988b) has argued that it would in any case prove impossible because such private ordering ignores the opposition between the world of contract and its natural foundation' within civil society. Furthermore, if marriage was to become truly contractual then, given its sexual basis, the boundaries between it and prostitution would be eroded. This has been challenged by Kymlicka (1991), who argues that the logic of contract is that people can choose between marriage and prostitution. Certainly, cohabiting relationships governed by contract are not necessarily reduced to contracts for body use.
4. However, providing recognition without creating a law of cohabitation is difficult.
5. Maclean and Eekelaar (1997) provide a full discussion of the distinction between legal and social obligations.
6. The Mass Observation Archive is located at the University of Sussex. Volunteers respond in writing to prompts or directives sent to them three or four times a year by the Archive.

Bibliography

Adams, J.M. and Jones, W.H. (1997) 'Conceptualization of Marital Commitment: an Integrative Analysis'. *Journal of Personali!y and Social Psychology* 72 (5): 1177–96.

Adams, M.A. (1998) 'How Does Marriage Matter? Individuation and Institutionalisation in the Trajectory of Gendered Relationships'. Unpublished paper, ASA Conference, 21–5 August, San Francisco.

Ahlander, N.R. and Bahr, K.S. (1995) 'Beyond Drudgery, Power and Equity: Towards an Expanded Discourse on the Moral Dimensions of Housework in Families'. *Journal of Marriage and the Family* 57: 54–68.

Akerloff, G.A. (1998) 'Men without Children'. *Economic Journal* 108 (March): 287–309.

Alcock, P. (1984) 'Remuneration or Remarriage? The Matrimonial and Family Proceedings Act, 1984'. *Journal of Law and Society* 11 (3): 357–66.

Alwin, D.F., Braun, M. and Scott, J. (1992) 'The Separation of Work and the Family: Attitudes towards Women's Labour-force Participation in Britain, Germany and the United States'. *European Sociological Review* 8: 13–38.

Anderson, E. (1993) *Value in Ethics and Economics*. Cambridge, Mass.: Harvard University Press.

Anderson, M., Bechhofer, F. and Gershuny, J. (1994) 'Introduction'. In M. Anderson, F. Bechhofer and J. Gershuny (eds), *The Social and Political Economy of the Household*. Oxford: Oxford University Press.

Anderson, O. (1999) 'State, Civil Society and Separation in Victorian Marriage'. *Past and Present* no. 163 (May): 161–201.

Arber, S. and Ginn, J. (1995) 'The Mirage of Gender Equality: Occupational Success in the Labour Market and Within Marriage'. *British Journal of Sociology* 46 (1): 21–43.

Archbishop of Canterbury (1967) *Standards of Morality: Christian and Humanist*. London: A.R. Mowbray.

Archbishop of Canterbury (1971) *Marriage, Divorce and the Church*. Report of a Commission appointed by the Archbishop of Canterbury to prepare a statement on the Christian doctrine of marriage. London: SPCK.

Askham, J. (1984) *Identity and Stability in Marriage*. Cambridge: Cambridge University Press.

Atkins, S. and Hoggett, B. (1984) *Women and the Law*. Oxford: Basil Blackwell.

Atkinson, R. (1965) *Sexual Morality*. London: Hutchinson.

Axinn, W.G. and Thornton, A. (1992) 'The Relationship between Cohabitation and Divorce: Selectivity or Causal Influence?' *Demography* 29 (3): 357–74.

Axinn, W.G. and Thornton, A. (1993) 'Mothers, Children, and Cohabitation: the Intergenerational Effects of Attitudes and Behavior'. *American Sociological Review* 58 (April): 233–46.

Backett, K.C. (1982) *Mothers and Fathers: A Study of the Development and Negotiation of Parental Behaviour*. London: Macmillan.

Baier, A. (1986) 'Trust and Anti-trust'. *Ethics* 1 (1): 231–60.

Bailey, D.S. (1952) *The Mystery of Love and Marriage: A Study in the Theology of Sexual Relations*. London: SCM.

Bainham, A. (1994) 'Divorce and the Lord Chancellor: Looking to the Future or Getting Back to Basics?.' *Cambridge Law Journal* 53 (2): 253–62.

Baker, L. and Emry, R. (1993) 'When Every Relationship is Above Average: Perceptions and Expectations of Divorce at the Time of Marriage'. *Law and Human Behavior* 17 (4): 439–50.

Baldock, J. (1999) 'Culture: the Missing Variable in Understanding Social Policy?' *Social Policy and Administration* 33 (4): 458–73.

Bane, M.J, (1976) *Here to Stay: American Families in the Twentieth Century*. New York: Basic Books.

Bane, M.J. and Jargowsky, P.A. (1988) 'The Links between Government Policy and Family Structure: What Matters and What Doesn't'. In A. Cherlin (ed.), *The Changing American Family and Public Policy*. Washington, DC: Urban Institute Press.

Barlow, A. and Duncan, S. (2000) 'New Labour's Communitarianism, Supporting Families and the "Rationality Mistake": Part II'. *Journal of Social Welfare and Family Law* 22 (2): 129–43.

Barnes, K.C. (1958) *He and She*. London: Darwen Finlayson.

Barnes, K.C. and Barnes G.F. (1938) *Sex and Friendship and Marriage*. London: Allen and Unwin.

Barr, O.S. (1969) *The Christian New Morality: A Biblical Study of Situation Ethics*. Oxford: Oxford University Press.

Barrett, M. and McIntosh, M. (1982) *The Anti-social Family*. London: Verso.

Bauman, Z. (1993) *Postmodern Ethics*. Oxford: Basil Blackwell.

Bauman, Z. (1995) *Life in Fragments*. Oxford: Basil Blackwell.

Beck, U. and Beck Gernsheim, E. (1995) *The Normal Chaos of Love*. Cambridge: Polity Press.

Beck Gernsheim, E. (1999) 'On the Way to a Post-familial Family: From a Community of Need to Elective Affinities'. *Theory, Culture and Society* 15 (34): 53–70.

Becker, G. (1981) A *Treatise on the Family*. Cambridge, Mass.: Harvard University Press.

Becker, G., Landes, E.M. and Michael, R.T. (1977) 'An Economic Analysis of Marital Instability'. *Journal of Political Economy* 85 (6l): 1141–87.

Behlmer, G. (1994) 'Summary Justice and Working-Class Marriage in England, 1870–1940'. *Law and History Review* 12: 229–75.

Bell, C. and Newby, H. (1976) 'Husbands and Wives: The Dynamics of the Deferential Dialectic'. In D. Leonard and S. Allen (eds), *Dependence and Exploitation in Work and Marriage*. London: Longman.

Bellah, R. (ed.) (1973) *Emile Durkheim on Morality and Society*. Chicago: University of Chicago Press.

Bellah, R., Madsen R., Sullivan, W., Swidler, A. and Tipton, S.M. (1985) *Habits of the Heart: Middle America Observed*. Berkeley: University of California Press.

Bennett, A. (1985 [1906]) *Whom God Hath Joined*. Stroud: Alan Sutton.

Bentley, G.B. (1965) 'The New Morality: a Christian Comment'. In R. Sadler (ed.), *Sexual Morality: Three Views*. London: Arlington Books.

Berger, P. and Kellner, H. (1964) 'Marriage and the Construction of Reality'. *Diogenes* no. 46: 1–25.

Bernard, J. (1976) *The Future of Marriage*. Harmondsworth: Penguin.

Berry, F.R. (1966) *Christian Ethics and Secular Society*. London: Hodder and Stoughton.

Bielby, W.T. and Bielby, D.D. (1992) 'Family Ties: Balancing Commitments to Work and Family in Dual Earner Households'. *American Sociological Review* 54 (5): 776–89.

Birkenhead, Earl of (F. E.Smith) (1927) *Law, Life and Letters*, Volume I. London: Hodder and Stoughton.

Black, S. and Sykes, M. (1971) 'Promiscuity and oral contraception: the relationship examined'. *Social Science and Medicine* 5: 637–43.

Blackstone, W. (1771) *Commentaries on the Laws of England*. Volume I, 4th edition. Dublin: John Exshaw, Henry Saunders, Boulter Grierson and James Williams.

Blakenhorn, D., Bayme, S. and Elshtain, J.B. (eds) (1990) *Rebuilding the Nest: A New Commitment to the American Family*. Milwaukee: Family Service America.

Bland, L. (1995) *Banishing the Beast: English Feminism and Sexual Morality. 1885–1914*. Harmondsworth: Penguin.

Blood, R.O. and Woffe, D.M. (1960) *Husbands and Wives: The Dynamics of Married Living*. Glencoe, Ill.: Free Press.

Blumstein, P. and Schwartz, P. (1983) *American Couples*. New York: William Morrow.

Blumstein, P. and Schwartz, P. (1991) 'Money and Ideology: Their Impact on Power and the Division of Household Labour'. In R. Lesser Blumberg (ed.), *Gender, Family and Economy: The Triple Overlap*. London: Sage.

Bone, M. (1986) 'Trends in Single Women's Sexual Behaviour in Scotland'. *Population Trends* 43: 7–14.

Booth, Mrs Justice (1985) *Report* of the Matrimonial Causes Procedure Committee. London: Lord Chancellor's Dept.

Bosanquet, H. (1906) *The Family*. London: Macmillan.

Bott, E. (1971) *Family and Social Network: Roles, Norms and External Relationships in Ordinary Urban Families*. London: Tavistock. 2nd edn 1957.

Bradshaw, J. (1997) 'Child Welfare in the UK: Rising Poverty, Falling Priorities for Children'. In C.A. Cornia and S. Danziger (eds), *Child Poverty and Deprivation in the Industrialized Countries*, 1945–1995. Oxford: Clarendon Press.

Bradshaw, J. and Millar, J. (1991) *Lone-parent Families in the UK*. Department of Social Security Research Report no. 6. London: HMSO.

Bradshaw, J., Stimson, C., Skinner, C. and Williams, J. (1999) *Absent Fathers?* London: Routledge.

Braine, J. (1990 [1957]) *Room at the Top*. London: Mondrain.

Bremer, C.S. (1912) *Divorce and Morality*. London: Frank Palmer.

Brewer, S.J. (1993) 'Reconceptualising Marital Commitment: an Interpretative Interactional Qualitative Study'. Unpublished PhD thesis, University of Connecticut.

Brickman, P. (1987) *Commitment, Conflict and Caring*. Englewood Cliffs, NJ: Prentice-Hall.

Briffault, R. (1931) 'The Origins of Patriarchal Marriage'. *The Listener*, 14 January: 51–2.

Brinig, M.F. and Crafton, S.M. (1994) 'Marriage and Opportunism'. *Journal of Legal Studies* 23: 869–94.

British Council of Churches (1966) *Sex and Morality: A Report to the British Council of Churches*. London: SCM Press.

Brophy, B. (1985) 'Law, State and the Family: the Politics of Child Custody'. Unpublished Phd thesis, University of Sheffield.

Brown, S.L. and Booth, A. (1996) 'Cohabitation versus Marriage: a Comparison of Relationship Quality'. *Journal of Marriage and the Family* 58 (August): 668–78.

Buchmann, M. (1989) *The Script of Life in Modern Society: Entry into Adulthood in a Changing World*. Chicago: University of Chicago Press.

Buck, N. and Ermisch, J. (1995) 'Cohabitation in Britain'. *Changing Britain.* (Newsletter of the ESRC Population and Household Change Research Programme), no. 3: 3–5.

Bumpass, L. (1990) 'What's Happening to the Family? Interactions between Demography and Institutional Change.' *Demography* 27 (4): 483–98.

Burgess, E.W. and Locke, H.J. (1953) *The Family from Institution to Companionship*, 2nd edn. New York: American Book Co. 1st edn 1945.

Burgoyne, C.B. (1990) 'Money in Marriage: How Patterns of Allocation both Reflect and Conceal Power'. *Sociological Review* 38 (4): 634–63.

Burgoyne, J., Ormrod, R. and Richards, M.P.M. (1987) *Divorce Matters.* Harmondsworth: Penguin.

Burke, P.J. and Reitzes, D.C. (1991) 'An Identity Theory Approach to Commitment'. *Social Psychology Quarterly* 54 (3): 239–51.

Burns, A. and Scott, C. (1994) *Mother-headed Families and Why They Have Increased.* Hillsdale, NJ: Lawrence Erlbaum.

Burrows, N. (1995) 'Cohabitation: the Church leads the Law'. *Family Law,* August: 439.

Caird, M. (1897) *The Morality of Marriage, and Other Essays on the Status and Destiny of Woman.* London: George Redway.

Cancian, F.M. (1987) *Love in America Gender and Self-Development.* Cambridge: Cambridge University Press.

Cancian, F.M. and Gordon, S.L. (1988) 'Changing Emotion Norms in Marriage: Love and Anger in US Women's Magazines since 1900'. *Gender and Society* 2 (3): 308–42.

Carbone, J. and Brinig, M.F. (1991) 'Rethinking Marriage: Feminist Ideology, Economic Change, and Divorce Reform'. *Tulane Law Review* 65 (5): 953–1010.

Carstairs, G.M. (1962) *This Island Now.* London: Hogarth Press.

Castles, F.G. and Flood, M. (1993) 'Why Divorce Rates Differ: Law, Religion, Belief and Modernity'. In F.G. Castles (ed.), *Families of Nations: Patterns of Public Policy in Western Democracies.* Aldershot: Dartmouth.

Cheal, D. (1991) *Family and the State of Theory.* Hemel Hempstead: Harvester Wheatsheaf.

Cherlin, A. (1981) *Marriage, Divorce and Remarriage.* Cambridge, Mass.: Harvard University Press.

Cherlin, A. (1992) *Marriage, Divorce, Remarriage*, 2nd edn. Cambridge, Mass.: Harvard University Press.

Chesser, E. (1964) *Love without Fear.* London: Arrow Books. 2nd edn 1941.

Chester, R. (1971) 'Contemporary Trends in the Stability of English Marriage'. *Journal of Biosocial Science* 3: 389–402.

Church of England (1971) *Marriage, Divorce and the Church*, Report of the Commission on the Christian Doctrine of Marriage. London: SPCK.

Clarkberg, M., Stolzenberg, R.M. and Waite, L.J. (1995) 'Attitudes, Values, and Entrance into Cohabitational versus Marital Unions'. *Social Forces* 74 (2): 609–34.

Clive, E.M. (1980) 'Marriage: an Unnecessary Legal Concept?' In J. Eekelaar and S.N. Katz (eds), *Marriage and Cohabitation in Contemporary Societies: Areas of Legal, Social and Ethical Change*. Toronto: Butterworths.

Cohen, L. (1987) 'Marriage, Divorce, and Quasi-rents; or, "I gave him the best years of my life" '. *Journal of Legal Studies* XVI (2): 267–304.

Cohen, M.R. (1933) 'The Basis of Contract'. *Harvard Law Review* XLVI (4): 553–92.

Coleman, D. and Chandola, T. (1999) 'Britain's Place in Europe's Population'. In S. McRae (ed.), *Changing British Families and Households in the 1990s*. Oxford: Oxford University Press.

Coleman, J.S. (1988) 'Social Capital in the Creation of Human Capital'. *American Journal of Sociology* 94 (Suppl.): S95–S120.

Collini, S. (1991) *Public Moralists: Political Thought and Intellectual Life in Britain, 1850–1930*. Oxford: Clarendon Press.

Coltrane, S. (1996) *Family Man. Fatherhood, Housework, and Gender Equity*. Oxford: Oxford University Press.

Comfort, A. (1963) *Sex in Society*. London: Gerald Duckworth.

Committee on One-parent Families (1974) *Report*, Cmnd 5629. London: HMSO.

Committee on Social Insurance and Allied Services (1942) *Report*, Cmd 6404. London: HMSO.

Conference on Christian Politics, Economic and Citizenship (COPEC) (1924) *The Relation of the Sexes*. London: Longman.

Convocations of Canterbury and York (1935) *The Church and Marriage: Report of the Joint Committees of the Convocations of Canterbury and York*. London: SPCK.

Cooper, D. (1972) *The Death of the Family*. Harmondsworth: Pelican Books.

Cooter, R. (1997) 'Normative Failure Theory of Law'. *Cornell Law Review* 82: 947–79.

Corti, L., Laurie, H. and Dex, S. (1995) *Highly Qualified Women*. Department of Employment, Research Series no. 50. University of Essex: Centre on Micro-social Change.

Creighton, C. (1999) 'The Rise and Decline of the "Male Breadwinner Family" in Britain'. *Cambridge Journal of Economics* 23: 519–41.

Cretney, S. (1996) 'Divorce Reform in England: Humbug and Hypocrisy or a Smooth Transition?' In M. Freeman (ed.), *Divorce: Where Next?* Aldershot: Dartmouth.

Cretney, S. (1998) *Law, Law Reform and the Family*. Oxford: Clarendon Press.

Crompton, R. (ed.) (1999) *Restructuring Gender Relations and Employment: The Decline of the Male Breadwinner*. Oxford: Oxford University Press.

Dalton, C. (1985) 'An Essay in the Deconstruction of Contract Doctrine'. *Yale Law Journal* 94 (5): 997–1114.

Dau-Schmidt, K. (1997) 'Economics and Sociology: the Prospects for an Interdisciplinary Discourse on Law'. *Wisconsin Law Review* 1997: 389–419.

Davidoff, L. and Hall, C. (1987) *Family Fortunes: Men and Women of the English Middle Class*. London: Hutchinson.

Davis, G. (1999) 'Monitoring Publicly Funded Mediation'. *Family Law* 29 (Sept.): 625–35.

Davis, G. and Murch, M. (1988) *Grounds for Divorce*. Oxford: Clarendon Press.

Davis, G., Cretney, S. and Collins, J. (1994) *Simple Quarrels*. Oxford: Clarendon Press.

Davis, K. (1985) 'The Future of Marriage'. In K. Davis (ed.), *Contemporary Marriage*. New York: Russell Sage Foundation.

Dawson, C. (1930) *Christianiiy and Sex*. London: Faber and Faber.

Deech, R. (1980) 'The Case Against Legal Recognition of Cohabitation'. In J.M. Eekelaar and S.N. Katz (eds), *Marriage and Cohabitation in Contemporary Societies*. Toronto: Butterworths.

Deech, R. (1993) 'The Rights of Fathers: Social and Biological Concepts of Parenthood'. In J. Eekelaar and P. Sarcevic (eds), *Parenthood in Modern Society: Legal and Social Issues for the 21st Century*. Dordrecht: Martinus Nijhoff.

Delphi, C. and Leonard, D. (1992) *Familiar Exploitation: A New Analysis of Marriage in ConternporM Western Society*. Cambridge: Polity Press.

Demant, V.A. (1963) *Christian Ethics: An Exposition*. London: Hodder and Stoughton.

Dench, G. (1994) *The Frog, the Prince and the Problem of Men*. London: Neanderthal Books.

Dennis, N. and Erdos, G. (1992) *Families without Fatherhood*. London: Institute of Economic Affairs.

Dennis, N., Henriques, F. and Slaughter, C. (1969) *Coal is Our Life: An Analysis of a Yorkshire Mining Community*. London: Tavistock.

De Rougemont, D. (1940 [1939]) *Passion and Society*. London: Faber and Faber.

De Singly (1996) *Modern Marriage and its Loss to Women: A Sociological Look at Marriage in France*. London: Associated University Presses.

Despert, L. (1953) *Children of Divorce*. New York: Doubleday

Deverson, J. and Kindsay, K. (1975) *Voices from the Middle Class: A Study of Families in Two London Suburbs*. London: Hutchinson.

Devlin, P. (1965) *The Enforcement of Morals*. Oxford: Oxford University Press.

Dewar, J. and Parker, S. (1992) *Law and the Family*. London: Butterworths.

Dex, S. and McCulloch, A. (1997) *Flexible Employment: The Future of Britain's Jobs*. London: Macmillan.

Dicey, A.V. (1948) *Lectures on the Relation between Law and Public Opinion in England during the Nineteenth Century*, 2nd edn. London: Macmillan.

Dingwall, R. (1999) ' "Risk Society": the Cult of Theory and the Millenium'. *Social Policy and Administration* 33 (4): 474–91.

Dingwall, R. and Eekelaar, J. (eds) (1998) *Divorce, Mediation and the Legal Process*. Oxford: Clarendon Press.

Dominian, J. (1991) *Passionate and Compassionate Love*. London: Darton, Longman and Todd.

Donzelot, J. (1980) *The Policing of Families*. London: Hutchinson.

Doucet, A. (1995) 'Gender Equality and Gender Differences in Household Work and Parenting'. *Women's Studies International Forum* 18 (3): 271–84.

Douglas, G. (1990) 'Family Law under the Thatcher Government'. *Journal of Law and Society* 17 (4): 411–26.

Drew, J.D. (1984) 'Covivance: Unmarried Cohabitation and the Negotiation of Commitment in the Intimate Dyad'. Unpublished PhD thesis, Boston University.

Dror, Y. (1959) 'Law and Social Change'. *Tulane Law Review* 33 (4): 787–802.

Duncan, G.J. and Hoffinan, S.D. (1985) 'A Reconsideration of the Economic Consequences of Marital Dissolution'. *Demography* 22 (4): 485–97.

Duncan, S. and Edwards, R. (1999) *Lone Mothers, Paid Work and Gendered Moral Rationalities*. London: Macmillan.

Duncomb, J. and Marsden, D. (1993) 'Love and Intimacy: the Gender Division of Emotion and "Emotional Work". A Neglected Aspect of the Sociological Discussion of Heterosexual Relations'. *Sociology* 27 (2): 201–41.

Dworkin, R. (1971) 'Lord Devlin and the Enforcement of Morals'. In R.A. Wasserstrom (ed.), *Morality and the Law*. Belmont, Cal.: Wadsworth.

Edgell, S. (1980) *Middle Class Couples: A Study of Segregation, Domination and Inequality in Marriage*. London: Allen and Unwin.

Edgworth, F.Y. (1992) 'Equal Pay to Men and Women for Equal Work'. *Economic Journal* 32: p. 431–57.

Edwards, D.L. (1963) 'A New Stirring in English Christianity'. In J.A.T. Robinson and D.L. Edwards (eds), *The Honest to God Debate*. London: SCM Press.

Eekelaar, J. (1978) *Family Law and Social Policy*. London: Weidenfeld and Nicolson.

Eekelaar, J. (1984) *Family Law and Social Policy*, 2nd edn. London: Weidenfeld and Nicolson.

Eekelaar, J. (1991) *Regulating Divorce*. Oxford: Clarendon Press.

Eekelaar, J. and Maclean, M. (1986) *Maintenance after Divorce*. Oxford: Clarendon Press.

Ehrenreich, B. (1983) *The Hearts of Men: American Dreams and the Flight from Commitment*. London: Pluto Press.

Eichler, M. (1981) 'Power, Dependency, Love and the Sexual Division of Labour'. *Women's Studies International Quarterly* 4 (2): 201–19.

Elias, N. (1991) *The Society of Individuals*. Oxford: Basil Blackwell.

Ellis, H. (1910) *Studies in the Psychology of Sex*, volume VI: *Sex in Relation to Society*. Philadelphia: F.A. Davis.

Ellman, I.M. (1989) 'The Theory of Alimony'. *California Law Review* 77 (1): 3–81

Ellman, I.M. (1997) 'The Misguided Movement to Revive Fault Divorce'. *International Journal of Law, Policy and the Family* 11 (2): 216–45

Ellman, I.M. and Lohr, S. (1997) 'Marriage as Contract, Opportunistic Violence and Other Bad Arguments for Fault Divorce. *University of Illinois Law Review* (3): 719–72.

Ellwood, D. and Bane, M.J. (1985) 'The Impact of AFDC on Family Structure and Living Arrangements'. In R.G. Ehrenberg (ed.), *Research in Labor Economics VII*. Greenwich, Conn.: JAI Press.

Elster, J. (1991) 'Rationality and Social Norms'. *Archives Européennes de Sociologie*. 32: 109–29.

Elshtain, J.-B. (1990) 'The Family and Civil Life'. In D. Blankenhorn, S. Bayme and J.B. Elshtain (eds), *Rebuilding the Nest: A New Commitment to the American Family*. Milwaukee: Family Service America.

Ermisch, J. and Francesconi, M. (1998) *Cohabitation in Great Britain: Not for Long. But Here to Stay*. Working Paper 98–1. University of Essex: ESRC Research Centre on Micro-social Change.

Estin, A.L. (1995) 'Love and Obligation: Family Law and the Romance of Economics'. *William and Mary Law Review* 36 (3): 989–1087.

Etzioni, A. (1994) *The Spirit of Community: The Reinvention of American Society*. New York: Touchstone Books.

Eurostat (1995) *Women and Men in the European Union: A Statistical Portrait*. Luxembourg: Office for Official Publications of the European Countries.

Farrell, C. (1978) *My Mother Said: The Way Young People Learned about Sex and Birth Control*. London: Routledge and Kegan Paul.

Fassinger, P.A. (1993) 'Meanings of Housework for Single Fathers and Mothers: Insights into Gender Inequality'. In J.C. Hood (ed.), *Men, Work and Family*. London: Sage.

Ferree, M. M. (1990) 'Beyond Separate Spheres: Feminism and Family Research'. *Journal of Marriage and the Family* 52: 866–84.

Ferri, E. and Smith, K. (1996) *Parenting in the 1990s*. London: Family Policy Studies Centre.

Finch, J. and Mason, J. (1993) *Negotiating Family Responsibilities*. London: Tavistock/Routledge.

Finch, J. and Summerfield, P. (1991) 'Social Reconstruction and the Emergence of Companionate Marriage'. In D. Clark (ed.), *Marriage, Domestic Life and Social Change: Writings for Jacqueline Burgoyne, 1944–1988*. London: Routledge.

Fineman, M.A. (1993) 'Our Sacred Institution: the Ideal of the Family in American Law and Society'. *Utah Law Review* (2): 387–405.

Fineman, M.A. (1994) 'The End of Family Law? Intimacy in the Twenty-first Century'. In S. Ingber (ed.), *Changing Perspectives of the Family: Proceedings of the 5th Annual Symposium of the Constitutional Law Resource Center*. Des Moines, Iowa: Drake University Law School.

Fineman, M.A. (1995) *The Neutered Mother, the Sexual Family and other Twentieth Century Tragedies*. London: Routledge.

Firth, R., Hubert, J. and Forge, A. (1970) *Families and Their Relatives*. London: Routledge and Kegan Paul.

Fiske, A. (1992) 'The Four Elementary Forms of Sociality: Framework for a Unified Theory of Social Relations'. *Psychological Review* 99 (4): 689–723.

Fitzpatrick, M.A. (1988) *Between Husbands and Wives: Communication in Marriage*. London: Sage.

Fletcher, G.P. (1993) *Loyalty: An Essay on the Moraliiy of Relationships*. Oxford: Oxford University Press.

Fletcher, J. (1966) *Situation Ethics: The New Morality*. London: SCM Press.

Fletcher, J. (1967) *Moral Responsibility: Situation Ethics at Work*. London: SCM Press.

Fletcher, P. (1938) *In Search of Personality*. London: Rich and Cowan.

Fletcher, R. (1966) *The Family and Marriage in Britai*n. Harmondsworth: Penguin.

Folsom, J.K. (1948) *The Family and Democratic Society*. London: Routledge and Kegan Paul.

Ford, R., Marsh, A. and McKay, S. (1995) *Changes in Lone Parenthood*. Department of Social Security Research Report no. 40. London: HMSO.

Fox Harding, L.M. (1999) 'Family Insecurity and Family Support: An Analysis of Labour's "Supporting Families" 1998'. Paper given to the Social Policy Association Annual Conference, London, July.

Freeman, M.D.A. and Lyon, C.M. (1983) *Cohabitation without Marriage*. Aldershot: Gower.

Fukuyama, F. (1999) *The Great Disruption: Human Nature and the Reconstitution of Social Order*. London: Profile Books.

Furlong, M. (1965) *With Love to the Church*. London: Hodder and Stoughton.

Furstenberg, F.F. and Cherlin, A.J. (1991) *Divided Families: What Happens to Children When Parents Part*. Cambridge, Mass.: Harvard University Press.

Galston, W. (1991) *Liberal Purposes. Good Virtues and Diversity in the Liberal State*. Cambridge: Cambridge University Press.

Garfinkel, I. and McLanahan, S. (1986) *Single Mothers and Their Children: A New American Dilemma*. Washington, DC: Urban Institute.

Gay, P. (1986) *The Bourgeois Experience: Victoria to Freud*, Volume II: *The Tender Passion*. Oxford: Oxford University Press.

Gergen, K.J. (1991) *The Saturated Self: Dilemmas of Identity in Contemporary Life*. New York: Basic Books.

Gershuny, J. (2000) *Changing Times Work and Leisure in post-Industrial Society*. Oxford: Oxford University Press.

Gershuny, J. and Berthoud, R. (1997) *New Partnerships? Men and Women in the 1990s*. Colchester: ESRC Research Centre on Micro-social Change, University of Essex.

Gershuny, L, Godwin, M. and Jones, S. (1994) 'The Domestic Labour Revolution: a Process of Lagged Adaptation?'. In M. Anderson, F. Bechhofer and J. Gershuny (eds), *The Social and Political Economy of the Household*. Oxford: Oxford University Press.

Gerson, K. (1993) *No Man's Land: Men's Changing Commitments to Family and Work*. New York: Basic Books.

Gibson, C. (1996) 'Contemporary Divorce and Changing Family Patterns'. In M. Freeman (ed.), *Divorce: Where Next?* Aldershot: Dartmouth.

Giddens, A. (1992) *The Transformation of Intimacy: Sexuality, Love and Eroticism in Modern Societies*. Cambridge: Polity Press.

Gilder, G. (1987) 'The Collapse of the American Family'. *Public Interest* (Fall): 20–5.

Giles, J. (1995) *Women, Identity and Private Life in Britain, 1900–1950*. New York: St. Martin's Press.

Gilligan, C. (1982) *In a Different Voice*. Cambridge, Mass.: Harvard University Press.

Gillis, J.R. (1986) *For Better, for Worse: British Marriages, 1600 to the Present*. Oxford: Oxford University Press.

Gillis, J.R. (1988) 'From Ritual to Romance: Towards an Alternative History of Love'. In C.-Z. Stearns and P.N. Stearns (eds), *Emotional and Social Change: Towards a New Psycho-history*. New York and London: Holmes Meier.

Gillis, J.R. (1997) *A World of Their Own Making: A History of Myth and Ritual in Family Life*. Oxford: Oxford University Press.

Glendon, M.A. (1976) 'Marriage and the State: the Withering Away of Marriage'. *Virginia Law Review* 62 (4): 663–720.

Glendon, M.A. (1981) *The New Family and the New Property*. Toronto: Butterworths.

Glenn, N.D. (1987) 'Continuity versus Change, Sanguineness versus Concern: Views of the American Family in the Late 1980s'. *Journal of Family Issues* 8 (4): 348–54.

Glenn, N.D. (1997) 'A Reconsideration of the Effect of No-fault Divorce on Divorce Rates'. *Journal of Marriage and the Family* 59 (November): 1023–30.

Goldstein, J. , Freud, A. and Solnit, A. (1973) *Beyond the Best Interests of the Child*. New York: Free Press.

Goldstein, L, Freud, A. and Solnit, A. (1980) *Before the Best Interests of the Child*, London: Burnett Books.

Goldthorpe, J.H., Lockwood, D., Beckhofer, F. and Platt, J. (1969) *The Affluent Worker: Industrial Attitudes and Behaviour*. Cambridge: Cambridge University Press.

Goode, W. (1956) *After Divorce*. Glencoe, Ill.: Free Press.

Goodnow, J.J. and Bowles, J.M. (1994) *Men, Women and Household Work*. Melbourne: Oxford University Press.

Gordon, L. (1988) *Heroes of their Own Lives: The Politics and History of Family Violence in Boston, 1880–1960*. New York: Viking.

Gorer, G. (1955) *Exploring English Character*. London: Cresset Press.

Gorer, G. (1971) *Sex and Marriage in England Today: A Study of the Views and Experience of the Under-45s*. London. Nelson.

Gottman, J.M. (1994) *What Predicts Divorce? The Relationship between Marital Processes and Marital Outcomes*. Hillsdale NJ: Lawrence Erlbaum Associates.

Gouriet, M. (2000) 'Cohabitation Update'. *Family Law* 30 (March): 210–11.

Gray, H. (1923) *Men, Women and God: A Discussion of Sex Questions from the Christian Point of View*. London: SCM.

Greatbatch, D. and Dingwall, R. (1989) 'Selective Facilitation: Some Preliminary Observations on a Strategy Used by Divorce Mediators'. *Law and Society Review* 23 (4): 613–41.

Greatbatch, D. and Dingwall, R. (1997) 'Argumentative Talk in Divorce Mediation Sessions'. *American Sociological Review* 62 (February): 151–70.

Gregson, N. and Lowe, M. (1994) 'Waged Domestic Labour and the Renegotiation of the Domestic Division of Labour with Dual Career Households'. *Sociology* 28 (1): 55–78

Griffiths, M. (1995) *Feminisms and the Self: The Web of Identity*. London: Routledge.

Gummer, J.S. (1971) *The Permissive Society: Fact or Fantasy?* London: Cassell.

Habermas, J. (1996) *Between Facts and Norms: Contributions to a Discourse Theory of Law and Democracy*. Cambridge, Mass.: MIT Press.

Hagan, E.J. (1946) 'Spiritual Foundations of the Family'. In J. Marchant (ed.), *Rebuilding Family Life in the Post-war World*. London: Odhams Press.

Hakim, C. (1996) *Key Issues in Women's Work: Female Heterogeneity and the Polarization of Women's Employment*. London: Athlone.

Hall, D.R. (1996) 'Marriage as a Pure Relationship: Exploring the Link between Pre-marital Cohabitation and Divorce in Canada'. *Journal of Comparative Family Studies* XXVII (1): 1–12.

Haller, M. and Hoellinger, F. (1994) 'Female Employment and the Change of Gender Roles: the Conflictual Relationship between Participation and Attitudes in International Comparison'. *International Sociology* 9 (1): 87–112.

Halsey, A.H. (1993) 'Changes in the Family'. *Children and Society* 7 (2): 125–36.

Hamilton, C. (1909) *Marriage as a Trade*. London: Chapman and Hall.

Harkness, S., Machin, S. and Waldfogel, J. (1996) 'Women's Pay and Family Incomes in Britain, 1979–1991'. In J. Hills (ed.), *New Inequalities: The Changing Distribution of Income and Wealth in the UK*. Cambridge: Cambridge University Press.

Harris, N, (1996) 'Unmarried Cohabiting Couples and Social Security in Great Britain'. *Journal of Social Welfare and Family Law* 18 (2): 123–46.

Hart, H.L.A. (1963) *Law, Liberty and Morality*. Oxford: Oxford University Press.

Haskey, J. (1993) 'Trends in the Numbers of One Parent Families in Great Britain'. *Population Trends* no. 71: 26–33.

Haskey, J. (1995) 'Trends in Marriage and Cohabitation: the Decline in Marriage and the Changing Pattern of Living in Partnerships'. *Population Trends* no. 80: 5–15.

Haskey, J. (1996) 'The Proportions of Married Couples who Divorce: Past Patterns and Current Prospects'. *Population Trends* no. 83 Spring: 25–36

Haskey, J. (1999) 'Cohabitation and Marital Histories of Adults in Great Britain'. *Population Trends* no. 96 Summer: 1–12.

Held, V. (1993) *Feminist Morality. Transforming Culture, Society and Politics*. Chicago: University of Chicago Press.

Heller, A. (1979) *A Theory of Feelings*. The Netherlands: Van Oorcum Assen.

Hemming, J. (1969) *Individual Morality*. London: Nelson.

Hennock, E.P. (1976) 'Poverty and Social Theory in England: the Experience of the 1980s'. *Social History* 1 (1): 67–91.

Henson, H.H. (1910) *Marriage and Divorce*. London: Hugh Rees.

Herbert, A.P. (1934) *Holy Deadlock*. London: Methuen.

Herbert, A.P. (1937) *The Ayes Have It: The Story of the Marriage Bill*. London: Methuen.

Hetherington, E., Cox, M. and Cox, R. (1978) 'The Aftermath of Divorce'. In J. Stevens and M. Matthews (eds), *Mother–Child, Father–Child Relations*. Washington, DC: National Association for the Education of Young Children.

Himmelfarb, G. (1986) *Marriage and Morals Among the Victorians*. London: Faber and Faber.

Hirschleifer, D. (1998) 'Informational Cascades and Social Conventions'. In P. Newman (ed.), *The New Palgrave Dictionary of Economics and the Law*, vol. 2. London: Macmillan.

Hirschman, A.O. (1970) *Exit, Voice and Loyalty: Responses to Decline in Firms, Organizations and States*. Cambridge, Mass.: Harvard University Press.

Hirschman, A.O. (1986) *Rival Views of Market Society and Other Recent Essays*. New York: Viking.

Hobhouse, L.T. (1906) *Morals in Evolution*. London: Chapman and Hall.

Hochschild, A. (1990 [1989]) *The Second Shift*. London: Piatkus.

Hoggett, B. (1980) 'Ends and Means: the Utility of Marriage as a Legal Institution'. In J.M. Eekelaar and S.N. Katz (eds), *Marriage and Cohabitation in Contemporary Societies*. Toronto: Butterworths.

Hollis, M. (1998) *Trust within Reason*. Cambridge: Cambridge University Press.

Holmes, A.S. (1986) 'Hard Cases and Bad Laws: Divorce Reform in England, 1909–37'. Unpublished PhD thesis, Vanderbilt University.

Holroyd, M. (1989) *Bernard Shaw. 1856–1950*, vol. 2. London: Chatto and Windus.

Home Office (1998) *Supporting Families*. London: Stationery Office.

Home Office and Department of Health and Social Security (1979) *Marriage Matters*. London: HMSO.

Honore, T. (1982) *The Quest for Security: Employees, Tenants, Wives*. London: Stevens and Sons.

Howard, M. (1993) 'Picking Up the Pieces'. Mimeo, Conservative Political Centre Fringe Meeting, Blackpool.

Hughes, G. (1962) 'Morals and the Criminal Law'. *Yale Law Journal* 71: 662–83.

Hunter, D.J. (1991) *Culture Wars: The Struggle to Define America*. New York: Basic Books.

Hunter, H.O. (1978) 'An Essay on Contract and Status: Marriage and the Meretricious Spouse'. *Virginia Law Review* 64: 1039–97.

Huxley, A. (1949) *Do What You Will*. London: Chatto and Windus.

Inge, W.R. (1930) *Christian Ethics and Modern Problems*. London: Hodder and Stoughton.

Ingleby, R. (1988) 'The Solicitor as Intermediary'. In R. Dingwall and J. Eekelaar (eds), *Divorce and Mediation and the Legal Process*. Oxford: Clarendon Press.

Inglehart, R. (1997) *Culture Shift in Advanced Industrial Society*. Princeton, NJ: Princeton University Press.

Ingram, K. (1922) *An Outline of Sexual Morality*. London: Jonathan Cape.

Jackson, E., Wasoff, F. with Maclean, M. and Dobash, R.E. (1993) 'Financial Support on Divorce: the Right Mixture of Rules and Discretion?' *International Journal of Law and the Family* 7: 230–54.

Jacob, H. (1989) 'Another Look at No-fault Divorce and the Post-divorce Finances of Women'. *Law and Society Review* 23 (1): 95–115.

Jacob, H. (1992) 'The Elusive Shadow of the Law'. *Law and Society Review* 26 (3): 565–90.

James, E.O. (1952) *Marriage and Society*. London: Hutchinson.

Jamieson, L. (1998) *Intimacy: Personal Relationships in Modern Society*. Cambridge: Polity Press.

Jarvis, H. (1997) 'Housing, Labour Markets and Household Structure: Questioning the Role of Secondary Data Analysis in Sustaining the Polarization Debate'. *Regional Studies* 31 (5): 521–31.

Jarvis, S. and Jenkins, S.P. (1997) *Marital Splits and Income Changes: Evidence for Britain*. Working Paper 97–4, ESRC Research Centre on Micro-social Change.

Jefferies, A. (1996) 'British Conservatism: Individualism and Gender'. *Journal of Political Ideologies* 1 (1): 33–52.

Joad, C.E.M. (1946) *The Future of Morals*. London: John Westhouse. 1st edn 1924.

Johnson, M.P. (1991) 'Commitment to Personal Relationships'. In W.H. Jones and D. Perlman (eds), *Advances in Personal Relationships: A Research Annual*. London: Jessica Kingsley, vol. 3, pp. 117–43.

Joshi, H. and Davis, H. (1992) *Child Care and Mothers' Lifetime Earnings: Some European Contrasts*. London: Centre for Economic Policy Research.

Kahn-Freund, 0. (195 5) 'England'. In W. Friedmann (ed.), *Matrimonial Property Law*. London: Stevens and Sons.

Karst, K.L. (1980) 'The Freedom of Intimate Association'. *Yale Law Journal* 89 (1): 624–92.

Kay, H.H. (1987) 'Equality and Difference: a Perspective on No-fault Divorce and its Aftermath'. *University of Cincinnati Law Review* 56 (1): 1–90.

Kay, H.H. (1990) 'Beyond No-fault: New Directions in Divorce Reform'. In S.D. Sugarman and H.H. Kay (eds), *Divorce Reform at the Crossroads*. New Haven, Conn.: Yale University Press.

Keeling, M. (1967) *Minds in a Free Society*. London: SCM Press.

Kerr, M. (1958) *The People of Ship Street*. London: Routledge.

Keyserling, Count Herman (1926) *The Book of Marriage: A New Interpretation by 24 Leaders of Contemporary Thought*. New York: Harcourt Brace.

Kiernan, K. (1992) 'The Impact of Family Disruption in Childhood on Transitions made in Young Adult Life'. *Population Studies* 46: 213–34.

Kiernan, K. (1993) 'Men and Women at Work and at Home'. In R. Jowell, L. Brook, G. Prior and B. Taylor (eds), *British Social Attitudes, the 9th Report. 1992–3*. Aldershot: Dartmouth.

Kiernan, K. (1996) 'Family Change: Parenthood, Partnership and Policy'. In D. Halpern, S. Wood, S. White and G. Cameron (eds), *Options for Britain*. Aldershot: Dartmouth.

Kiernan, K. (1999a) 'Cohabitation in Western Europe'. *Population Trends* no. 96 (Summer): 25–32.

Kiernan, K. (1999) 'Childbearing Outside Marriage in Westerm Europe'. *Population Trends* no. 98 (Winter): 11–20.

Kiernan, K. and Estaugh V. (1993) *Cohabitation, Extra-Marital Childbearing and Social Policy*. London: Family Policy Studies Centre.

Kiernan, K., Land, H. and Lewis, J. (1998) *Lone Mother Families in Twentieth Century Britain*. Oxford: Oxford University Press.

Kilpatrick, W. (1975) *Identity and Intimacy*. New York: Delacorte Press.

King, D. (1986) *The New Right: Politics, Markets and Citizenship*. Basingstoke: Macmillan.

Kingdom, E. (1988) 'Cohabitation Contracts: a Socialist-Feminist Issue'. *Journal of Law and Society* 15 (1): 77–89.

Kingdom, E. (1990) 'Cohabitation Contracts and Equality'. *International Journal of the Sociology of Law* 18: 287–98.

Kohli, M. (1986) 'The World We Forgot: a Historical Review of the Life-course'. In V.W. Marshall (ed.), Later Life: The Social Psychology of Ageing. London: Sage.

Komarovsky, M. (1962) *Blue-collar Marriage*. New Haven, Conn.: Yale University Press.

Komter, A. (1989) 'Hidden Power in Marriage'. *Gender and Society* 3 (2): 187–216.

Kuijsten, A.C. (1996) 'Changing Family Patterns in Europe: a Case of Divergence?' *European Journal of Population* 12 (2): 115–43.

Kymlicka, W. (1991) 'Rethinking the Family'. *Philosophy and Public Affairs* 30 (1): 77–97.

Lacey, T.A. (1947) *Marriage in Church and State*. London: SPCK.

Lambeth Conference (1930) *Report*. London: SCM.

Land, H. (1980) 'The Family Wage'. *Feminist Review* no. 5: 55–77.

Lasch, C. (1977) *Haven in a Heartless World*. New York: Basic Books.

Laslett, B. (1973) 'The Family as a Public and Private Institution: an Historical Perspective'. *Journal of Marriage and the Family* 35 (3): 480–91.

Lauer, J.C. and Lauer, R.H. (1986) *Till Death Do Us Part, How Couples Stay Together*. New York: Haworth Press.

Lauerman, N. J. (1987) 'A Step Towards enhancing Equality, Choice and Opportunity to Develop in Marriage and at Divorce'. *University of Cincinnati Law Review* 56 (2): 493–520.

Law Commission (1996) *Reform of the Grounds of Divorce: The Field of Choice*, Cmnd 3123. London: HMSO.

Law Commission (1969) *Family Law: Report on Financial Provision on Matrimonial Proceedings* no. 25. London: HMSO.

Law Commission (1988) *Facing the Future: A Discussion Paper on the Grounds for Divorce*, no. 170, HC 479. London: Law Commission.

Law Commission (1990) *Family Law: The Grounds for Divorce*, no. 192 HC 636. London: Law Commission.

Lawson, A. (1988) *Adultery: An Analysis of Love and Betrayal*. Oxford: Basil Blackwell.

Leach, E. (1967) *A Runaway World?* Oxford: Oxford University Press.

Lecky, W.E.H. (1884) *History of European Morals*, Volume II. London: Longman. 3rd edn 1869.

Lees, S. (1993) *Sugar and Spice: Sexuality and Adolescent Girls*. Harmondsworth: Penguin.

Le Grand, J. (1997) 'Knights, Knaves or Pawns? Human Behaviour and Social Policy'. *Journal of Social Policy* 26 (2): 149–70

Leonard, D. (1980) *Sex and Generation: A Study of Courtship and Weddings*. London: Tavistock.

Leonard, D. (1990) 'Sex and Generation Reconsidered'. In C. C. Harris (ed.), *Family, Economy and Community*. Cardiff. University of Wales Press.

Lessig, L. (1996) 'Social Meaning and Social Norms'. *University of Pennsylvania Law Review* 144: 2181–9.

Lessig, L. (1998) 'The New Chicago School'. *Journal of Legal Studies* 27 (June): 661–91.

Lesthaeghe, R. (1995) 'The Second Demographic Transition in Western Countries: an Interpretation'. In K. Oppenheim Mason and A.-M. Jensen (eds), *Gender and Family Change in Industrialized Countries*. Oxford: Clarendon Press.

Lesthaeghe, R. and Surkyn, J. (1988) 'Cultural Dynamics and Economic Theories of Fertility Change'. *Population and Development Review* 14 (1): 1–45.

Levinger, G. (1976) 'A Social Psychological Perspective on Marital Dissolution'. *Journal of Social Issues* 32 (1): 20–47.

Lewis, J. (1980) *The Politics of Motherhood: Child and Maternal Welfare 1900–1939*. London: Croom Helm.

Lewis, J. (1984) *Women in England, 1871–1945*. Brighton: Harvester Wheatsheaf.

Lewis, J. (1986) 'Anxieties About the Family and the Relationships Between Parents, Children and the State in Twentieth-century England'. In M. Richards and P. Light (eds), *Children of Social Worlds*. Cambridge: Polity Press.

Lewis, J. (1992a) *Women in Britain since 1945*. Oxford: Basil Blackwell.

Lewis, J. (1992b) 'Gender and the Development of Welfare Regimes'. *Journal of European Social Policy* 2 (3): 159–73.

Lewis, J. (1995) 'Intimate Relationships between Men and Women: the Case of H.G. Wells and Amber Pember Reeves'. *History Workshop Journal* no. 37: 76–98.

Lewis, J. and Kiernan, K. (1996) 'The Boundaries between Marriage, Non-marriage and Parenthood: Changes in Behaviour and Policy in Post-war Britain'. *Journal of Family History* 21 (3): 372–87.

Lewis, J. and Maclean, M. (1997) 'Recent Developments in Family Policy in the UK: the Case of the 1996 Family Law Act'. In M. May, E. Brunsdon and G. Craig (eds), *Social Policy Review 9*. London: Social Policy Association.

Lewis, J. and Wallis, P. (2000) 'Fault, Breakdown and the Church of England's Involvement in Divorce Law Reform'. *Twentieth Century British History* 11 (3) 308–32.

Lewis, L, Clark, D. and Morgan, D.H.J. (1992) *Whom God Hath Joined Together: The Work of Marriage Guidance*. London: Routledge.

Lewis, J. with Datta, J. and Sarre, S. (1999) *Individualism and Commitment in Marriage and Cohabitation*. London: Lord Chancellor's Department.

Lindsey, B.B. and Evans, W. (1928) *The Companionate Marriage*. London: Brentano's.

Lippmann, W. (1929) *A Preface to Morals*. London: George Allen and Unwin.

Lord Chancellor's Department (1985) *Report of the Matrimonial Causes Procedure Committee*. London: HMSO.

Lord Chancellor's Department (1993) *Looking to the Future. Mediation and the Grounds for Divorce*, Cm 2424. A Consultation Paper. London: Stationery Office.

Luhmann, N. (1986) *Love as Passion: The Codification of Intimacy*. Cambridge: Polity Press.

Lukes, S. (1973) *Individualism*. Oxford: Basil Blackwell.

Lundberg, S. and Pollak, R.A. (1996) 'Bargaining and Distribution in Marriage'. In I. Persson and C. Jonung (eds), *Economics of the Family and Family Policies*. London: Routledge.

Lye, D.N. and Waldron, I. (1997) 'Attitudes Toward Cohabitation, Family, and Gender Roles: Relationships to Values and Political Ideology'. *Sociological Perspectives* 40 (2): 199–225.

Lystra, K.I. (1989) *Searching the Heart: Women, Men and Romantic Love in Nineteenth Century America*. Oxford: Oxford University Press.

Mace, D. (1945) *The Outlook for Marriage*. London: Marriage Guidance Council.

Macfarlane, A. (1986) *Marriage and Love in England. 1300–1840*. Oxford: Blackwell.

Mackinnon, D.M. (1963) 'Moral Objections'. In A.R. Vidler (ed.), *Objections to Christian Belief*. London: Constable.

Maclean, M. (1991) *Surviving Divorce: Women's Resources after Separation*. London: Macmillan.

Maclean, M. and Eekelaar, J. (1986) *Maintenance after Divorce*. Oxford: Clarendon Press.

Maclean, M. and Eekelaar, J. (1997) *The Parental Obligation: A Study of Parenthood Across Households*. Oxford: Hart.

Maclean, M. and Wadsworth, M.E.J. (1988) 'The Interests of Children after Parental Divorce: a Long Term Perspective'. *International Journal of Law and the Family* 2: 155–66.

Macmillan, A.T. (1944) *What is Christian Marriage?* London: Macmillan.

Macmurray, J. (1935) *Reason and Emotion*. London: Faber and Faber.

Maine, H. (1861) *Ancient Law: Its Connection with the Early History of Society and its Relation to Modern Ideas*. London: John Murray.

Malinowski, B. (1931) 'The Present Crisis in Marriage'. *The Listener* 7 January: 7–8.

Mansfield, P. (1999) 'Developing a Concept of Partnership'. Paper given to the ESRC Marriage and Divorce Seminar Group, 10 December, London School of Hygiene and Tropical Medicine.

Mansfield, P. and Collard, J. (1988) *The Beginning of the Rest of Your Life? A Portrait of Newly-wed Marriage*. London: Macmillan.

Manting, D. (1996) 'The Changing Meaning of Cohabitation and Marriage'. *European Sociological Review* 12 (l): 53–65.

Marchant, J. (1904) *Public Morals*. London: Morgan Scott.

Marchant, J. (ed.) (1946) *Rebuilding Family Life in the Post-war World*. London: Odhams Press.

Marks, L. (1994) *Model Mothers: Jewish Mothers and Maternal Provision in East London*, 1870–1939. Oxford: Oxford University Press.

Marris, P. (1991) *Attachment Across the Life Cycle*. London: Routledge.

Marsh, A., McKay, S., Smith, A. and Stephenson A. (2001) *Low Income Families in Britain: Work, Welfare and Social Security in 1999*. DSS Report no. 138. London: Stationery Office.

Maslow, A. (1987) *Motivation and Personality*, 3rd edn. New York: Harper and Row 1st edn 1954.

Mead, L. (1997) *The New Paternalism.* Washington, D.C.: Brookings Institution.

Mattinson, J. (1988) *Work, Love and Marriage: The Impact of Unemployment.* London: Duckworth.

McCarthy, P., Walker, J. and Hooper, D. (2000) 'Saving Marriage: A Role for Divorce Law?' *Family Law* 30: 412–16.

McDougall, W. (1912) *Introduction to Social Psychology*, 5th edn. London: Methuen.

McGregor, O.R. (1957) *Divorce in England: A Centenary Study.* London: Heinemann.

McIntyre, A. (1967) *Secularization and Moral Change.* Oxford: Oxford University Press.

McLanahan, S. and Booth, K. (1989) 'Mother-only Families: Problems, Prospects and Politics'. *Journal of Marriage and the Family* 51 (Aug.): 557–80.

McLanahan, S. and Sandfur, G. (1994) *Growing Up with a Single Parent.* Cambridge, Mass.: Harvard University Press.

McLelland, D. (1996) 'Contract Marriage: The Way Forward or Dead End?' *Journal of Law and Society* 23 (2): 234–46.

McRae, S. (1993) *Cohabiting Mothers: Changing Mothers and Motherhood?* London: Policy Studies Institute.

McRae, S. (1997a) 'Cohabitation: a Trial Run for Marriage?' *Sexual and Marital Theory* 12 (3): 259–73.

McRae, S. (1997b) 'Household and Labour Market Change: Implications for the Growth of Inequality in Britain'. *British Journal of Sociology* 18 (3): 384–405.

Merrivale, Rt Hon. Lord (1936) *Marriage and Divorce: The English Point of View.* London: George Allen and Unwin.

Meulemann, H. (1994) 'Matrimony and Cohabitation: Old and New Normalcies'. Unpublished paper given at the International Sociological Association World Congress of Sociology, 18–23, July Bielefeld.

Miles, M.B. and Huberman, M.A. (1994) *Qualitative Data Analysis: An Expanded Sourcebook*, 2nd edn. London: Sage.

Millar, J. (1996) 'Poor Mothers and Absent Fathers'. Paper given at the SPA Annual Conference, July, University of Liverpool.

Millar, J. and Whiteford, P. (1993) 'Child Support in Lone-parent Families in Australia and Britain'. *Policy and Politics* 21 (1) 59–72.

Ministry of National Insurance (1954) *Report of the National Assistance Board for the Year ended December 1953*, Cmd 9210. London: HMSO.

Mitchell, A. (1985) *Children in the Middle: Living through Divorce.* London: Tavistock.

Mitchell, B. (1967) *Law, Morality and Religion in a Secular Society*. Oxford: Oxford University Press.

Mnookin, R.H. (1979) *Bargaining in the Shadow of the Law: The Case of Divorce*. Working Paper no. 3. London: Law Commission.

Mogey, J.M. (1956) *Family and Neighbourhood: Two Studies in Oxford*. Oxford: Oxford University Press.

Moore, G.E. (1968) *Principia Ethica*. Cambridge: Cambridge University Press.

Moore, K.A. and Burt, M.R. (1982) *Private Crisis, Public Cost: Policy Perspectives on Teenage Childbearing*. Washington, DC: Urban Institute Press.

Morgan, D.H.J. (1985) *The Family, Politics and Social Theory*. London: Routledge and Kegan Paul

Morgan, D.H.J. (1996) *Family Connections*. Cambridge: Polity Press.

Morgan, D.H.J. (1999) 'Risk and Family Practices: Accounting for Change and Fluidity in Family Life'. In E.B. Silva and C. Smart (eds), *The New Family*. London: Sage.

Morgan, P. (1995) *Farewell to the Family: Policy and Family Breakdown in Britain and the USA*. London: Institute of Economic Affairs.

Morgan, P. (2000) *Marriage-lite: The Rise of Cohabitation and its Consequences*. London: Institute for the Study of Civil Society.

Morris, L.D. (1985) 'The Renegotiation of the Domestic Division of Labour in the Context of Male Redundancy'. In R. Roberts, R. Finnegan and D. Gallie (eds), *New Approaches to Economic Life. Economic Restrictions: Unemployment and the Social Division of Labour*. Manchester: Manchester University Press.

Mount, F. (1983) *The Subversive Family*. London: Allen and Unwin.

Moyse, C.A. (1996) 'Reform of Marriage and Divorce Law in England and Wales, 1909–3 7'. Unpublished PhD thesis, University of Cambridge.

Muller-Lyer, F. (1931) *The Evolution of Modern Marriage: A Sociology of Sexual Relations*. London: Allen and Unwin. 1st edn 1913.

Mullins, C. (1954) *Marriage Failures and the Children*. London: Epworth Press.

Munby, D.L. (1963) *The Idea of a Secular Society and its Significance for Christians*. Oxford: Oxford University Press.

Murch, M. (1980) *Justice and Welfare in Divorce*. London: Sweet and Maxwell.

Murray, C. (1984) *Losing Ground: American Social Policy 1950–1980*. New York: Basic Books.

Nakonezny, P.A., Shull, R.D. and Rodgers, J.L. (1995) 'The Effect of No-fault Divorce Law on the Divorce Rate across the 50 States and its Relation to Income, Education and Religiosity'. *Journal of Marriage and the Family* 57: 477–88.

Neale, B. and Smart, C. (1997) 'Experiments with Parenthood'. *Sociology* 31 (2): 210–19.

Newcomb, M.D. (1981) 'Heterosexual Cohabitation Relationships'. In S. Duck and R. Gilmour (eds), *Personal Relationships: Studying Personal Relationships*. London: Academic Press.

Newcomb, M.D. (1987) 'Cohabitation and Marriage: a Quest for Independence and Relatedness'. In S. Oskamp (ed.), *Family Process and Problems: Social Psycological Aspects*. Applied Social Psychology Annual 7. Newbury Park, Cal.: Sage.

Newman, P. and Smith, A. (1997) *Social Focus on Families*. London: Stationery Office.

Newsom, G.E. (1932) *The New Morality*. London: Ivor Nicholson and Watson.

Nock, S.L. (1995a) 'Commitment and Dependency in Marriage'. *Journal of Marriage and the Family* 57 (May): 503–14.

Nock, S.L. (1995b) 'A Comparison of Marriages and Cohabiting Relationships'. *Journal of Family Issues* 16 (1): 53–76.

Nordstrom, B. (1986) 'Why Men Get Married: More and Less Traditional Men Compared'. In R.A. Lewis and R.E. Salt (eds), *Men in Families*. London: Sage.

Norton, A.J. and Glick, P.C. (1976) 'Marital Instability: Past, Present, and Future'. *Journal of Social Issues* 32 (1): 5–19

Nye, I.F. (1957) 'Child Adjustment in Broken and in Unhappy Unbroken Homes'. *Journal of Marriage and Family Living* 19: 356–61.

Oakley, A. (1974) *The Sociology of Housework*. Oxford: Martin Robertson.

O'Connor, P. (1992) *Friendships between Women: A Critical Review*. Hemel Hempstead: Harvester Wheatsheaf

O'Donovan, K. (1993) *Family Law Matters*. London: Pluto Press.

Offer, A. (1996) *Between the Gift and the Market: The Economy of Regard*. Discussion Papers in Economic and Social History no. 3, University of Oxford, Oxford.

Office for National Statistics (ONS) (1997a) *Living in Britain: 1995 General Household Survey*. London: Stationery Office.

—— (1997b) *Population Trends* no. 87 Spring. London: Stationery Office.

—— (1997c) *Population Trends* no. 88 Summer. London: Stationery Office.

—— (1998) *Living in Britain: Results from the 1996 General Household Survey*. London: Stationery Office.

Office of Population Censuses and Surveys (OPCS) (1987a) *Birth Statistics: Historical Series 1837–1983* Series FMI. London: HMSO.

—— (1987b) Population Trends no. 47 Spring. London: HMSO.

—— (1993a) *Population Trends* no. 71 Spring. London: HMSO.

—— (1993b) *Population Trends* no. 83 Spring. London: HMSO.

—— (1995a) *Population Trends* no. 81 Autumn. London: HMSO.

—— (1995b) *Marriage and Divorce Statistics: Historical Series 1837–1983* Series FM2. London: HMSO.

Okin, S.M. (1979) *Women in Western Political Thought*. Princeton, NJ: University of Princeton Press.

Okin, S.M. (1989) *Justice Gender and the Family*. New York: Basic Books.

Olsen, F.E. (1983) 'The Family and the Market: a Study of Ideology and Legal Reform'. *Harvard Law Review* 96 (7): 1497–1578.

Oppenheim Mason, K. and Jensen, A.-M. (1995) 'Introduction'. In K. Oppenheim Mason and A.-M. Jensen (eds), *Gender and Family Change in Industrialized Countries*. Oxford: Clarendon Press.

Oppenheimer, H. (1962) *Law and Love*. London: Faith Press.

Oppenheimer, V.K. (1994) 'Women's Rising Employment and the Future of the Family in Industrialised Societies'. *Population and Development Review* 20 (2): 293–342.

Oppenheimer, V.K. and Lew, V. (1995) 'American Marriage'. In K. Oppenheim Mason and A.-M. Jensen (eds), *Gender and Family Change in Industrialized Countries*. Oxford: Clarendon Press.

O'Reilly, J. and Fagan, C. (1998) *Part-time Prospects: An International Comparison of Part-time Work in Europe, North America and the Pacific Rim*. London: Routledge.

Pahl, J. (1989) *Money and Marriage*. London: Macmillan.

Pahl, J.M. and Pahl, R.E. (1971) *Managers and Their Wives. A Study of Career and Family Relationships in the Middle Class*. London: Allen Lane.

Pahl, R. (1995) *After Success: Fin de Siècle Anxiety and Identity*. Cambridge: Polity Press.

Pahl, R. (1996) 'Friendly Society'. In S. Kraemer and J. Roberts (eds), *The Politics of Attachment: Towards a Secure Society*. London: Free Association Books.

Pahl, R. and Wilson (1988) 'The Changing Sociological Construct of the Family'. *Sociological Review* 36 (2): 233–66.

Parker, S. (1990) *Informal Marriage, Cohabitation and the Law*. 1750–1989. London: Macmillan.

Parsons, T. (1949) *Essays in Sociological Theory Pure and Applied*. Glencoe, Ill.: Free Press.

Parsons, T. and Bales, R.F. (1955) *Family Socialization and Interaction Process*. Glencoe, Ill.: Free Press.

Pateman, C. (1988a) 'The Patriarchal Welfare State'. In A. Gutman (ed.), *Democracy and the Welfare State*. Princeton, NJ: Princeton University Press.

Pateman, C. (1988b) *The Sexual Contract*. Cambridge: Polity Press.

Peters, H.E. (1986) 'Marriage and Divorce: Informational Constraints and Private Contracting'. *American Economic Review* 76 (June): 437–54.

Pfau-Effinger, B. (1998) 'Gender Cultures and the Gender Arrangement: a Theoretical Framework for Cross-national Gender Research'. *Innovation* 11 (2): 147–66.

Phillips, M. (1997) *The Sex Change State*. London: Social Market Foundation.

Phillips, M. (1999) *The Sex Change Society*. London: Social Market Foundation.

Phillips, R. (1988) *Putting Asunder: A History of Divorce in Western Society*. Cambridge: Cambridge University Press.

Pickford, R. (1999) *Fathers, Marriage and the Law*. London: Family Policy Studies Centre and the Joseph Rowntree Foundation.

Pildes, R.H. (1991) 'The Unintended Cultural Consequences of Public Policy: a Comment on the Symposium'. *Michigan Law Review* 89 (3): 936–78.

Piper, C. (1993) *The Responsible Parent: A Study in Divorce Mediation*. Brighton: Harvester Wheatsheaf.

Pittenger, W.N. (1967) *Love is the Clue*. London: A.R. Mowbray.

Pleck, J.H. (1985) *Working Wives/Working Husbands*. London: Sage.

Popenoe, D. (1988) *Disturbing the Nest: Family Change and Decline in Modern Societies*. New York: Aldine de Gruyter.

Popenoe, D. (1993) 'American Family Decline, 1960–1990: a Review and Appraisal'. *Journal of Marriage and the Family* 55 (August): 527–55.

Posner, E.A. (1996) 'Law, Economics and Inefficient Norms'. *University of Pennsylvania Law Review* 144 (5): 1697–1744.

Posner, R. (1992) *Sex and Reason*. Cambridge, Mass.: Harvard University Press.

Prinz, C. (1995) *Cohabiting, Married or Single: Portraying, Analyzing and Modeling, New Living Arrangements in the Changing Societies of Europe*. Aldershot: Avebury.

Putnam, R.D. (1993) *Making Democracy Work: Civic Traditions in Modern Italy*. Princeton, NJ: Princeton University Press.

Queensberry, Marquess of (n.d.) *Marriage and the Relation of the Sexes*. London: Watts and Co.

Quilter, H. (ed.) (1888) *Is Marriage a Failure?* London: Swann Sonnschein.

Quinn, N. (1982) ' "Commitment" in American Marriage: a Cultural Analysis'. *American Ethnologist* 9 (4): 775–98.

Rapoport, R. and Rapoport, R.N. (1971) *Dual-career Families*. Harmondsworth: Penguin.

Rapoport, R. and Rapoport, R.N. (1976) *Dual-career Families Re-examined: New Integrations of Work and Family*. Oxford: Martin Robertson.

Regan, M.C. (1999) *Alone Together: Law and the Meanings of Marriage*. Oxford: Oxford University Press.

Regan, P.C. and Sprecher, S. (1995) 'Gender Differences in the Value of Contributions to Intimate Relationships: Egalitarian Relationships Are Not Always Perceived to Be Equitable'. *Sex Roles* 33 (3–4): 221–38.

Rehbinder, M. (1971) 'Status Contract and the Welfare State'. *Stanford Law Review* 23: 941–55.

Reibstein, J. and Richards, M. (1992) *Sexual Arrangements: Marriage and Affairs*. London: Heinemann.

Reynolds, J. and Mansfield, P. (1999) 'The Effect of Changing Attitudes to Marriage on its Stability'. In J. Simons (ed.), *High Divorce Rates: The State of the Evidence on Reasons and Remedies*. London: Lord Chancellor's Department.

Reynolds, S. (1910) 'Divorce "for the Poor" '. *Fortnightly Review* 94 (Sept.): 487–96.

Rheinstein, M. (1972) *Marriage, Stability, Divorce and the Law*. Chicago: University of Chicago Press.

Rhymes, D. (1964) *No New Morality*. London: Constable.

Richards, M.P.M. (1982) 'Post-divorce Arrangements for Children: a Psychological Perspective'. *Journal of Social Welfare Law* (May): 133–151.

Richards, M.P.M. and Dyson, M. (1982) *Separation, Divorce and the Development of Children: A Review*. London: Department of Health and Social Security.

Richards, M.P.M. and Elliot, F. (1991) 'Sex and Marriage in the 1960s and 1970s'. in D. Clark (ed.), *Marriage, Domestic Life and Social Change: Writings for Jacqueline Burgoyne, 1944–1988*. London: Routledge.

Rindfuss, R.R. and VandenHeuvel, A. 'Cohabitation: a Precursor to Marriage or an Alternative to Being Single?' *Population and Development Review* 16 (4): 703–26

Roberts, E. (1984) *A Woman's Place: An Oral History of Working Class Women*. Oxford: Basil Blackwell.

Roberts, E. (1995) *Women and Families: An Oral History 1940–1970*. Oxford: Basil Blackwell.

Robinson, J.A.T. (1963) *Honest to God*. London: SCM Press.

Robinson, J.A.T. (1970) *Christian Freedom in a Permissive Society*. London: SCM Press.

Robinson, J.A.T. and Edwards, D.L. (eds) (1963) *The Honest to God Debate*. London: SCM Press.

Rodgers, B. and Pryor, J. (1998) *Divorce and Separation: The Outcomes for Children*. York: Joseph Rowntree Foundation.

Rodgers, H. (1999) 'Cohabitation Committee Report to the National Committee'. *Solicitors Family Law Association Review*, no. 79 (June): 3–9.

Rolph, C.H. (ed.) (1961) *The Trial of Lady Chatterley*. London: privately printed.

Ross, C. (1987) 'The Division of Labor at Home'. *Social Forces* 65 (3): 816–33.

Ross, E. (1993) *Love and Toil: Motherhood in Outcast London, 1870–1918*. Oxford: Oxford University Press.

Rostow, E.V. (1960) 'The Enforcement of Morals'. *Cambridge Law Journal* (Nov.): 174–98.

Rowntree, G. (1964) 'Some Aspects of Marriage Breakdown in Britain During the Last Thirty Years'. *Population Studies* 18 (2): 147–63.

Rowntree, G. and Carrier, N. (1958) 'The Resort to Divorce in England and Wales, 1838–1957'. *Population Studies* 11 (3): 188–233.

Rowthorn, R. (1999) 'Marriage and Trust: Some Lessons from Economics'. *Cambridge Journal of Economics* 23: 661–91.

Royal Commission on Divorce and Matrimonial Causes (1912a). *Report*, Cd 6478. London: HMSO.

Royal Commission on Divorce and Matrimonial Causes (1912b). *Minutes of Evidence*, Cd 6480. London: HMSO.

Royal Commission on Marriage and Divorce (1956a) *Minutes of Evidence*. London: HMSO.

Royal Commission on Marriage and Divorce (1956b) *Report*, Cmd 9678. London: HMSO.

Royden, A.M. (1921) *Sex and Commonsense*. London: Hurst and Blackett.

Rubery, L, Smith, M. and Fagan, C. (1998) 'National Working-time Regimes and Equal Opportunities'. *Feminist Economics* 4 (1): 71–10 1.

Rusbult, C.E. (1987) 'Responses to Dissatisfaction in Close Relationships: the Exit–Voice–Loyalty–Neglect Model'. In D. Perlman and S. Duck (eds), *Intimate Relationships: Development, Dynamics, and Deterioration*. London: Sage.

Rusbult, C.E. (1991) 'Commentary on "Commitment to Personal Relationships"'. In W. Jones and D. Perlman (eds), *Advances in Personal Relationships: A Research Annual*. London: Jessica Kingsley.

Rusbult, C.E. and Buunk, B.P. (1993) 'Commitment Processes in Close Relationships: an Interdependence Analysis'. *Journal of Social and Personal Relationships* 10: 175–204.

Russell, B. (1916) *Principles of Social Reconstruction*. London: Allen and Unwin.

Russell, B. (1985) *Marriage and Morals*. London: Unwin Paperbacks (1st. edn. 1929).

Safilios Rothschild, C. (1970) 'The Study of Family Power Structure: a Review 1960–69'. *Journal of Marriage and the Family* 32 (4): 539–52.

Safilios Rothschild, C. (1976) 'A Macro- and Micro-examination of Family Power and Love: an Exchange Model'. *Journal of Marriage and the Family* 38 (2): 355–62.

St John-Stevas, N. (1964) *Law and Morals*. London: Burns and Oates.

Sandel, M. (1996) *Democracy's Discontent: America in Search of a Public Philosophy*. Cambridge, Mass.: Belknap Press of Harvard University Press.

Scanzoni, J. (1972) *Sexual Bargaining Power Politics in the American Marriage*. Englewood Cliffs NJ: Prentice-Hall.

Scanzoni, J., Polanko, K., Teachman, J. and Thompson, L. (1989) *The Sexual Bond: Rethinking Families and Close Relationships*. Newbury Park, Cal.: Sage.

Schneider, C. (1985) 'Moral Discourse and the Transformation of American Family Law'. *Michigan Law Review* 83 (6):1803–79.

Schoen, R. (1992) 'First Unions and the Stability of First Marriage'. *Journal of Marriage and the Family* 54 (May): 281–4.

Schoen, R. and Weinick, R. (1993) 'Partner Choice in Marriages and Cohabitations'. *Journal of Marriage and the Family* 55 (May): 408–14.

Schofield, M. (1968) *The Sexual Behaviour of Young People*. Harmondsworth: Penguin.

Schultz, M. (1982) 'Contractual Ordering of Marriage: a New Model for State Policy'. *California Law Review* 70 (2): 204–334.

Schwartz, P. (1994) *Peer Marriage: How Love between Equals Really Works*. New York: Free Press.

Scott, E.S. (1990) 'Rational Decision-making about Divorce'. *Virginia Law Review* 76 (1): 9–91.

Scott, J. (1997) 'Changing Households in Britain: Do Families Matter?' *Sociological Review* 45 (4): 591–620.

Scott, J., Alwin, D. and Braun M. (1996) 'Generational Changes in Gender-role Attitudes in a Cross-national Perspective'. *Sociology* 30 (3) 471–92.

Scott, J., Braun, M. and Alwin, D. (1999) 'Partner, Parent, Worker: Family and Gender Roles'. In *British Social Attitudes Survey, 15th Report*. Aldershot: Ashgate.

Scott, S. (1999) 'Family Change: Revolution or Backlash in Attitudes?'. In S. McRae (ed.), *Changing British Families and Households in the 1990s*. Oxford: Oxford University Press.

Seccombe, C.E. (1933) *The Basis of Christian Marriage*. London: SCM Press.

Seligman, A.B. (1997) *The Problem of Trust*. Princeton, NJ: Princeton University Press.

Selznik, P. (1992) *The Moral Commonwealth: Social Theory and the Promise of Community*. Berkeley: University of California Press.

Sennett, R. (1985) *The Fall of Public Man*. London: Faber and Faber.

Shaw, G.B. (1913) *Getting Married: A Disquisitory Play*. London: Constable.

Silberstein, L. (1992) *Dual-career Marriage*. Hillsdale, NJ: Lawrence Erlbaurn Asssociates.

Sillitoe, A. (1994 [1958]) *Saturday Night and Sunday Morning*. London: Flamingo.

Singer, J.B. (1989) 'Divorce Reform and Gender Justice'. *North Carolina Law Review* 67 (5): 1103–21.

Singh, S. (1997) *Marriage Money: The Social Shaping of Money in Marriage and Banking*. St Leonards, NSW: Allen and Unwin.

Skolnick, A. (1991) *Embattled Paradise: The American Family in an Age of Uncertainty*. New York: Basic Books.

Smart, C. (1982) 'Justice and Divorce: the Way Forward?' *Family Law*, vol. 12: 135–7.

Smart, C. (1984) *The Ties that Bind: Law, Marriage and the Reproduction of Patriarchal Relations*. London: Routledge and Kegan Paul.

Smart, C. (1985) *The Family and Social Change: Some Problems of Analysis and Intervention*. Research Working Paper 13, Gender Analysis and Policy Unit, University of Leeds.

Smart, C. (1991) 'The Legal and Moral Ordering of Child Custody'. *Journal of Law and Socieiy* 18 (4): 485–501.

Smart, C. and Neale, B. (1997) 'Good Enough Morality? Divorce and Post-modernity'. *Critical Social Policy*. 53: 3–27..

Smart, C. and Neale, B. (1997) 'Wishful Thinking and Harmful Tinkering? Sociological Reflections on Family Policy'. *Journal of Social Policy* 26 (3): 301–21.

Smart, C. and Neale, B. (1999) *Family Fragments*. Cambridge: Polity Press.

Smart, C. and Stevens, P. (2000) *Cohabitation Breakdown*. York: Joseph Rowntree Foundation.

Smelser, N.J. (1980) 'Vicissitudes of Work and Love in Anglo-American Society'. In N. Smelser and E.H. Erikson (eds), *Themes of Work and Love in Adulthood*. London: Grant McIntyre.

Smith, B.A. (1990) 'The Partnership Theory of Marriage: a Borrowed Solution Fails'. *Texas Law Review* 68 (4): 689–743.

Smock, P.J. (2000) 'Cohabitation in the US: an Appraisal of Research Themes, Findings and Implications'. *Annual Review of Sociology* 26: 1–20.

Smock, P.J. and Manning W.D. (1997) 'Cohabiting Partners' Economic Circumstances and Marriage'. *Demography* 34 (3): 331–41.

Somerset Maugham, W. (1926) *The Constant Wife*. London: George H. Doran.

Sorensen, A. and McLanahan, S. (1987) 'Married Women's Economic Dependency, 1940–1980'. *American Journal of Sociology* 93 (3): 659–87.

Sorokin, P.A. (1941) *Social and Cultural Dynamics*, Volume 4. New York: American Book Co.

South, S.J. and Spitze, G. (1994) 'Housework in Marital and Nonmarital Households'. *American Sociological Review* 59 (June): 327–47.

Spence, J.C. (1946) *The Purpose of the Family*. London: National Children's Homes.

Spencer, H. (1876) *The Principles of Sociology*, Volume I. London: Williams and Norgate.

Spencer, H. (1892) *The Principles of Ethics*, Volume I. London: Williams and Norgate.

Stacey, J. (1990) *Brave New Families: Stories of Domestic Upheaval in Late Twentieth Century America*. New York: Basic Books.

Stamp, P. (1985) 'Research Note. Balance of Financial Power in Marriage: An Exploratory Study of Breadwinning Wives'. *Sociological Review* 33 (3): 546–57.

Stanley, L. (1995) *Sex Surveyed 1949–1994: From Mass Observation's Little Kinsey to the National Survey and the Hite Reports*. London: Taylor and Francis.

Stanley, S.M. and Markman, H.J. (1992) 'Assessing Commitment in Personal Relationships'. *Journal of Marriage and the Family* 54 (August): 595–608.

Stedman Jones, G. (1974) 'Working Class Culture and Working Class Politics in London, 1870–1900. *Journal of Social History* no. 7: 460–508.

Stephen, J.F. (1873) *Liberty, Equality, Fraternity*. London: Smith, Elder.

Stone, L. (1979) *The Family, Sex and Marriage in England, 1500–1800*. Harmondsworth: Penguin.

Stone, L. (1990) *Road to Divorce, England 1530–1987*. Oxford: Oxford University Press.

Stopes, M. (1918) *Married Love*. New York: Critic and Guide Co.

Strathern, M. (1992) *After Nature: English Kinship in the Late Twentieth Century*. Cambridge: Cambridge University Press.

Straver, C.J., van der Heiden, Ab M. and Robert, W.C.J. (1980) 'Lifestyles of Cohabiting Couples and Their Impact on Juridical Questions'. In J.M. Eekelaar and S.N. Katz (eds), *Marriage and Cohabitation in Contemporary Societies*. Toronto: Butterworths.

Suchman, M.C. (1997) 'On Beyond Interest: Rational, Normative and Cognitive Perspectives in the Social Scientific Study of Law'. *Wisconsin Law Review* 1997: 475–501.

Sugden, R. (1998a) 'Conventions'. In P. Newman (ed.), *The New Palgrave Dictionary of Economics and the Law*, vol. 1. London: Macmillan.

Sugden, R. (1998b) 'Normative Expectations: the Simultaneous Evolution of Institutions and Norms'. In A. Ben Ner and L. Putterman (eds), *Economics, Values and Organisations*. Cambridge: Cambridge University Press.

Sunstein, C.R. (1987) 'On the Expressive Function of Law'. *University of Pennsylvania Law Review* 144: 2021–53.

Sunstein, C.R. (1997) *Free Markets and Social Justice*. Oxford: Oxford University Press.

Supplementary Benefits Commission (1971) *Cohabitation*. London: HMSO.

Susman, W.I. (1979) ' "Personality" and the Making of Twentieth Century Culture'. In J. Higham and P. Cankin (eds), *New Directions in American Intellectual History*. Baltimore, MD: Johns Hopkins University Press.

Sweet, J.A. and Bumpass, L. (1990) *American Families and Households*. New York: Russell Sage.

Swidler, A. (1980) 'Love and Adulthood in American Culture'. In N.J. Smelser and E.H. Erikson (eds), *Themes of Work and Love in Adulthood*. London: Grant McIntyre.

Tannen, D. (1992) *You Just Don't Understand: Women and Men in Conversation*. London: Virago.

Taylor, C. (1989) *Sources of the Self: The Making of the Modern Identity*. Cambridge: Cambridge University Press.

Taylor, C. (1992) *Men versus the State: Herbert Spencer and Late Victorian Individualism*. Oxford: Clarendon Press.

Thair, T. and Risdon, A. (1999) 'Women in the Labour Market: Results from the Spring 1998 LFS'. *Labour Market Trends* (March): 103–29.

Thatcher, M. (1995) *The Downing Street Years*. London: HarperCollins.

Thèry, I. (1994) *Le Démarriage*. Paris: Editions Odile Jacob.

Thèry, I. (1998) *Couple, filiation et parente aujourd'hui*. Paris: La Documentation Française/Odile Jacob.

Thomas, K. (1959) 'The Double Standard'. *Journal of the History of Ideas* no. 20: 195–216.

Thompson, L. (1991) 'Family Work: Women's Sense of Fairness'. *Journal of Family Issues* 12 (2): 181–96.

Thompson, L. and Walker, A.J. (1989) 'Gender in Families: Women and Men in Marriage, Work and Parenthood'. *Journal of Marriage and the Family* 51 (November): 845–71.

Thompson, P. (1988) *The Voice of the Past*. Oxford: Oxford University Press. 2nd edn. 1978.

Thomson, E. and Colella, U. (1992) 'Cohabitation and Marital Stability: Quality or Commitment?' *Journal of Marriage and the Family* 54: 259–67.

Thornton, A. (1989) 'Changing Attitudes Towards Family Issues in the United States'. *Journal of Marriage and the Family* 51: 873–93.

Traugott, M. (ed.) (1978) *Emile Durkheim and Institutional Analysis*. Chicago: University of Chicago Press.

Treas, J. (1991) 'The Common Pot or Separate Purses? A Transaction Cost Interpretation'. In R. Lesser Blumberg (ed.), *Gender, Family and Economy*. London: Sage.

Treas, J. (1993) 'Money in the Bank: Transaction Costs and the Economic Organisation of Marriage'. *American Sociological Review* 58: 723–34.

Tronto, J. C. (1993) *Moral Boundaries: A Political Argument for an Ethic of Care*. London: Routledge.

Turner, C. (1967) 'Conjugal Roles and Social Networks: a Re-examination of an Hypothesis'. *Human Relations* 20 (2): 121–30.

Unjern Steinberg, L. (1926) 'The Marriage of the Future'. In H. Graf von Keyserling (ed.), *The Book of Marriage: A New Interpretation by Twenty-four Leaders of Contemporary Thought*. New York: Harcourt Brace.

Van de Kaa D.J. (1987) 'Europe's Second Demographic Transition'. *Population Bulletin* 42: 1–59.

Van Deth, J. and Scarborough, E. (eds) (1995) *Beliefs in Government*, vol, 4: *The Impact of Values*. Oxford: Oxford University Press.

Vaughan, D. (1986) *Uncoupling: Turning Points in Intimate Relationships*. Oxford: Oxford University Press.

Vicinus, M. (1985) *Independent Women: Work and Community for Single Women*, 1850–1920. London: Virago.

Vidler, A.R. (ed.) (1963) *Objections to Christian Belief*. London: Constable.

Vogler, C. (1998) 'Money in the Household: Some Underlying Issues of Power'. *Sociological Review* 46 (4): 687–713.

Vogler, C. and Pahl, J. (1993) 'Social and Economic Change and the Organisation of Money within Marriage'. *Work. Employment and Society* 7 (1): 71–95.

Vogler, C. and Pahl, J. (1994) 'Money, Power and Inequality within Marriage'. *Sociological Review* 42 (2): 263–88.

Waite, L. (1995) 'Does Marriage Matter?' *Demography* 32 (4): 483–507.

Walby, S. (1997) *Gender Transformations*. London: Routledge.

Walker, J. and Hornick, J.P. (1996) *Communication in Marriage and Divorce: A Consultation on Family Law*. Leeds Castle: BT Forum.

Walker, J., McCarthy, P. and Timms, N. (1994) *Mediation: The Making and Re-making of Cooperative Relations. An Evaluation of the Effectiveness of Comprehensive Mediation*. Newcastle: Relate Centre for Family Studies, University of Newcastle.

Walker, K. (1957) *Your Marriage*. London: Transworld Pubs. 1st edn 1951.

Wallerstein, J.S. and Kelly, J.B. (1980) *Surviving the Breakup: How Children and Parents Cope with Divorce*. London: Grant McIntyre.

Ward, M. (1909) *Daphne, or Marriage à la Mode*. London: Cassell.

Ward, M. (1915) *Eltham House*. London: Cassell.

Warde, A. and Hetherington, K. (1993) 'A Changing Domestic Division of Labour? Issues of Measurement and Interpretation'. *Work, Employment and Society* 7 (l): 23–45.

Wax, A. (1989) 'Bargaining in the Shadow of the Market: Is There a Future for Egalitarian Marriage?'. *Virginia Law Review* 84 (4): 509–672.

Webster, W. (1999) *Imagining Home: Gender, 'Race' and National Identity*, 1945–1964. London: UCL Press.

Weeks, J., Donovan, C. and Heaphy, B. (1999) 'Everyday Experiments: Narratives of Non-heterosexual Relationships'. In B. Silva and C. Smart (eds), *The New Family*. London: Sage.

Weitzman, L.J. (1981) *The Marriage Contract: Spouses, Lovers and the Law*. New York: Free Press.

Weitzman, L.J. (1985) *The Divorce Revolution*. New York: Free Press.

Wells, H.G. (1902) *Anticipations of the Reaction of Mechanical and Scientific Progress upon Human Life and Thought*. London: Chapman and Hall.

Wells, H.G. (1906) *Socialism and the Family*. London: A.C. Fifield.

Wells, H.G. (1930) 'Divorce is Inhuman'. In B. Russell *et al.* (eds), *Divorce*. New York: John Day.

Wells, H.G. (1933) *The World of William Clissold*. London: Waterlow.

Wells, H.G. (1966 [1934]) *Experiment in Autobiography: Discoveries and Conclusions of a Very Ordinary Brain (since 1866)*, Volume II. London: Victor Gollancz and Cresset Press.

West, R. (1912) 'The Gospel According to Mrs Humphry Ward'. *Freewoman* 15 Feb.: 249–50.

Westermarck, E. (1926) *The Origin and Development of Moral Ideas*. London: Macmillan. 1st edn 1908.

Westermarck, E. (1929) *Marriage*. London: Ernest Benn.

Westermarck, E. (1936) *The Future of Marriage in Western Civilisation*. London: Macmillan.

Wheelock, J. and Oughton, E. (1994) *The Household as a Focus for Comparative Research*. Working paper 4. Centre for Rural Economics, University of Newcastle upon Tyne.

Whitehead, A. (1976) 'Sexual Antagonism in Herefordshire'. In D. Leonard and S. Allen (eds), *Dependency and Exploitation in Work and Marriage*. London: Longman.

Whitehouse, M. (1977) *Whatever Happened to Sex*? London: Wayland.

Williams, J. (1994) 'Is Couverture Dead? Beyond a New Theory of Alimony'. *Georgetown Law Journal* 82 (7): 2227–90.

Wilson, E. (1977) *Women and the Welfare State*. London: Tavistock.

Wilson, G. (1987) *Money in the Family*. Aldershot: Avebury.

Wilson, J.Q. (1993) *The Moral Sense*. New York: Free Press.

Wilson, P. and Pahl, R. (1988) 'The Changing Sociological Construct of the Family'. *Sociological Review* 36 (2): 233–66.

Wilson, W.J. (1987) *The Truly Disadvantaged: The Inner City, the Underclass and Public Policy*. Chicago: Chicago University Press.

Winnett, A.R. (1968) *The Church and Divorce*. London: A.R. Mowbray.

Wolfe, A. (1989) *Whose Keeper? Social Science and Moral Obligation*. Berkeley: University of California Press.

Wolfram, S. (1987) *In-laws and Out-laws: Kinship and Marriage in England*. New York: St. Martin's Press.

Wolheim, R. (1959) 'Crime, Sin, and Mr Justice Devlin', *Encounter* 13 (74): 34–40.

Wright, H. (1968) *Sex and Birth Control*. London: Allen and Unwin.

Wright, M. (1984) 'Marriage: From Status to Contract?' *Anglo-American Law Review* 13: 17–31.

Wright, T.R. (1986) *The Religion of Humanity: The Impact of Comtean Positivism on Victorian Britain.* Cambridge: Cambridge University Press.

Yankelovich, D. (1981) *New Rules: Searching for Self-fulfillment in a World Turned Upside Down.* New York: Random House.

Young, I.M. (1995) 'Mothers, Citizenship and Independence: a Critique of Pure Family Values'. *Ethics* 105: 535–56.

Young, M. and Willmott, P. (1973) *The Symmetrical Family.* London: Routledge and Kegan Paul.

Zelig, K.C. (1993) 'Putting Responsibility Back into Marriage: Making a Case for Mandatory Prenuptials'. *Universijy of Colorado Law Review* 64: 1223–45.

Zimmerman, C.C. (1949) *The Family of Tomorrow.* New York: Harper.

Index